CW00553122

To Stacey
lov

x x

1

In a World of My Own

by
James Christie &
Stephen Holbrook

In a World of My Own
Mage Publishing ISBN: 9780952710943
Mage Publishing 2020 © James Christie and
Stephen Holbrook. No part of this book may be
reproduced by any means without the written
consent of Mage Publishing and the authors. All the
usual copyright conditions apply.

For Margaret Holbrook

25/8/1939 – 24/2/2018

Sleep softly sweet butterfly.
Let me hold you one more night
for in the morning you will wake,
spread your wings and fly
with the gentle beating
of a new born heart.

Infused with the spirit
of your kind,
you are always guiding
and always loving
these fragile flowers left behind,
and we are bathed in the gossamer light
of God's bright rainbow.

Chapter One
Acorns

Hollywood legend James Stewart and our national treasure Dame Judi Dench have one thing in common inasmuch that at different times they have both told me that it is very uncool to name drop. Nevertheless, despite their sound advice, I am going to drop a name here, which is that of Jane McDonald, star of half a dozen TV shows and who, in my opinion, is one of the finest female vocalists this country has ever produced. Her name is relevant because she and Steve Holbrook (who is the subject of this book) have been best friends for most of their lives, and how they met and became such bosom buddies could be the subject of an entire book in its own right.

Some friendships ignite immediately while others need a little time to mature; some are based on sexual attraction while others are based on synchronicity and common interests: in Steve and Jane's case, it was most definitely the latter. They met for the first time in the early 1980s. Steve's father was the manager of the prestigious Wakefield Theatre Club and while Steve was too young to work behind the bar, he was given a part-time job as a glass collector. Jane was doing her work experience in the promotions department, so this in effect was their 'first contact'.

They met again a year or so later after the Wakefield Theatre Club had closed and re-opened under the name of 'Pussycatz'. By this time Jane had given up on the idea of working in an office and was performing at the club as a dancer. They exchanged a few words and the occasional smile, and that was about the sum total of their 'second contact'.

Their 'third' and more significant contact is a little more complicated to narrate and involves a weird element of synchronicity, so look, I'll write it slowly in the hope that you will read it slowly, because it's quite important, and I don't want anything to get lost in the translation. If that sounds a bit patronising, I honestly don't mean it to be, but go ahead and shoot me anyway!

Joanne, Steve's sister, and her boyfriend, Paul, had got into the habit of accompanying Steve to the spiritualist church services at Peterson Road, and on one particular night, the guest medium failed to show up. Pardon the old joke, but she was delayed by unforeseen circumstances!

"Don't worry," Paul exclaims in a loud voice to all and sundry, "Steve here is good enough to take the service and put on a demonstration!"

Stephen could have cheerfully killed him, but by then it was too late. A lovely lady called Janet Ferguson, who was the president of the church, could see how nervous Stephen was at the prospect and put his mind at rest by suggesting that they could take the evening through together. Stephen reluctantly agreed but said that first he needed to get some fresh air to clear his mind… Instead of getting the fresh air to clear his mind he scuttled down the road to the nearest pub and downed a rapid pint to settle his nerves!

Anyway, this was the night he stood on a public platform for the very first time and, much to his own amazement, he thoroughly enjoyed it – and, indeed, to such an extent that he found himself wondering when he might be able to do it again!

And now we come to Stephen's third contact with Jane McDonald. He was very surprised to find her sitting in the congregation one night, and thought to himself *what the heck is she doing here?* Obviously they knew each other from the Theatre Club and Pussycatz, and it was only when they said hello to each other at the end of the evening, that he learned that Janet Ferguson who had facilitated Steve's first public appearance, was in fact Jane's grandmother, and that Jane's mum, Jean, was on the church committee!

This led to them meeting on frequent occasions at the spiritualist church, and they often commented that they were the only people present under the age of sixty! They both grumbled about how the spiritualist movement should be opened up to a younger demographic and, in part, this set Steve on his pathway; he wasn't being evangelical, but just wanted to spread the word to new people rather than preaching to the converted.

After one particular service Jane invited Steve along to one of her gigs, which was the first time he'd ever heard her sing and perform as a solo act. To say that he was impressed is putting it mildly, and this first invitation led to Steve attending Jane's concerts whenever he could. In effect, he became her most ardent and enthusiastic fan! On one such occasion he had a peculiar vision that made no sense to him at the time – or indeed to Jane when he told her about it afterwards.

She'd been performing at The Barracks Hotel in Pontefract and was in the middle of the stage belting out one of her big ballads, when gradually he became aware of the fact that the background around her seemed to be diffusing into an out of focus haze. Within the haze he had an image the American flag and of a cruise liner amid blue skies and turquoise seas: there was also an impression of TV cameras and Jane singing, not from the stage of the club where she was performing, but from within the frame of a television set.

These kind of visions do not impinge upon the psychic mind in glaring technicolour with surround sound… they are much more muted and subtle and are frequently confusing and ambiguous. Nevertheless, Steve felt sufficiently certain of what he'd seen to give Jane a formal prophesy. *'I can see you doing some kind of TV show where you're on board a cruise ship in America, and there'll be cameras on board doing some filming and recording, and this show is going to make you famous!'*

Like anyone else who might have been on the receiving end of such a prediction, Jane asked the obvious question – "when is this going to happen?" Steve told her the truth and said he hadn't got a clue, only he was quite certain that it *would* happen one day. Needless to say, it *did* happen, and the rest, as they say, is history!

Over the years Steve has had a number of sittings with Jane, always on a very casual and unofficial basis, because he positively hates doing private readings – to the extent that he simply won't do them! He *did* do them when he was first starting out at the Peterson Road Spiritualist Centre and he was very much in demand, but he very quickly declined to accept the responsibility inherent with these one-to-one sessions, mainly because he felt it *was* such a responsibility. People came to his table expecting to be able to communicate with a departed loved one, but, of course, there was no guarantee that this would happen. Therefore a sitting could be over in less than five minutes, which would inevitably have been a profound disappointment to the client who hoped to have a long and detailed conversation with their Mum or Dad. In his defence, Stephen never charged for these sessions – or if he did the money went straight into the church coffers and never into his own pocket – but as far as he was concerned, this wasn't the point.

He was quick to learn that for his clairvoyance to work as well as it could, he needed the group energy of an audience/congregation, and thus if a message came through which only lasted for a couple of minutes, he could move on to the next recipient with a clear conscience.

Now here is an oddity. It is quite possible to be psychic without being clairvoyant, but I have never met a clairvoyant yet who has not also had some psychic ability. Psychism and clairvoyance are related, but they are not at all the same thing. If someone is giving a clairvoyant reading (using the modern definition of the word 'clairvoyant') it infers that the information is coming from the spiritual presence of a third party. In a purely psychic reading there is no third party, and whatever information is made available comes from the interaction of the psychic's mind with the psychic emanations of the client. I suppose it could be said that what happens here is that the psychic consciously makes contact with the *sub*conscious of the sitter.

So, if Steve had a few sittings with Jane, they were conducted spontaneously and very much on the psychic vibration. He was able to tell her about the cruise and the TV cameras and her budding stardom, and at another session he confirmed that she would marry Henrik Briksen. A few years later he mentioned her hosting a prime time TV show (there were several) and spoke of her performing in the most prestigious venue in Las Vegas. Yet none of this information came through in any kind of formal session... rather it was drip-fed into a general conversation.

I remember one evening in Todmorden when he cheerfully informed my wife Jo (who was very nervously waiting for some exam results) that she would be delighted with the results but would not, however, take up a new career as a landscape gardener. Instead, she would join me in running our small promotions company. Jo was less than chuffed because after three years studying horticulture as a mature student, with a gap year spent attending the herbaceous borders at Harewood House, working 24/7 with me was definitely not on her agenda. And yet things worked out exactly the way Stephen had told her.

There is a phrase doing the political rounds at the moment, when various politicians, usually from the south, are making reference to the Northern Powerhouse. Well, I've got news for you guys, the North has *always* been a powerhouse, although sadly it is not nearly as powerful today as it was when Steve Holbrook and Jane McDonald were starting out upon their respective careers back in the early 1980s. The abysmal three day week of the mid '70s had receded into history to be replaced with a new energy, and nowhere was this more apparent than in the entertainments industry.

While there were still working men's clubs virtually on every street corner, there were also cabaret bars and night clubs opening up all over the place, not least of which was the Wakefield Theatre Club, and a few miles down the road, the Batley Variety Club. You might think that such venues were a bit parochial, Oop North and miles away from the sophisticated hotspots to be found in London and the Home Counties, and yet they played host to the top stars of the day. Artists such as Michael Jackson, Bob Monkhouse, Les Dawson,

Ray Charles, Lulu, Shirley Bassey and even Roy Orbison topped the bills on a weekly basis and tickets for these shows (in pre-internet days) would sell out within a few hours of the adverts appearing in the local newspapers.

And yet, despite these two particular venues, it was in the rough and tumble of the WMCs that Jane cut her teeth and learned her craft – and while she was doing it, Steve was also stepping out onto the public platform for the first time, demonstrating his skills as a medium in a host of small spiritualist churches and a plethora of draughty village halls. Too many times had he sat in a spiritualist congregation listening to the medium pass out messages from the 'other side' and too many times had he found himself thinking that the messages were just a little bit vague and generalised and wondered, especially after that first night at Peterson Road with Janet Ferguson, if he could do any better?

There was only one way to find out, and in the end, he decided to put it to the test and billing himself as 'Britain's Youngest Medium' (he was still only in his late teens) he booked a small hall over in the West Riding, and shaking like an aspen leaf in a bowl of unset jelly, confronted an audience as a professional clairvoyant for the very first time. He doesn't remember any of the details of that first demonstration, only that he came off the platform to very warm round of applause, and collapsed into a convenient arm chair bathed in sweat, with no real idea of how good (or how bad) he had been.

Either way, he was encouraged to continue with his crusade. He trained to be a hairdresser and after working an eight hour day in the salon, he would jump into his car and drive all over Yorkshire presenting evening demonstrations of clairvoyance; he must have been good, probably far better than he thought he was, for his reputation spread quickly and rare was the evening when he did not demonstrate to a packed hall.

In those days his business operation was very informal... He'd put an advert in the local paper, inviting people to come along and pay on the door – and they would arrive in droves, pay a few quid to get in, and then sit spellbound for the better part of two hours while night after night Stephen Holbrook provided hard evidence for post mortem survival. Or at least, *most* of them would...

Generally speaking, you can divide an audience attending an evening of clairvoyance into a number of distinctly different groups. About 50% are convinced that life *does* carry on after death, and they go along in the hope of being shown evidence of this fact. If they receive a message from a loved one, then that's a bonus, but even if they don't, they're happy enough to share the experience with those who do.

Maybe 20% of the audience attend because they are quite *desperate* to receive a message from the other side; very frequently they are those people who have been recently bereaved. They are not sure whether they believe in post mortem survival, but they *want* to believe, even *need* to believe, and they expect (or at least hope) that Stephen will deliver the goods and come up with some proof for them.

Maybe another 25% come along with open minds, wanting to know what the whole thing is about, with no firm opinions on the subject one way or the other. It would be quite wrong to say they were just looking for an evening's entertainment, because they have an interest in the subject and are looking to learn more.

This leaves the odd 5% and sad to say these are the doubters, the disbelievers, the dyed in the wool sceptics. They come along hoping that Stephen will fail and fall flat on his face, for in so doing, it will validate their own minority opinion. Anyone and everyone is entitled to their own opinion but when that opinion is based on fear and ignorance, things do not bode well for the majority. Even when Steve delivers the most precise and accurate message imaginable, the sceptics still cry fraud and foul. Two of their favourite angles is that Stephen is (a) cold reading, or (b) that he has got plants in the audience. This is clearly quite preposterous, and here is the reason why!

Taking the second criticism first, namely that of having plants in the audience. Say Steve does four demonstrations a week, and at each demonstration there are a 100 people in the audience. Take into consideration that over a two hour demonstration he will bring, on average, ten messages through, so over one week that would be 40 messages. Thus, he would need to have 40 people on his payroll, or one way or the other, would have to suborn the services of 10 people per night prior to going out onto the platform. I need to tell you that even if he was only paying audience plants a peppercorn fee, he'd be broke within a month simply because he does not have that flexibility of budget to finance such an endeavour. Furthermore, remember that on Monday he might be in Glasgow, Tuesday in Newcastle, Wednesday in Leicester, Thursday in Torquay... How on earth could he organise and maintain such a network of accomplices? The answer is that he couldn't! Stephen Holbrook has been demonstrating for more than 35 years, and if he did have plants in the audience, don't you think that the word would have got out by now and that he would have been rumbled? He has never been "rumbled" because there is nothing to rumble.

I met Steve in 1999. I have written three books about the man (this will be the fourth) and for 11 years I worked as his tour and promotions manager. I have witnessed more than 2000 of his demonstrations both in this country and abroad, and if hc'd bccn chcating in any way, believe me, I'd have known about it!

On the second charge, that of 'cold reading' – this is actually quite an interesting one, because if you asked Steve about cold reading he would assume that you wanted him to do an open air demonstration in the middle of a North Yorkshire winter! If you'll excuse a slight diversion, I *do* know a bit about cold reading, because with my work with palmistry and the Tarot, I have been accused of it myself.

Now, listen up, because I'll share a secret with you. To do a cold reading, you have to be very *very* clever, and you have to work for many years to acquire the skills which are needed to pull it off with sufficient panache and confidence to fool the person you're trying to read. Steve and I are both Taureans, neither of us is particularly clever, and neither of us has the patience or the dedication needed to master these skills. Frankly, it is much easier to have faith in our natural abilities and leave the cold readers where they belong... Out in the cold!

Also, in Steve's case, there is an obvious point to be made. Namely, it's bloody difficult to do a cold reading on someone who is sat a hundred feet away in the dimly lit stalls of a small theatre or right at the back of a hotel lounge. For this 'cold reading' thing to work, you have got to be able to see who you're talking to; you need to judge and monitor their reactions to get your next lead. Like a lot of mediums, Steve works on the vibration of the voice, and even if you were to blindfold him, it wouldn't affect his abilities in the slightest.

"Ah," someone might bleat, "When I saw Mr Holbrook demonstrate at the Kenton Theatre in Henley, all the house lights were full on!"

Yes sir, but so were the stage spotlights, and speaking here as someone who has stood on many such stages, albeit only with a guitar across his chest and a handful of songs waiting to be sung, believe me, you still can't see the audience clearly... It's just a splurge of faces and shapes, and although you can pick out a few individual faces on the front row, by the second or third rows you're as blind as the proverbial bat.

Steve's detractors accuse him of being vague, so let me pick a transcript at random from my filing cabinet, and you tell me what you think!

Retford Little Theatre, September 2006

Steve: "I want to talk to a lady, maybe towards the middle of the theatre, who has lost her husband in the last five or six months..."
Seven hands go up from around the middle of the theatre.

Steve: "The gentleman I'm pulling in here died of cancer. Does that apply to any of you?"
Four hands go down, leaving three.

Steve: "The gentleman who is talking to me is saying that he died of bowel cancer. Does this apply to any of you?"
Two hands go down, leaving only one.

Steve: "Hello my love. Can I hear your voice please? Just a straight yes or no... Has your husband passed over with bowel cancer within the last half year?"

Lady:	"Yes, it's me over here. My husband died of bowel cancer in April."
Steve:	"Thank you, my love. Can you tell me, who is Dorothy?"
Lady:	"That's me. My name is Dorothy!"
Steve:	"So who is Tom or Tommy?"
Lady:	"My husband's name was Tom, but most of his friends always called him Tommy."
Steve:	"Well Dorothy, I've got Tommy here with me and he's saying he wants to thank you for all the love, care and attention you gave to him, especially during his last few weeks. He's also giving me the number 40 and he's telling me this should be a very significant number, and should prove that it's really him. So, is the number 40 important in any way?"
Lady:	"This year would have been our fortieth wedding anniversary."
Steve:	"Dorothy, my love, he's telling me that he's seen Daisy and that he meets Paul every day. Also that he takes a walk every morning with Charley. Do these names mean anything to you?"
Lady:	"Yes! Daisy was his mother's name, and Paul is our son... He got killed in a motor bike accident five years ago. Charley was the name of our dog, and Tom always took him out for a walk every morning before he went to work."
Steve:	"He's telling me that three o'clock is very important...?"
Lady:	"He passed away at three o'clock in the afternoon and that's what it says on the death certificate."
Steve:	"And can you tell me why the name of Catherine should be so important?"

Lady: "He died in Saint Catherine's Hospice."

This is just a part of a much longer transcript and it conveys nothing of the raw emotion that was inherent to the message. I have only given you the exchange of dialogue and have made no mention of the kindness and sympathy in Stephen's voice or the tears of amazement and gratitude in Dorothy's eyes. In this message Stephen went on to say that Tommy liked the way Dorothy had redecorated the house, that he loved the new curtains, but thought that the expensive 42 inch HD television was a bit of an indulgence. He told her that he was very proud of the way she had coped since his departure, and congratulated her on her recent promotion at work.

I interviewed Dorothy at length after the demonstration, and she confirmed the fact that she had never met Stephen Holbrook prior to this evening, and she also confirmed the accuracy of everything Stephen had said. She *had* redecorated the house, she *had* bought new curtains, and she *had* splashed out on a new TV. Furthermore, despite the fact that while some women of her age were winding down and looking forwards to retirement, she *had* accepted a new job position which gave her more authority and a substantial increase in salary.

I know beyond a shadow of a doubt that Dorothy was not 'planted' in the audience, and I do not believe that any cold reading techniques were used in bringing through the messages from her late husband. The question then is, how does he do it? The sceptics would still maintain it was some kind of trick or con, while Stephen is quite serene in the knowledge that he has made some kind of contact with the spiritual entity of the departed. Now, another question is this, and it is a question which the sceptics in particular are duty bound to answer... Namely, if they are right and Stephen is wrong, how *does* he do it? What are the mechanics? How does he know a husband's name, the nature and even the precise *time* of his death, the names of his mother and his son and his dog, the fact that he walked the dog every morning? How can he possibly know that his wife has just redecorated the house even down to the detail of buying new curtains and splashing out on a new TV?

Dear Mr & Mrs Sceptic, answers please on a postcard, directly to me c/o Mage Publishing.

Chapter Two
Roots

Stephen Holbrook is a product of the North, as is Jane McDonald, and come to think of it, I suppose you could say the same about me. Steve and Jane were both born in the Wakefield area of Yorkshire, and like a lot of Yorkshire folk they are extraordinarily proud of their roots and their Northern heritage. Typical of those who have this Northern background, they dispense with airs and graces and what you see 'off' the stage is exactly the same as what you see 'on' the stage. Jane McDonald's persona is that of the working class girl from down the road while Steve Holbrook could be fairly described as a typical Yorkshire Tyke; they do not trade on their Northerness, but neither do they seek to hide it. Indeed, as I've said, they are both proud of it, and to them it is something to be celebrated.

Having said all that, in their own ways, they are very astute business people. Both have learned the value of maintaining an independent grip on their own careers, and in different ways, both have learned the wisdom of the old Yorkshire adage that says "if tha wants summat done proper, do it thee bloody sen!"

Back to the 'Northern Powerhouse' cliché… Perhaps it is no accident that some of the nation's top entertainers come from the North, and curiously, so do (and did) some of the very best British mediums. I think here of Ossie Rae from Bishop Auckland, Billy Belton from Newcastle upon Tyne, Donna Rathbone of Osmotherley, and of course, Steve Holbrook from Wakefield. It is interesting to note that the spiritualist church was founded in the North (Darlington 1853) and it was only with the advent of the First World War that it was embraced by the rest of the country at large. But if you were to ask where exactly *is* 'The North' you're going to get a variety of answers – some of them very silly and some of them ill-informed and even arrogant.

To your typical Londoner or someone from the Home Counties, The North begins just after Watford Gap services on the M1… To others it encompasses Coventry and Birmingham, and even Leicester, which causes the residents of those conurbations to scream treason as they point out that they live in *The Midlands!* I've heard Derby and Stoke-on-Trent described as being 'Northern' which I suppose they are if compared with Folkestone and Dover, but residents of Derby would say they're in The Peak District, while people living in Stoke would point out that they are living in the heart of The Black Country.

A Northerner would make a more realistic assessment of the geographical situation, suggesting that The North begins just south of Sheffield, stretching over to The Wirral and Liverpool in the west, Grimsby and Hull in the east, then heading north to Blackpool, Manchester, Bradford and Leeds, then on up to Teesside and Tyneside before petering out somewhere around Berwick-on-Tweed and the Scottish Borderlands.

The North is a vast tract of land, not always pretty, but when occasionally you do find beauty, it is a rare beauty indeed. One need only think of the North Yorkshire Moors, The Dales and The Lake District.

Having made that last reference, it must also be said that there is also some truth in the saying that 'It's grim up North' – our transport infrastructure is terrible, the weather is mostly bloody awful, wages are significantly lower than they are in the south, unemployment is significantly higher, the heart has been ripped out of our industry, and anyone who achieves anything up here has got to work a damned sight harder to achieve it than their brethren in the Londoncentric south. Little wonder then that both Steve and Jane McDonald have had a hard slog getting to where they are today! Like anybody else from this part of the world, they don't bleat about it or make complaint, but it is always there, subliminally simmering beneath the subconscious of the psyche.

Nevertheless it must be acknowledged that Stephen had a safe and happy childhood, surrounded by the love of his parents, Margaret and Eric, and supported by the presence of his characterful grandfather, John. Indeed, a special relationship seemed to develop between grandfather and grandson, more akin to a tight bond of pure friendship rather than any kind of familial relationship. In the fullness of time, Stephen was presented with two baby sisters, Joanne first and then Adele. From what I can gather there were no sibling rivalries or jealousies and Steve took on the role of 'big brother' with great pride and aplomb.

He was a bright and energetic boy who revelled within the security of his family, and although not an outstanding academic student at primary school, his wit and personality won him many friends. This is not to say he was a 'goody two shoes' because he certainly wasn't, and there were times when he overplayed his hand and fell flat on his face. Stephen told me a story quite recently which illustrates this point perfectly.

As part of his multifaceted job as manager of the Wakefield Theatre Club, Eric Holbrook was charged with the care and maintenance of the three company cars, owned by the directors. Thus, on one day Eric would drop Stephen off at school in a Rolls Royce. On another day it would be in a Ferrari, and on a third day it would be in a Porsche. This cavalcade of exotic motor transport did not go unnoticed by Stephen's school friends, and when he was asked "Hey Steve, are all these cars yours?" he answered truthfully, and said no – they were his Dad's!

Now whether this was a totally innocent response or whether he was being just a wee bit disingenuous, I don't know and Stephen isn't saying, but for a while the other members of his class assumed that these beautiful motor cars belonged to Mr Holbrook Senior, and they were suitably impressed. Then, of course, the theatre club closed, the high flying cars disappeared, and Eric started ferrying Stephen to school in a rather dilapidated Morris Minor. To save face, Stephen brazened it out and told his classmates that the Roller, the Ferrari and the Porsche were "off the road at the moment", but he was fairly sure that he wasn't really fooling anybody!

As Stephen progressed through his early teens his schoolwork began to suffer. It seemed that he could not concentrate on any of the lessons, and indeed many a school report stated quite bluntly "Stephen is a bright boy but suffers from a marked absence of concentration."

What is interesting is the *cause* of this absence of concentration. Steve remembers that – "It was sometimes very difficult to hear what the teachers were saying. There were other voices in my head, a babble of words that were there more as thought-forms than actually spoken words. I didn't know where the words were coming from, and I certainly didn't know what they were saying. There were times when I thought I was going mad, but I didn't want to tell anyone else about what was happening to me in case *they* thought I was going mad too. There would be times when the babble of voices would be still and quiet for a while, but sooner or later they always came back, and when they did, they were always more strident and insistent than they had been before."

Listening to Stephen tell this story now, I marvel that he managed to survive his school days at all. Few kids, especially in these later years of academic education where there is a sustained force-feeding of facts designed to get them through specific exams with grades that are a credit to the school if not to the child, find the educational process easy. In Stephen's case he was working with a profound handicap and it is all credit to his resourcefulness and determination that he got grades as good as he did. By his own admission they were not *good* grades, but they got him through, albeit at a price.

At 16 years old Stephen took the brave and unprecedented step of going to see his local doctor. "I had to do something! The voices in my head were becoming unbearable. I couldn't sleep properly, I wasn't eating and I couldn't think straight. I thought I might be having some sort of nervous breakdown, so I reckoned that if I could get some tranquillisers or something, I might be able to turn things around a bit."

Now you could say that God looks after his own, or you could just say that Stephen was extremely lucky in his choice of doctor. What is fairly clear is the fact that most doctors would either have prescribed the requested tranquillisers or passed their patient on for some kind of psychiatric assessment... Stephen's GP, a much more enlightened soul, listened to everything Stephen had to say, before offering a prescription.

"I think," said the good doctor, "that before I start filling your system with drugs, you should pay a visit to Peterson Road."

"Er, yes, of course," young Stephen stammered in response, thinking that perhaps he was being passed on to some kind of specialist clinic. "But what's at Peterson Road?"

"The local spiritualist church," the doctor had replied soberly. "But there's just one thing, if you *do* decide to pay them a visit, don't tell anyone that I sent you!"

In Stephen's first book 'The Light in the Darkness' we discuss this incident in more detail and give an in-depth insight into the philosophy of The Spiritualist Church. Suffice to say that this was his first formal contact with the spiritualist movement, and it has to be said that the church at Peterson Road served him well. They were quick to realise that they had a budding medium on their hands, and over a number of months they taught him how to control the insistent babble of voices which so frequently filled his young and inexperienced mind, and eventually to such an extent that he could hear *individual* voices, and ultimately he came to understand much of what they were saying to him.

He was taught that these voices were spirit voices trying to make contact with the earth plane, and because through a quirk of genes and DNA, Stephen was a natural clairaudient medium, it was inevitable that the voices should home in on the psychic signal which, unbeknown to him, he had been emitting since the onset of puberty. Inevitably he was exposed to the beliefs and teachings of the church, and because they made total sense to him, he had no problem in embracing them with an open mind and an open heart. He sensed rather than intellectualised the fundamental truth that death is a natural transition from one life to another, and was unbelievably excited by the idea that it might be possible to communicate between the two worlds. He took this not just from his mentors at Peterson Road, but also from those voices speaking quietly inside his head.

Nevertheless, the ever practical side of his nature said that he had to do something to earn a living, and after much thought, he enrolled at a hair dressing college, where he proved to be a natural! This was a brilliant career pathway because it gave him first-hand experience in interacting with the public and he realised that he could communicate on all sorts of different levels with the people who sat in his chair. I suppose it was kind of inevitable that after a while he started picking up thought form messages for his clients, and the word quickly went round that if you wanted to talk to your late Uncle Alfred or Auntie Mary while having your hair done, Steve Holbrook was the man to see. When I met him all those years ago his first client of the day was often booked in at 7.30 am and he was lucky to get out of the salon much before 6.30 pm, and indeed, much later than that on nights when he didn't have a demonstration of clairvoyance to go to. I have often speculated as to how many of Stephen's clients came to see him because he was a very good hairdresser, and how many came to see him because he was turning out to be a very good medium.

Chapter Three
Mentors

As we go through our lives, especially perhaps when we are younger, we meet a lot of people. This is particularly true if one is working with the public at large. Inevitably then, in Stephen's early years as a medium, *he* met a whole host of different people... There were those folk who had received messages from him, there were newspaper editors and advertising managers; on top of that there were friends that he made in a purely social environment, and just as I, as a musician, would gravitate towards other musicians, so quite naturally did Stephen gravitate towards other spiritualists and mediums.

One of the first contacts Stephen made was with a medium called Una Pierce from Huddersfield. When he phoned her to arrange a consultation, she told him that her appointments book was full, almost through till the end of the year, but then proceeded to give him a devastatingly accurate reading over the telephone, answering all the questions he'd wanted to ask and describing the clothes he was wearing, even down to the fact that he had his grandfather's old watch on his wrist. Sometime later Una and Stephen did meet up and she became a close ally and teacher.

However, of far greater influence was Stephen's relationship with Eric Hatton, who was the doyen of the Stourbridge Spiritualist Church and a leading light within the Spiritualists National Union down at Stanstead Hall in Essex. Stephen would only have been in his early 20s when he first met him, while Eric was over 60. Despite the disparity in ages, Eric took Stephen under his wing and the two men became firm friends. Eric was very pleased and impressed with

Stephen's work, and he was always on hand with spiritual guidance and helpful advice... and I suppose Eric's recommendation and sponsorship did nothing to harm Steve's already growing reputation. In return, over the years, Steve brought through a number of messages for Eric, including a communication from a dead friend who had died in a mysterious car accident. The crash investigation team had been unable to identify the cause of the accident, but retelling the events from the driver's point of view, Stephen was able to pinpoint the precise cause of the accident and thus, in Eric's mind at least, the mystery was solved.

Old age comes to us all (as I know too damned well from personal experience) and in Eric Hatton's later years he became increasingly frail in body, although still bright in mind. The last time Stephen saw him was at Wolverhampton Civic Theatre, when escorted by a lady called Sue Farrow from the *Psychic News* newspaper, he joined Stephen on stage at the end of the demonstration to receive a round of applause for his outstanding services to spiritualism. Later on that same evening, Sue Farrow asked if Stephen would be prepared to do an in depth interview for the paper, and when Stephen promptly said that he would be delighted, Sue promised to send him a questionnaire, which would set the template for the interview. A short while later Stephen was deeply saddened to hear that his old friend Eric had passed away, and two weeks after that, he received the questionnaire from *Psychic News*.

Now, for you to understand the significance of what happened next, we need to backtrack a little and take a look at how the business side of Stephen's work has changed over the last 20 years.

When I met him in 1999 he was demonstrating in small halls, mainly around his home county of Yorkshire, but with occasional forays across the border into Lancashire and down to the Midlands. The admission price was £4, and people would pay on the door. Certainly, they could phone and reserve a seat, but even then they were asked to turn up on the night and pay on the door – and while some of them did, some of them didn't, creating a situation whereby Stephen never knew exactly how many seats he might have spare, or in a worst case scenario, how many people he might have to turn away. This was always a tense state of affairs, which occasionally caused some resentment among Stephen's customers who thought they had booked a seat, arrived a bit late, and then found that their seat was not available.

And yet, having said that, the method, while not perfect, still worked reasonably well, and it suited Stephen to do things in this way. Remember, at that time he was a one man band, and had to do all the arranging himself... Booking the hall, placing the adverts in the local papers, manning the box office, then changing personas, and marching onto the stage as the star of the show.

When it was mooted that I should promote him in some of his venues, the business plan for those venues changed slightly: for the sake of ease and simplicity we maintained the pay on the door policy, but advance bookings had to pay in advance and tickets were issued. On the evening of the events, we would keep careful note of how many ticket holders arrived at the venue, and always held back the requisite number of seats that might be required until the very last minute. We felt we could get away with this by telling the people who bought tickets that they had to be there at least fifteen minutes before the demonstration started, otherwise their reservations might be forfeit.

In promoting Stephen I felt that my brief was quite simple. First, I had to get him into bigger and more prestigious venues, and I had to introduce him to a wider public. Stephen had two friends who arranged events for him in the south-west, which left me with pretty well the rest of the country to play with. Over a three year period we introduced him to venues on Tyneside, Scotland, the North Yorkshire coast, East Anglia, Essex and Kent, Gloucestershire, Warwickshire and Hampshire. We forsook the caverns of old town halls, and instead used the function rooms of three or four star hotels and small theatres like Retford Little Theatre, the Newark Palace Theatre, The Spa Centre in Leamington, The Quay Theatre in Brighton and the Kenton Theatre in Henley-on-Thames.

We usually played to full houses, and there were two good reasons for this. Clairvoyance and mediumship was suddenly the flavour of the month on TV, and mediums like Colin Fry and Derek Acorah were becoming household names. Secondly, instead of spending a hundred quid on a couple of little 3x4 adverts, we would frequently spend the better part of £1,000 on bigger and bolder adverts. Also, by then, my wife Jo and I were equipped to take credit card payments over the phone, which put paid once and for all to the chaos frequently experienced at the box office on the actual nights of the demonstrations.

One of the first things that I did was raise the price of entrance from £4 to £6... Stephen was very dubious about this, not thinking that people would be prepared to pay that kind of money. However, they did, and when the ticket price increased over an 11 year period to a whacking great £13, no one ever complained and indeed, many people told me to my face that Stephen's evidence would have been worth twice the price.

Let me reiterate, that at no time was I ever responsible for *all* of Stephen's demonstrations, and indeed the events that were promoted by myself only ever accounted for about 20% of his overall workload. And yet, there was an obvious knock on effect. With his own venues, he realised that he was seriously undercharging for his tickets, he also realised the advantage of letting someone else take the bookings for his various demonstrations, which brought his mother Margaret into the Holbrook Business Plan, and it was she, who for many years, took bookings over the phone for him. The other thing that dawned on him was just how tiring it was driving the better part of 40,000 miles a year across the land to and from his various venues, and how much nicer it was to be driven in a comfortable car (either by me or my wife Jo) while he curled up and fell asleep in the back. Eventually, this led to him finding a full time manager-cum-chauffeur – but that is another story for later on in this book.

In 2010 I was persuaded, primarily by my wife Jo, with some gentle encouragement from Steve, to give up the promoting business. I wasn't happy about it at first – in fact I felt very low and rejected, but with hindsight, I can see why it had to happen. I was getting old, and stale, and grumpy... I'd had major heart surgery and had had two subsequent heart attacks. I had run out of patience with clients if I thought they were being rude and out of order, and was finding the whole business very stressful. In effect, I was no longer being much help to Stephen and his work, and in many respects I had become something of a hindrance.

With the benefit of hindsight and objectivity, I now see very clearly that it was the right thing to do, and I take some mischievous solace in the thought that in my own way, maybe I was a minor mentor in Stephen's kaleidoscopic world, for if I made the man realise that he was worth more than four quid a seat, and that there were a whole load of other people out there in Britain who could benefit from his remarkable gifts, then I did him no harm.

Concomitant to all this, there is another factor which is most relevant. Jumping on the bandwagon of TV mediumship, the newspapers who had been taking Steve's money for years (mine too!) suddenly saw a way in which they could *make* some money out of Stephen's gifts, and the Readers' Services and Readers' Holidays departments suggested that they present him in a variety of venues. All the advertising costs and ticket sales would be down to them, and all he would have to do was turn up, do the demonstrating, then take a percentage of the profit as his fee.

Initially this sounded like a deal sent from Heaven, and so it was. Instead of placing 5x3 adverts, the papers would splash out with half a flaming page, and if bookings were a bit slow, well they'd put in another couple of half pages! If Steve and I had had to do that, we'd have been broke and out of business in a fortnight! So, for a while, this worked very well... but then after a year or so of this being the status quo, Stephen began to feel uneasy, and he was hard pressed to know exactly why.

Now then, let's get back to Eric Hatton. Stephen missed him. He'd been an anchor point in Steve's life for many years, and now he wasn't there any more... Not in the flesh anyway. When Sue Farrow's questionnaire arrived in the post it was a particularly busy morning. Stephen glanced at it, thought that some of the questions were totally irrelevant, and threw it across the desk to Rob Green.

"Here," he said, "Rob, sort this out for me will you, just put whatever you think is right, then get it back in the post."

At that point, he heard Eric Hatton's voice speaking clearly in his ear... Not as some discarnate entity, but as though the man was standing right next to him in the flesh.

"Stephen, I am very disappointed in you!" The voice sounded stern – and, well, very disappointed! And Stephen knew why.

"Rob," he called across the office. "Changed my mind. Bring the questionnaire back and let's have a look at it together and do the best we can with it."

Thus, with due diligence and care the questionnaire was filled in and dispatched back to Stanstead Hall.

Sometime later, after Sue Farrow's article had been written, she phoned him one morning, sounding very flustered and confused. There had been a séance at Stanstead Hall the previous night and Eric had come through, asking to speak to Stephen Holbrook. Stephen, of course had not been there, and Ms Farrow was less than pleased when Stephen had to tell her several times that he had no idea what Eric wanted to talk to him about. Also, although he didn't mention it over the phone, Stephen couldn't understand why Eric might want to talk to him through a medium when it was glaringly apparent that he could talk to Stephen directly if he so chose, the business with the questionnaire proving the point.

A few weeks after this incident, Stephen and Rob were sunbathing on a beautiful Spanish beach. It was a much deserved, and in Stephen's case, *necessary* holiday. He'd been working six days a week for the better part of six months without any kind of break, and he was fairly exhausted. After three days of unpressurised relaxation he finally found himself beginning to unwind, and without any formal agenda, looked back over the last few years of his life. On the surface, he had everything going for him, but on the inside, he was far from happy – and maddeningly, he couldn't find a coherent reason for this state of mind. He told himself that maybe he was just tired, but in his heart of hearts, he knew it was more than that.

Eric Hatton was still fresh in his mind, and as is always the case when you think of dead friends, you remember the times you shared with them, both the good and the bad, and you become aware of that hollow spot in your solar plexus that feels so empty without them. Look, I can't even begin to prove this, but I think that Man does have a soul, and it resides not in the heart or the mind, but in the solar plexus. This is where we hold and nurse our pain, and until you tell me otherwise, I suspect it is the same for all of us.

So, Steve is lying there, stinking of Ambre Solaire, and unbidden, Eric Hatton's voice is suddenly speaking in his ear. Just as had been the case with the questionnaire, it is not a discarnate voice coming from within his head, but rather from someone sitting next to him, speaking directly into his ear.

"Stephen," says Eric's voice, "go back to your roots!"

The message was not repeated, and nor did it need to be, for Stephen understood quite perfectly what Eric meant.

As soon as he got home Stephen began to put Eric's advice into action, and during the following months he divested himself of the lucrative but mercenary newspaper contracts, and started booking his own venues again, this time taking on a much higher percentage of engagements at spiritualist churches and committing himself to a far greater number of charity events. He did not revert to the 'pay on the door' system, but made a point of finding smaller venues, perhaps a bit off the beaten track, and in so doing, picked up his initial quest of bringing the evidence of post mortem survival to people who otherwise might never hear it. On the downside, he sacrificed a major chunk of his income, but on the upside, he became a significantly happier man, knowing that Eric Hatton had been right, and that by following the arrow Eric had drawn in the sand, he had done the right thing.

Chapter Four
Evidence I

Within the contents of Stephen's first three books there are pages and pages of evidence of post mortem survival. This evidence has been collected from the first hand testimony of those who have received messages from their loved ones, confirmed by family members and friends. Between us, Stephen and I have received many hundreds of letters and emails which have provided detailed corroboration, and I have 11 years' worth of notes and tape recordings which fill a very large filing cabinet in the corner of my office, taken or recorded from recipients of messages on the night upon which they were received.

Some of the evidence (frequently accompanied by photographs) is poignantly sad, some of it is a bit weird and even spooky, and some of it is hilariously funny – which just goes to prove that occasionally there is humour in tragedy. However, Stephen cannot always be relied upon to see the humour, and I well remember the night in Darlington when he told a gentleman on the front row that "it's really nice to meet a man who comes more than once" and asked a lady in Stratford if she was "hot in bed?" On both occasions the audience rocked with laughter, leaving Stephen standing on the stage wondering what on earth he'd said to create such hilarity. I had to explain it to him afterwards, but even then he didn't quite get it. Then there was the occasion when he was talking to a lady on the front row, and told her that he had her late husband with him who wanted to say hello. The lady cut him off sharply and told him to "send him back 'cos I couldn't stick the old bugger!"

Probably one of the funniest things I heard at a demonstration (and forgive me, because I know I have told this story before!) happened at a demonstration in Retford. Stephen was struggling to get a message through from somebody called Richard, a gentleman who wanted to talk to a lady in the audience. No one claimed the message, and Steve had to edge his way forwards to establish the identity of the man who was trying to make the contact.

"He's telling me that he passed over quite some time ago, at least five or six years ago, after a long illness…"

Still no one could claim the message from Richard.

"He's telling me that he was always a snappy dresser, and you hardly ever saw him without a suit and a tie…"

Still no audience response.

"He's shouting his name at me now, and he's saying 'tell her it's Richard' over and over again, and I know for certain that there is someone in this audience tonight who knew a smart looking man called Richard who passed over a few years ago!"

Tentatively a busty looking young woman with a short skirt and fishnet tights stands up over to the left of the auditorium and waves her hand nervously in the air.

"I can't take a Richard," she calls out, "but I can take a Dick!"

It took the better part of five minutes for some semblance of levity to return to the theatre, and I promise you, this tale is neither apocryphal nor a joke. It really did happen, and I was there at the time to bear witness to the event!

I was talking to Stephen a couple of weeks ago, and he told me the following tale which just goes to prove that Spirit occasionally sees the funny side of things. If they didn't, then this evidence might never have seen the light of day.

Stephen was demonstrating in Salford, and half way through his introduction, two ladies arrived late, and shuffled their way to the only two free seats in the building which were halfway down a long row of seats. Stephen paused in the presentation to allow for the scuffing of chairs and the repeated raised whispers of "Sorry." At one point, the second of the two ladies looked up at Stephen, and apologised directly. "Sorry we're late! The flaming car wouldn't start!"

Stephen, not in the least bit perturbed, grinned down at them. "Don't worry," he said. "I'm just glad you could make it, because I've got a message for you and I'll be coming to you in a minute!"

Steve finished the introduction then honed in directly on the two late arrivals. "I've got a message here from your Dad… At least, I have if your Dad's name is Brian…"

The two ladies look at each other in mutual shock, and admit that their late father's name was, in fact Brian.

"And he's telling me," Stephen continued, "that he's got a message for the twins. Do you know who the twins are, my loves?"

"We're twins…" the first lady replied. "Twin sisters!"

They were obviously not identical twins, for there was a marked difference in their appearance.

"Okay," Stephen continues, unflustered. "Now, he's telling me something about a lilac coloured car and fish and chips. Does this make any sense to you?"

Now, you might think that reference to a lilac coloured car and fish and chips is a bit of a parochial thing to say if one is seeking to provide evidence of post mortem survival, but for these twin sisters, it was totally incontrovertible evidence. When you hear the back story, you'll understand why.

There was not a lot of money in the family, and to save a few quid, the ladies forewent the usual hearse, but dropped the back seats down of their lilac coloured estate car, and slid their father's inexpensive basket weave coffin in behind the driver's seat. Half way to the crematorium, they realised that they were going to be far too early, so stopped off at the local Morrison's café for a fish and chip lunch, leaving the car and the coffin parked in Morrisons' car park! Their father had obviously joined them for lunch, if not in the flesh, than certainly in spirit!

It is the *little* things like this, the little seemingly inconsequential *details* that make Stephen's evidence so strong. If you were going to fake a message or whatever, how on earth would you conjure up a scenario like that? Stephen followed up this introductory evidence with a host of other information, but a lilac coloured car and fish and chips does it for me.

When Stephen was approached by tour operator Jean Merry and offered the chance to go cruising, initially in the Mediterranean and then subsequently in the Caribbean, his first inclination was to say no. Nevertheless, after some pushing and encouragement from yours truly, he did go and meet Ms Merry, which led to a happy and fruitful shipboard collaboration and led to the establishment of 'The Clairvoyant Cruises'. Stephen is an absolute sun bunny and Rob, his manager, needs to phone a cloud therapist even if there is only the faintest smudge on the distant horizon, and I suspect that the thought of ten days in the sun in the middle of an English winter was no small incentive to give it a try.

During the third cruise, Steve and Rob thought it would be a nice gesture to buy Jean a very special present, just to thank her for all her hard work, which they would present to her at the end of his last shipboard demonstration. Jean had absolutely no idea that this plan was afoot, and the boys thought that she might like the rather jazzy (and rather expensive) novelty watch that they'd chosen from the ship's duty free shop.

Prior to that last demonstration Jean found herself in conversation with a couple from Canada who were taking the cruise as part of a bereavement process as they mourned the loss of their beautiful young daughter. Quite logically, Jean started talking to them about Stephen's gift, and invited them along to that evening's demonstration. She was rather surprised when they turned up, because despite her invitation, she'd quietly thought that they looked like people who might not be interested in Stephen's line of work.

Now, to clarify things. Jean had never met this couple before. The couple had never heard of Stephen Holbrook, and didn't even realise that there was this 'clairvoyant thing' happening on board ship. Jean had no idea that the boys had bought her a watch a couple of days before, and neither Steve nor Rob had met the Canadian couple before. One other thing I would ask you to take into consideration is the fact that when Stephen is demonstrating he becomes detached from the 'real' world and wouldn't even know what he'd eaten for dinner that night, let alone what he might have bought in the duty free shop two or three days previously.

During the demonstration, he brought a detailed message through for the Canadian couple from a young girl who had passed into spirit late in the previous year, who he identified as being their daughter. He described her appearance, provided details of her passing and, after some initial struggling, came up with her name. He thought it sounded like Dominique, but then corrected himself, and settled on the more unusual name of Domino.

The grieving couple were delighted and amazed by this message, and perhaps it could be said that this was when their healing process really began, knowing that their daughter was still alive, albeit in another realm and dimension.

The real punch of this story comes when half an hour later, Jean Merry was presented with her gift, and opened it there and then, to find a most unusual wristwatch attached to a broad strap covered in dominos!

Stephen believes that this was Domino's way of saying thank you to Jean for talking to her parents and persuading them to attend the demonstration, just so that she could make contact and give them the strength and courage they needed to press on without her. Could this be just a coincidence? Well, it *could* have been, I suppose, but in my opinion it would be stretching all credulity, and I don't know what you think, but I am inclined to agree with Stephen. One thing I have learned is that if spirit wants to make contact with you they will go to some extraordinary lengths to get their message through. This we shall see in greater detail later on in the book.

Our first visit to Sunderland was an extremely tense affair because we had booked a room at the local leisure centre with 200 seats, but when we arrived we were told that there had been a double booking and that the 200 seat room was no longer available, but not to worry, there was another room available. The trouble was that this 'other room' could only seat 100 and we had already sold 200 tickets. Despite the fact that we had a contract which stipulated and confirmed a 200 seat room, the local official was completely intransigent and we were told to take it or leave it because it wasn't *his* fault. So, we did our best to cram 200 people into the smaller room, which meant that many people who had been told over the phone that they could just come along and pay on the door, had to be turned away. This caused a lot of anger and ill-will, which was not a good start to a spiritual event.

Nevertheless, Steve took to the stage and did his best in these very adverse circumstances. He brought through some good evidence, but quite honestly it was hard going. The room was hot, stuffy and overcrowded and the audience didn't seem to be in much of a mood to give him any kind of help. Despite all this, one message sticks out very clearly.

"I want," Stephen began cautiously, "to talk to a lady who lost her husband a number of years ago, and although this gentleman would have passed over in hospital, he passed as a result of some kind of accident, rather than natural causes. He's giving me the name of Barbara…?"

A lady called out from the back of the room… "My name is Barbara, and I lost my husband a few years back in the way that you describe."

"All right m'love… He's telling me something about a pipe, so did your husband smoke a pipe?"

"No definitely not."

"Okay, erm, he's mentioning the letter C, so does that mean anything to you?"

"No."

"I wonder if I've got that wrong," Stephen mused, "so tell me, did he have anything to do with the sea? Was he a fisherman?"

"Yes and no," came the tight reply. Obviously the lady was determined not to give anything away.

This caused Stephen to pause for a long few seconds, then when he spoke again it was as though some sort of green light had gone on in his brain.

"No, he wasn't a fisherman but he did work on the sea?"

"Yes."

Stephen: "Now I'm getting a whiff of oil, so did he work on one of the drilling platforms?"

"Yes, that's right?"

"Who is Pat or Patrick?"

"That was his name, but no one ever called him that."

Stephen inclined his head to one side as though listening to an unseen voice. "What about George or Georgy?"

"You're close. He was known as Geordie."

Stephen smiled sadly. "But I don't think he ever liked being called that, did he, bearing in mind he was a Sunderland man and wasn't born anywhere near Tyneside."

"You're right about that."

"What's the significance of a red car?"

The lady cracked her face and smiled for the first time. "That's where he was from. Redcar."

"And what does the number 88 mean to you? All the eights, two fat ladies, 88?"

"He died in 1988."

"Did he have anything to do with Bingo?"

"No, that were me. I used to play every week but he hated the bloody game."

Stephen: "He's telling me about the 4th of August. Does that date mean anything to you?"

"Ay, it does. That's the day we buried him."

"And were there a lot of people there? A lot of people you didn't know and had never met?"

"Half the town turned up and we couldn't get 'em all inside the church. He was a popular lad, was our Pat."

Stephen: "I'm feeling very hot and cold at the same time, and I've got that oily smell again and I can taste salt in my mouth. Please, m'love, does this mean anything to you at all?"

"Ay, more or less."

There was another pregnant pause while Stephen gathered his thoughts together, then, to use one of his own euphemisms, decided he was trying to push a snowball up hill, and brought the contact to a close.

"All right, m'love, just to finish off with, he's telling me that he's feeling fit and fine and that he's finally got his swimming pool, complete with the dolphins on the bottom, oh, and that he never expected to see you in a place like this... So anyway, thanks and good night... And are you sure he didn't ever smoke a pipe?"

"No never, sorry, only..." Barbara shook her head and fell silent. Stephen closed down the link and went to the next message.

On the surface, this seems like a relatively weak contact – and it certainly was a hard message to get over – but when I spoke to the lady at the end of the demonstration, she was able to throw light on the subject which indicated that Stephen had been absolutely on target with his words.

Her husband Patrick had died in 1988 on the Alpha Piper drilling platform in the North Sea. He'd been very badly burned and had jumped into the sea, where he'd been picked up by one of the rescue boats. Sadly, he had died a few hours later in hospital. When armed with this information it makes sense of just about everything Stephen said... Being hot and cold at the same time, smelling oil, tasting salt, the number 88, the mention of pipes linking with Alpha *Piper*, referencing a red car in connection with his place of birth which turned out to be Redcar, identifying two principle names, Patrick and Barbara… And for Barbara the absolute clincher was Steve's reference to a swimming pool with a dolphin design decorating the bottom. Patrick had been going on about wanting his own swimming pool for ages, and he'd always said that when he got it, it would have to have dolphins on the bottom. Indeed, he'd been working extra tours of duty on Alpha Piper to facilitate the purchase of such a luxury.

The lady called Barbara had been very tense and negative about the whole evening and had only gone along to keep her friend company. It is rather ironic that, in the circumstances, she got a message while her friend (who would have loved one) did not. I suppose it's also rather sad that had Barbara been a bit more open to what was going on around her, she might have got a lot more information and evidence out of the message. In her defence, she had been very surprised when Stephen had picked on her, and hey, sometimes that's just the way it goes.

Chapter Five
Guides

Stephen and I both thought it would be a good idea if we spent a few moments talking about guides – not the girl guides or tour guides, but the spirit guides who help mediums bring through the messages from the 'other' world and protect them while they are in the process of facilitating such messages.

Sad to say, spirit guides have become a bit of a cliché, no small thanks to the media's representation of such entities and not helped by people who are *not* mediums but who would so very much like to be one.

It has become de rigour to claim that one's spirit guide is either a Native American Indian, Chinese Mandarin or a Tibetan Monk and I even know of one self-professed clairvoyant lady who, while on a flight to Egypt, informed her companions that she had been contacted by both Isis and Nefertiti who had volunteered their services as spirit guides for the duration of her stay in Cairo and Luxor. There was even one man working in Yorkshire who claimed that his spirit guide was no less a personage than St. Peter himself! And yet, in our experience, spirit guides are usually quite ordinary souls, made extraordinary by their willingness to serve the cause of spiritual enlightenment.

With a smile, I remember one lady who firmly believed that her spirit guide was a priest from the lost city of Atlantis. When I asked her if she knew his name, she told me it was "Santorini" and when I asked her where she thought Atlantis might be, she looked at me scornfully and said: "Santorini, of course!".

Now, while it is true that many archaeologists think that if Atlantis ever existed, it was probably on the island of Santorini in the eastern Mediterranean, destroyed in 1646 BC by the eruption of one of the most violent detonations ever recorded, there is no hard evidence to indicate that this had anything to do with Atlantis. There is no doubt that there was such an eruption and that, indeed, it totally wiped out the Minoan civilisation. Sadly, as any advanced psychic investigator will tell you, with regard to Atlantis, the location is totally wrong! There is powerful evidence, albeit from spiritual knowledge rather than anything archaeological, which suggests that Atlantis was located many thousands of miles away on the eastern sea board of Lemuria, which at that time was a small continent slap bang in the middle of the Atlantic Ocean! Go in search of your own evidence – it's not that hard to find – and failing all else, ask the flaming lemmings!

Stephen has a number of guides, some of which are known to him, but others who are simply there for a few minutes to introduce him to a spiritual entity which wishes to pass on a message or messages to someone here on the earth plane, who just happens to be in Stephen's audience on any given night. There are, however, three clearly identifiable guides who are with Stephen almost on a permanent basis.

The first is an army Sergeant called Archie May who was killed in the Great War circa 1917. Because records, including census records, were available to us, we did some quite extensive research, the results of which were published in our earlier book 'Survival'. Archie was blown up in the trenches, and subsequently died from his wounds. Before the war he had been a hairdresser from Lancashire (an amazing coincidence when you consider that Steve's early career was also as a hairdresser) and furthermore Archie was also a committed spiritualist. He is quite a dour taciturn character, marshalling his spiritual contacts in rather a militaristic way. Whenever he joins with Stephen, Stephen's left arm becomes deformed into a cold rictus, and there is some evidence which suggests that Archie lost his left arm in the explosion which ultimately ended his time down here on the earth plane.

The second of Stephen's guides is a young boy of about 10 or 11 years old. His name is Christopher, and Stephen visualises him as being something of a street urchin from the very early part of the 20th or late 19th century. Invariably Christopher connects with spirit children who have passed before their time, who are trying to convey messages to their parents. These messages are understandably laced with drama and emotion and yet Christopher seems to handle things from his side of the veil with a calm and cheerful disposition. Stephen is convinced that he "sees" Christopher as he was at the time of his passing. He certainly died very young and did not, as they say, make old bones. Despite this, the young boy's aura and persona seem to be very mature, and certainly beyond his years. In his time on earth, he would, perhaps, have been regarded as 'a very old spirit'.

Stephen's third guide is a large black man called Warren. Steve thinks that Warren might have spent many years incarcerated in a prison. Warren seems to be particularly connected with people who have died sudden and violent deaths, including suicides, and those who have experienced the earth bound agonies of depression, substance abuse and mental disorders. Whenever Warren makes his presence felt, Stephen knows that he might be in for a rough ride. Warren also provides hard evidence for the fact that despite the traditional teachings of the Christian church, there is no purgatorial penance paid by those who, for whatever reason, have come to the conclusion that they have no choice other than to take their own lives. Logically, the suffering these souls have undergone to cause them to take such sad and drastic action, is penance enough!

When we speak of spirit guides we immediately think of those entities who work in partnership with clairvoyants and mediums, but there is another kind of spirit guide whose duties and purposes are less well defined, but no less important. We believe that everyone has at least one spirit guide, and on many occasions more than just one, but in the vast majority of cases we mortals are unaware of their presence except on those rare occasions when they do make themselves known to us. Furthermore, we do not have to be clairvoyant to experience this phenomena.

An example of this might be seen in the story of Sergeant Burt Watts, who after being evacuated from Dunkirk in 1940 was given a few months' recuperation in England before being posted to Singapore just in time to be taken prisoner by the Japanese. He spent a year in the notorious Changi jail, and then was dumped in the middle of the jungle where he became one of the tortured POWs who were forced to build the famous Burma railway line. He was actually one of the men who built the bridge over the River Kwai and, without going into detail, suffice to say that his four years of suffering beneath the Japanese bayonet were quite profound.

Burt was a stoic East Anglian man from farming stock, and not at all given to flights of fancy; indeed, he was a professional soldier, well-disciplined in keeping his emotions tightly in check. In the face of inhumane barbarity during his captivity, there were many times when he felt that he was never going to get out of Burma alive and he seriously considered taking his own life. And yet, when he was at his very lowest ebb he had visions, both sleeping and waking, of a beautiful Chinese girl who spoke to him in a language he could not understand. Nevertheless, he knew she was telling him to hold on and to be strong, because one day he would be rescued from this hell on earth. Over a forty month period she visited him at least a dozen times, and each visitation brought him a quality of calmness, along with a renewed sense of determination to survive. He describes her as being a tall willowy girl with long black hair, always wearing a silver cheongsam, with a black motif on her breast which looked like *Li* … He doesn't know if this was her name or if the motif had some other more obtuse meaning, but over the months he came to think of her as being Li.

Burt returned home in late 1945 and was discharged from the army three or four years later having reached the rank of RSM. He never spoke of his ordeal or his experience, except on one occasion when, in the most stressful and extraordinary circumstances, he spoke at length to me. Burt was my uncle, and acted as a father figure on the single occasion in my life when I needed a father figure. The story of his torture did much to alleviate the torture I myself was going through at the time, and I have never forgotten what he told me. Burt was not any kind of spiritualist, but he was an intelligent man, and recognised the Chinese girl as being someone or something not of this world.

A very sad anecdote in association with Burt Watts is that after spending four years of living on stale rice boiled in urine, his wife could never understand why he refused to eat the rice pudding she served on a regular basis at least twice a week!

I go to great lengths in telling people that while I have some psychic ability, I am *not* a clairvoyant. And yet there are times in my life, especially if I am struggling with a reading for a client, when my grandmother makes her presence felt in my mind. She gives me a nudge, maybe a clue, a small boost of fresh energy, which usually gets me over the hump. Sometimes, after having lost sleep over a difficult decision, I finally *make* a decision, and then I get a mental picture of an early mentor called Ossie Rae (professionally known as The Great Zareada, and one of the best mediums I have ever come across) – Ossie shakes his head vigorously to tell me it is the wrong decision and I should think again, or nods his head in approval. My memories of this remarkable man come flooding back, but no words ever pass between us. I recognise my grandmother and Ossie as being spiritual entities who are watching over me, and I am thankful for their presence, even though they only ever make their presence known within my mind.

Spirit guides are never malevolent, but evidence suggests that sometimes they can be highly mischievous, and a case in point involves a medium called Michael, whom Steve and I both knew well a few years ago and who, in our separate ways, tried to help along his pathway.

Michael grew up in a care home in North Wales and was systematically sexually abused from a very early age. Little wonder then that his teens and early 20s were tense and turbulent years, and little wonder that he turned to drugs and alcohol for sustenance. Inevitably, shifting from squat to squat and living his life on the very outside edge of society, he fell in with the wrong people, who did nothing at all to assist him in his desire for a normal and stable life style.

After one disastrous night of excess, he collapsed on the street and huddled into the nearest doorway for shelter. The doorway in question was the front door of a leading light in the local spiritualist church: she found him on her steps the following morning, shivering with cold, and barely conscious. Cutting a long story short, she took him in, clothed him, fed him, found him a job and introduced him to the spiritualists in her group. These were the first acts of kindness and compassion that Michael had ever experienced in his life, and it was natural that in the fullness of time, he too became a spiritualist. Sitting in a number of psychic circles, it soon became apparent that he had some clairvoyant ability of his own that he was extremely eager to develop... and it was around this time that he came into contact with Stephen and myself. If you were being unkind, you could say that he became a Stephen Holbrook groupie, but he was desperately eager to learn, and he didn't have to be 'Brains of The North' to realise that if he was going to learn anything at all, he might as well learn from the best.

Perhaps because he had been exposed to the traditions of the spiritualist church, he took it as a norm that all mediums should have a spirit guide. Thus, it was somewhat inevitable that he 'found' one of his own. No Red Feathers here, or Tibetan monks, but rather an odd-bod of an entity which Michael always referred to as 'The Jester'. Michael described him to me once as being a wizened old hunchback dressed in a mediaeval jester's costume of red and green. He had a care worn face, but with youthful dark eyes, that were, in Michael's own words, "full of love and laughter". To all intents and purposes, there was no malice in The

Jester, but he certainly did have a wicked sense of humour.

I clearly remember the night that I went to see Michael's first professional evening of clairvoyance, which was being held in the function room of a local pub. It was quite a decent sized room, and there were about 30 people in attendance. As you can imagine, Michael was extremely nervous, and for my part I thought the least I could do was to go along and lend a bit of moral support.

At the appointed time, Michael walked out onto what could be described as a small cabaret floor or performance area.

"Good evening," he said, "my name is Michael and…"

At that point there was a very loud and extremely shrill ringing which sent the man behind the bar scuttling over to a bank of switches on the wall behind him. "Sorry," he shouted, once the ringing ceased. "Bloody fire alarm!"

"Good evening," Michael began again. "Like I was saying, my name is Michael and I'd like to welcome you to this demonstration of clairvoyance…"

Once again the fire alarm exploded into life, this time seemingly more loud and strident than it had been before. Again the barman did a mid-stride Irish jig over to the bank of switches, cut the power, causing the alarm to fall silent.

"As I was saying," Michael forced a smile to his flustered face, "I'd like to welcome you to this demonstration of…"

For a third time the fire alarm kicked off, causing a few of the customers to burst into giggles while others just sat there with their fingers in their ears and painful expressions on their faces.

This happened twice more – five times in all – before Michael was able to begin. I can't be sure of the connection, but after the fifth interruption two hard faced Goth girls, covered in tattoos and body piercings, got up from their seats and made a scornful exit from the room. Michael says, and I can believe him, that they represented a very negative energy and his Jester wasn't going to let him begin until they had gone. All in all, Michael's debut demonstration wasn't very good, but in his defence, it was no worse than some of the demonstrations I have seen from other more experienced and 'celebrity' mediums, and with a start like the one that he'd had, who could blame him if he was nervous and rattled?

On another occasion Michael was sitting in a pub with a group of friends and was just about to leave when a mate plonked a fresh pint of beer down in front of him. Michael, who knew he'd already had more than enough and who was well aware of the fact that he'd told his new wife that he was just popping out for half an hour for a 'quick' drink, looked at the dark amber liquid with a degree of desperation and trepidation.

"Can anyone else drink this?" he begged, "because I really do have to get back home."

"Oh get it down you," his so called mate challenged. "One more pint isn't going to do you any harm!"

Michael was about to reach out to take the drink, but at that point, as though swiped by an unseen hand, the pint toppled over, spilling the contents all over Michael's lap and totally ruining his new cream trousers. He had no choice other than to leave the pub, and got home just in time to avert a nasty domestic accident caused by his wife falling asleep on the sofa while a couple of live coals had fallen out of the fire and were smouldering merrily on the rug in front of her. Michael assures me that no one had touched the pint of beer and takes it as a sign that his Jester was looking after him that night. Unbeknown to us all, Michael's Jester was destined to have a much more important role in Michael's life a few years down the road.

An interesting point to be made here is that most mystics, psychics and shamans need solitude to make contact with their inner spiritual strength. Sometimes they seek this solitude quite willingly, but on many occasions, it is forced upon them. This can be a painful and lonely process, but the darker the cloud, the more brightly shines the silver lining.

A question which both Stephen and I frequently get asked is "how do you recognise your spirit guide?" For some people the answer is easy, for others a little more difficult, and for a small minority, it is *very* difficult bordering on the impossible. So, let's start with some basic training!

In the same way that you can't hear what your best friend is saying if you're trying to communicate in a crowded room with flashing lights and a pounding disco, you can't hear what spirit might be trying to say to you if you're surrounded by noise and distraction. Therefore you have to learn how to be quiet and calm, and I would be the first to admit that this is easier said than done. If you can learn how to meditate this will help enormously, but you don't have to go that far. If you can take just 20 minutes every day to find a quiet place, sit back in a chair, close your eyes and relax, then sooner or later (and don't worry too much if it turns out to be a *lot* later) something or someone will start filtering through. You'll start recognising a familiar face or start hearing a familiar voice, and in time will come to realise that this face and voice is a frequent and regular visitor. Listen to what is being said to you, even if you don't understand it, because with repetition it will eventually start to make sense. Do not be totally surprised if you recognise this face or voice as belonging to a relative who has passed over, or even a close friend or other loved one... So, no, don't be surprised, but on the other hand, don't go into this experiment with preconceptions. Ultimately spirit is the soul of God, and God moves in mysterious ways.

Some people take to this like a duck to water while others have to exercise more patience and, as I say, there are a few who could spend three hours a day every day in the attempt, but who will still not get anything because they are unable to find that core of inner calmness and silence, or who give up after the first week of trying, especially if they don't get immediate results. It takes time, and it is the discipline required to find that time which is a key part of the process.

Look, give it a try, and if you need any help, feel free to contact me through Mage Publishing. Also, it is worth remembering that we are *all* born with some innate psychic ability which is why children, and especially very young children, seem to have this spiritual ability; in their own way, they are already communicating before they even learn to talk. As they grow older and are distracted by school work, boyfriends, girlfriends, exams, job interviews, career pathways, social media etc., this ability is forced into the background of everyday life. But nevertheless, it is still there within us, waiting to reconnect and to become a conscious, rather than just a subliminal part of our lives.

I have never had a problem with the idea of spirit guides, and indeed my grandmother introduced me to this concept when I was still in my early teens. *"Always,"* she said, *"be careful about what you say and what you do in this life because there's always an angel looking over your shoulder keeping a record."* I was told that our guides offer us a degree of protection, but I always questioned this, on the basis of if there is such an element of spiritual protection, why are the dreadful and painful things that cause us such distress allowed to happen? I waited many years to get an answer, but in the end, I *did* get an answer.

In the December of 2003 I met a remarkable woman called Edith Schiff. At the time of our meeting she would have been more than 90 years old, but was fit, hail, healthy and hearty, marched like a soldier, drank like a fish and smoked like a chimney. She had spent three years in Auschwitz concentration camp during the holocaust and still had that dreadful tattoo on her left forearm to prove it. Sadly Edith passed away at the ripe old age of 101, but I am informed she was still drinking half a litre of vodka every day, and still smoking 20 strong Spanish cigarettes.

Edith was a very powerful clairvoyant medium. She used her abilities sparingly, only ever when, in her opinion, 'the time was right'. I remember an occasion when we were discussing spirit guides, I broached the question to her that I have just made reference to, and her answer made a lot of sense. She pointed out that these lives that we all live, are only ever on loan from a Higher Spiritual Authority and, like a term at school, we are supposed to learn from them and carry our new found knowledge into the spirit world with us when we go home at the end of the term for a holiday. She further pointed out that although we all get hurt in our lives, how much worse might that hurt be if the element of spiritual protection was *not* there? As her coup d'etat she went on to point out that generally speaking people learn a lot more from pain than they ever do from pleasure!

Food for thought, ladies and gentlemen. Food for thought!

Chapter Six
Séance

Séance is a French word which simply means 'a meeting' but as with that other French word 'clairvoyance' which means having 'clear vision' both have been corrupted by their absorbance into the English language and have come to mean somewhat different things; a séance being a gathering of people who are attempting to make contact with the dead, and clairvoyance representing the ability to communicate with people from the world of spirit.

I had a meeting with Stephen a few days ago at the Wetherby Services on the A1. It's a convenient place to meet up for a light lunch or just a cup of coffee, especially if Steve is heading north for a demonstration.

In an odd way, I like this location because it reminds me of service stations from my distant past which used to be meeting places for touring musicians and entertainers, particularly on the north/south and south/north axis. Leicester Forest East was probably the most famous rendezvous, positioned as it was, half way between London and York, a third of the way up north from London towards Tyneside and the Scottish borders. Also it was dead centre for the east/west and west/east traffic. I remember a night in 1962 when The Beatles were sat at one table, The Kinks were sat at another, Gerry and the Pacemakers were larking around by the service counter, and me and my crap little band were sat in the middle, gobs hitting the floor and far too shy to go over to anyone and say hello.

However, I digress, and as I was saying, I met Steve a few days ago at Wetherby, and without much prompting from either of us, the conversation turned to the subject of séances. Oddly, for a clairvoyant,

Stephen hasn't had much experience with séances, while I am somewhat ambivalent. I have attended a few gatherings over the years, and quite honestly, I have not been impressed with the results... quite possibly because because they have been conducted by the wrong people for the wrong reasons.

However, over the last couple of decades there has been a growing degree of interest in physical mediumship, and indeed, many churches now have a specifically designated 'séance room' to facilitate this aspect of spiritual communication. These sessions are conducted by dedicated spiritualists who know what they are doing, and go about doing it in a safe and secure environment.

Unfortunately, there is another kind of séance, much loved by horror movie producers, which could be described as the 'do it yourself' version and invariably involves the planchette, better known in this country as the Ouija board. Now, in much the same way that you wouldn't give a child a loaded gun to play with, the Ouija board can be a very dangerous tool to play with unless you've had the training and the discipline to master some of the spiritual energies associated with it.

Stephen does *not* like the Ouija board and I can fully understand why. Believe it or not, if you are seriously trying to make contact with a spirit, it isn't nearly as difficult as you might imagine. The problem can come when you're trying to get rid of it afterwards. If the spirit doesn't want to be dismissed, it can (no pun intended) be the Devil's own job to send it away, and you have got to be a strong medium and powerful clairvoyant to exorcize it back to its own domain. Most people playing with the Ouija board are *not* strong mediums and clairvoyants, and inevitably there are problems – some of them very long lasting and psychologically damaging!

The upside of the Ouija board is that this technique *can* attract the attention of a spiritual entity, but the downside comes in the fact that you don't have much control (if any) over the identity of that entity. You might want to talk to your lovely old Auntie Mary, but if Auntie Mary is on holiday somewhere on The Costa del Heaven, or she hasn't got her celestial hearing aid plugged in, you might easily attract the attentions of Mad Alice, the axe murdering maniac from Manchester! So the message here is simple – *you have been warned* – and if you are interested in séances etc., go and have words with your local spiritualist church who will provide safety, security, support and training.

To bring a little lightness to the subject, some very funny things have happened in séances, and I do mean funny *ha ha* rather than funny in the sense of being scary or weird. The first séance I ever attended was in Whitby in 1961. I was 14 years old, doing my first professional summer season, and the star of the show was 'The Great Zareada' – clairvoyant and mind reader.

Zareada, better known to his friends as Ossie Rae, presented his clairvoyance in the form of a theatre and cabaret act, but this should not be allowed to detract from the man's phenomenal gift of mediumship. Anyway, about half way through the summer he decided to hold a séance on the stage of the theatre after the show was over, and once the audience had gone home. I suspect he may have been pressurised into this (a) by my mother, (b) by his landlady and (c) half the other female members of the cast. At the duly appointed time, about fifteen of us sat around in a circle on the stage: we couldn't find a table big enough, so we just held hands, and waited for Ossie to begin.

It was a great night to hold such an event – something straight out of a Hammer Horror film. Outside there was a half-moon hiding behind swathes of mist and fog; the streets of the little seaside town had suddenly become deserted, and somewhere in the distance a dog was howling quite pitifully.

Ossie explained that during the séance he was going to go for something called 'transfiguration'. I'd never sat in a séance before and had no idea what transfiguration meant. I wasn't alone in this, and Ossie explained that if he managed to get a strong contact with a spirit, he would allow the spirit's face to transfigure his own features so that he, Ossie, would be wearing the face of the spirit who would be talking through him. It was all very exciting, and for a 14 year old boy with a wild imagination, just a little bit scary.

Ossie began with a short prayer, then got into the business of what he called 'the summoning'.

"Oh spirit," he began quietly, "if you are with us, give us a sign."

Silence. Total and absolute.

"Oh spirit," Ossie said again, this time with a little more determination, "if you are with us, give us a sign."

Silence. Absolute and total.

"Oh spirit," Ossie incanted, this time allowing some impatience to creep into his voice, "I say again, if you are present, give us a sign!"

Nothing. Not a whisper and you could have heard a pin drop.

"Spirit," Ossie half shouted, "if you are with us, give us a bloody sign, and for heaven's sake, give it to us *now*!"

Then half the world fell apart. There was a thunderous roaring groan that sounded like URRRRRN URRRRRN URRRRRN. The walls of the little theatre seemed to tremble and the air was filled with motes of dust.

One lady screamed and fled from the stage, almost everyone else dropped hands, looking furtively and fearfully over their shoulders, I nearly pooped in my pants and my mother looked as white as the proverbial sheet.

Needless to say, that was the end of Ossie's transfigurational séance, and although I can laugh about it now, it was terrifying at the time.

Remember I mentioned that outside it was very foggy and misty? Well, the coastguard or harbour master decided it was so bad that they needed to start sounding the fog horn, someone somewhere pressed a button and the foghorn burst into life. None of us had any idea that the main speaker for the fog horn was mounted on the roof of the building immediately adjacent to the theatre! Less than 30 feet as flies the crow from where we were holding our meeting! I have no idea of just how loud a fog horn can be, but to us on that half-moon misty night, it sounded absolutely deafening!

As I mentioned earlier, Stephen is relatively inexperienced on the subject of séances but, nevertheless, he was invited to attend one a few years ago and, against his better judgement, he decided to go. In some ways, it would have been difficult for him to refuse because he'd been promising a friend called Jill that one day he would take her to see a proper séance, and also because the medium taking the séance was a man of great reputation and he and Stephen were more than just passing acquaintances. Stephen had received a specific invitation from this clairvoyant, and as the séance was 'by invitation only' Steve found it difficult to say no, for fear that this might have been misinterpreted as some kind of slight.

The invitation had come from none other than the incredible physical medium Stewart Alexander, who some time earlier had referred to Stephen in glowing terms within an article he had written for the Psychic Press. Stewart has been one of this country's leading physical mediums with more than forty years' experience. He has written a number of authoritative books on the subject and is the custodian of a phenomenal archive of material appertaining to all things of a spiritual and psychic nature. I think, for the sake of clarity and context, it is worth quoting from the article, word for word... And so...

From Stewart Alexander...

Often I have heard it said that student mediums have been taught not to do this or not to do that, because 'it' (whatever 'it' may be) is unacceptable in the public demonstration of mediumship. If that wasn't tragic it would be laughable! Mediumship – where it truly exists – should not be shackled. It should not be limited by rules and regulations. In my considered opinion its gradual unfoldment depends wholly first upon an inborn ability and second upon the cooperation of the Spirit World.

Mediumship cannot be taught: it can only be encouraged and possible guidelines suggested. It would seem however that today individualism is no longer acceptable – according to man-made rules which apparently must not be broken. There are far too many 'Do's and Don'ts' – far too many restrictions which stand firmly in the way of natural ability by shackling and stifling promising potential. Mediumship is, or at least should be, a perfectly natural expression of the individual.

What really matters is the result and nothing else. Not the manner in which it is presented by the evidential value. For me what is and what is not acceptable is restrictive nonsense. As far as I am concerned, mediums can stand on their heads if the evidence they present benefits as a result.

I would cite the international medium Stephen Holbrook who has to be one of the finest demonstrators in the UK. I have been privileged to see him work on numerous occasions over a twenty year period. Unquestionably unorthodox in his work and yet he is a literal breath of fresh air.

Although some may consider his work unpalatable because of the unique manner in which his mediumship functions, there can be no doubt that he enthrals his audience and, as a result, he has, over the years, built up a legion of admirers in respect of his undoubted talents. Highly entertaining and often comical, he embraces and captivates his audience, who cannot help but appreciate the highly evidential aspect of his high energy charged demonstrations.

Now – the point that I am making here is that his mediumship has developed and functions in a manner best suited to him and his Spirit helpers but if it were to be shackled then undoubtedly it would suffer as a result.

I have never met Stewart (although I would very much like to) but I have to say that I totally agree with his views and opinions. Stephen feels the same way and, on the strength of this, he duly attended the séance. This is what happened.

Stephen on The Séance:

I had recently learnt through my friend and colleague, Sandy Ingham - a wonderful Psychic Artist - that I had delivered a message to a lady in the audience at the Station

Hotel in Hull, and the message was from her sister who had passed in particularly tragic circumstances. Unbeknownst to me, this also happened to be the sister of the very well respected Physical Medium, Stewart Alexander.

Sandy had said to me several times throughout that year, that if I ever got a Thursday night off, Stewart had kindly said that I would be welcome to attend one of his private home circles/séances. To be honest, I think for my sins I am a plodder, reluctant to change, and it always takes me a long time to think things through. It may be a total surprise but I had never sat in a physical circle and, to be honest, had not been that keen to do so.

After trying to pin me down with no joy, one day Sandy was looking over at me, and saw that I had my diary open, she shot across the room with the speed of a bullet, and said "Right, look at the diary whilst it's open because you said if you had a Thursday free you would join us for Stewart's circle." I was cornered and so agreed to my next Thursday night off, if Stewart was free, to make the journey over to Hull. At that particular time, I was very nervous! What a wuss!! I was familiar with my own mental Mediumship and well within my comfort zone, but this is typical of me when it comes to pushing boundaries.

I had been told that I could take a friend with me, and I know a Medium called Jill from the North East who always said that if the chance ever came up, she would love to attend. So, we liaised with Stewart and arranged the date. When we arrived at Stewart's, straight away I knew I had made the right decision, his home was so welcoming and the six or seven other sitters were lovely engaging people. Any of my previous nervousness had now turned to excitement.

After exchanging general conversations, we all made our way to the séance room and made ourselves comfortable. Stewart was put into cable ties which bound him to his chair; the lights were low, and there were some illuminated trumpets at the centre of the room. I think some of this recollection may be a little sketchy, but I will try and remember everything to the best of my ability. After singing, to raise the vibration, and a little prayer, Stewart's spirit helpers started to communicate. First there was a little boy with the cutest voice I've ever heard; he seemed jovial and happy to be in attendance. To my surprise, the trumpets were literally lifting off the ground, almost as if they were dancing. Then they were going up so high and tapping the ceiling, then swooping down and gently stroking peoples' faces. One came to me and very softly pushed against my forehead, this was a spectacular vision to see but also to feel. All this was being done by the energy of spirits using Stewart as their medium.

It was then that Mike (Sandy Ingham's husband) was called to sit next to Stewart, and we could all hear Mike's dad calling him. So many personal details were mentioned, and his Dad made reference to a Carp... "We saw you with the carp", and also the word "rhinoceros" was mentioned. Mike was quite emotional at this, but obviously it meant nothing to the rest of us at the time, but I made a mental note to ask him later.

Almost immediately after this, a doctor came through who works with Spirit, and came over to me and asked my permission to take my hands. I said yes rather shakily, and at that point, I felt my hands being lifted, and from nowhere came a calm reassuring voice. It said "We are so truly grateful for all the work you do to help both us and our loved ones. It is with all our love and gratitude that we come through this evening, and you may not realise the great importance to us from the higher side of life to have that connection. As you spend so much time in the material world conveying these messages back from us, but our words need to be heard and our needs are often not recognised. We understand you have a wonderful way with your connections, and please accept our heartfelt thanks from our side too."

By this time, tears were streaming down my face. I had suddenly realised that this was of massive importance to the spirit world, just as it is to people in the audience hoping to receive messages from their loved ones! It seems so obvious, but when we live in our own world, and go out each night to face a room full of expectant faces, we sometimes forget how important all this is to those actually doing the work on the other side! They want to make contact with us just as much as we want to make contact with them.

I think the fact that he took my hands physically, and lifted them was itself an unnerving sensation, but the words he spoke to me seemed to take my mind off what was actually happening, and it felt somehow natural! And if this wasn't breathtaking enough, as we sat round a small table with our hands just touching by our little fingers, we were told to watch, as a small marble-sized ball of light appeared, and from the light came what looked like little spindles! Not knowing what to expect, I suddenly realised that these were the finger joints in a hand, and within minutes they had manifested into an actual hand and moved across the table. They touched Jill's hand, and she made a sharp intake of breath and I am sure her face would have been a picture! She told me later that she had secretly kicked out her legs beneath the table in case someone was pulling a stunt, but the only thing her legs came into contact with was fresh air. Anyway, then the hand simply disappeared back into a little ball of light and vanished. This was something I had only heard about, and my senses were bombarded! In a very good way of course. But I can honestly say I was in deep shock as to what I had experienced.

After the circle, my first port of call was Mike, and I walked up to him to ask him about the carp and the rhinoceros! He told me that only two days before, he was on a family outing to a big old Edwardian house, and he volunteered to look after Farrah, his grand-daughter, while the rest went to look around the house. Outside, Mike noticed a pond with carp in, and he was holding Farrah by the edge, letting the carp come to the surface to touch her fingers. And bizarrely enough, the day before, he had been teaching her to spell the word Rhinoceros! Both these facts had been relayed through Stewart's fantastic Mediumship. The information given might not have changed the world, but it certainly changed *Mike's* world!

To say I was delighted to have been there to witness this is an understatement. I felt, and still feel to this day, totally privileged to have experienced such a remarkable display of evidence. Thank you Stewart Alexander, for giving me an experience I will never forget! It's funny how it left me feeling; I know this may sound strange, but I felt as though someone had switched a light on! And all of a sudden, my life had become coloured. It was a very emotional experience and I can see why people like to do this in the privacy of their own home. It's somehow very personal, all the way home I felt elated and so very grateful at the same time. However, it also made me feel like I had so much to learn.

Stewart certainly is a master of his craft and, if anything, made me feel as though my Mediumship was, in comparison, pedestrian. I know Stewart would say "each to his own", and we shouldn't compare things that are so different because it doesn't give a true reflection, but that is honestly how I felt.

Now, ladies and gentlemen, I have known Steve Holbrook for a very long time, and I can tell you he is one of the most honest and sincere men that I have ever met. He is totally without guile, but at the same time, he is no man's fool, and if he says this is what happened at Stewart Alexander's séance – then it happened. However, for the sake of objectivity and

70

balance, I must confess that had I been one of Christ's disciples, I would most certainly have been Doubting Thomas, needing to put my hand in the wound before I could allow myself to believe. Against that, well, quite frankly, I would have loved to have been in Steve's shoes, experiencing what he experienced. My doubt is a weight on my back, and I'd be grateful to have it lifted and dispensed with. So, if there are any physical mediums out there who would like to help me in this quest, please get in touch through Mage Publishing.

Chapter Seven
Revelations

In the early summer of 2005 Stephen was scheduled to do a demonstration in Gloucester. Gloucester is a long way from Wakefield, so my wife Jo and I picked Steve up around 11 o'clock in preparation for the long drive down to the venue. It was a lovely sunny morning, but Jo and I were feeling a bit low. A few days earlier we had just had to have one of our precious pussy cats put to sleep, and her loss had affected us both more deeply than either of us cared to admit.

Now, whenever you come into contact with Stephen, no matter how tired or fed up you might be feeling, the bubbling Holbrook good humour gives you an immediate lift, and within a very short time you become invigorated by his infectious sense of fun and laughter.

However, on this particular morning, he seemed strangely quiet and withdrawn and there was a tension within him which was extremely unusual. I was aware of the fact that he must have been tired after a dozen consecutive nights on the road, but I also sensed that it was more than this. On a psychic level he was twanging like an over-tuned guitar string. And I was right. We'd no sooner turned the corner out of his street, when he asked Jo, who was driving, to stop the car because he had something to tell us.

Instead of saying anything, he just sat there on the back seat, looking pale and distressed, and staring down at his hands which he held tightly together on his lap.

"Come on Steve," Jo coaxed, "what's the problem?"

Stephen didn't answer, and I remember looking at him through the rear view mirror, and realising that he was almost in tears. Jo also realised that whatever this was, it was something serious.

"Come on Steve," she said soothingly. "It can't be all that bad."

"It might be," he muttered in a low croaky voice. "God knows what you're going to think of me when I tell you."

"Whatever it is, James and I are behind you all the way. Now what's wrong? Have you murdered Caroline and the kids, or have you suddenly discovered that you're gay and this is your 'coming out' speech?"

There was a long silence, followed by an even longer sigh. Then finally he glanced up at us. "It's the latter," he said.

Jo gave me a swift look with a raised eyebrow, and I remember squeezing her leg with one hand, while reaching over with the other, to give Stephen a reassuring pat on the knee. I suppose the bottom line here was that I wasn't at all surprised by Stephen's revelation.

"Is this something sudden," Jo asked, "or has it been going on for a while? Have you met someone?"

Steve nodded in assent to both questions.

"And, by any chance," Jo continued, "does this chap drink white wine?"

Steve looked up, startled. "Yes, as a matter of fact he does, but how did you know that?"

"Because until a few months ago you wouldn't touch the stuff. You always drank red. Then suddenly you switched…"

I know what some of you might be thinking at this point. How could Stephen be gay? He's got a beautiful wife and three gorgeous kids, and although he might have been a hairdresser for a while, not all hairdressers

73

are gay, are they? He doesn't walk around with a mince, one hand on his hip, the other wafting in the air at the end of a limp wrist. One *might* just think he was slightly effeminate because of the long wavy blond hair which was his chosen style of the day, but gay? Bloody hell, he wasn't even remotely camp, so no, no way could he be gay!

Well, I can see how you might arrive at this conclusion, but you would, of course, be wrong.

My mother was the archetypal 'lady of the theatre' and after being born in a dressing room, I grew up in the environment of the theatre before gravitating into the wider environs of the entertainments industry. This is a world which then, as now, is full of gay people, and I've mixed with gay people all my life. I have had (and still have) many gay friends, and despite the fact that I am totally heterosexual (talk to my wife) I have always been happy in gay company. Like I say, I'm a straight guy, but believe me, when I'm in the mood or I've had a few Spanish brandies, I can do 'camp' to such a convincing extent that would put most Old Queens to shame, and in the 1970s this could get me into any one of a dozen London night clubs that the general public didn't even know existed. Ah, I remember well The Sombrero Club on Kensington High Street, Eugene Dear and Simon Darling, the amazing Jean Fredericks – but that's another story! Actually, it's a whole flaming book of stories, so watch this space!

It is broadly assumed by people who don't know any better that the gay scene is a hotbed of promiscuity and, of course, there *is* a degree of promiscuity, but no more than you would find in heterosexual relationships and, indeed, since the 1980s, probably an awful lot less! Generally speaking (and research bears this out) gay relationships last longer and are more stable than heterosexual unions and some of the media depictions of gay relationships are so far wide off the mark that they have become cartoonish caricatures pandering to the preconceived notions of the heterosexual majority.

There are a number of different types of gay men. For example, there are those who know from a very early age, sometimes even prepubescent, that they are inhabiting the wrong body. There are those who become gradually aware of the fact that they can enjoy a deeper relationship with another man than they can with a woman. Some of these men accept and celebrate the fact, while others clam up in denial and fight an awful battle with themselves, sometimes to their grave; there are even some who will hang their heads in despair and shame, while others will go through the motions of heterosexuality, hiding what they see to be their dark secret. Then, there is another kind of man who sincerely believes that he is heterosexual until such time as he comes into contact with someone who causes him to change his mind. This can be an absolute bombshell of an incident which can turn a man's life upside down and onto its head within a matter of hours, and indeed, sometimes even minutes!

Whichever way it occurred for Stephen, knowing him as I do, I can only begin to imagine the agony and the anguish that he went through before he finally came to terms with his new sexual identity, and being the ever pragmatic Taurean that he is, do something practical about it. I'll let him tell you the story from here in his own words...

From Stephen:
It was manic! The traffic through Leeds at the best of times is horrendous, but this particular Friday teatime was worse than ever! Traffic was at a standstill. My mobile rang, it

was James, so I pulled over to take the call. He was just informing me that we had sold out for Portsmouth on April 28th but we still had a four week window for the adverts left to run. It would have been easy to stop them; we wouldn't have got a refund, but the money could be held on account for the following year. For some strange reason, I found myself saying "Why don't we try and see if the Marriott Hotel is available again on the 29th, and we can use the adverts to promote that? We can do two nights back to back."

James had always joked about Matinee performances, and I had always said "Absolutely not!" I never liked the idea of doing two nights at the same venue either. He knew that only too well, but rather than question me, he just said "Well, that's very unlike you Steve, but I will call them and see if they are free. Oh, wait a minute, that's your birthday!" I replied. "Well, never mind, we can have a nice meal afterwards". Five minutes later he called me back and said "They aren't free on the 29th, they have another function on" so I said "Why not try another hotel?" At that point I could hear Joanna (James' wife) in the background "Steve, what ARE you thinking about, it's your birthday! Surely you have better things to do...?"

Well, maybe I did, but I was still insistent that James tried to find somewhere else. Another five minutes went by, and when I pulled in to get some petrol, the phone rang again. This time we had success: James had booked the Hilton Hotel, literally ten minutes down the road from the Marriott, for the 29th April, and he was going to get the adverts amended with the new date on. Two hours later, everything was confirmed and I distinctly remember James saying "For once, I will not go against your better judgement, there's clearly a reason why you have to be in Portsmouth on the 29th. It could be that there is a special connection, or a special message, something that could be life-changing."

Well, it was, but no-one could ever, in their wildest dreams, have imagined that it would be the life-changing scenario that was to come!

The 28th came and my demonstration went smoothly. It was, as always, a wonderful evening in Portsmouth, with varying emotions and by this time, our second evening was also sold out. The day of the 29th April (my birthday), we arrived to check in at the Hilton. After checking the function room was set up correctly, I went to my room to make a cuppa. As I got to my room, the guy in the room next door was just locking his door. To my surprise, he had exactly the same shirt on that I had at home, and it is quite an unusual one at that!

Me, being me, said "Hey, I've got that shirt!" and he replied "You must have good taste then!" Nothing more was said, and I proceeded to boil the kettle. After my tea, I laid on the bed and drifted off, remembering to set my alarm for 6pm, to give me time to come round and get changed, ready for 7pm to meet James and Jo in the function room. It was then it dawned on me, as I walked down the corridor, that this was the particular night that I had insisted on doing.

As I walked through the bar, there were lots of people waiting to go through to the function room, one or two familiar faces, but the majority of them I hadn't seen before. After navigating through the busy bar, just as I got to main door, I saw that familiar shirt, instantly thinking "Oh God, I hope he's not going in, when he's in the room next door." It appeared to be quite the opposite, as he said "Hi again, do you have any idea what's going on in there? All these women!" Those that know me will understand what I said in return. "There must be some sort of book publishing event going on" which was my stock in trade answer to this particular question.

"Oh right" he said "I just wondered why it was so busy!" I then quickly shot into the room as he turned back to the bar. After helping Joanna to seat everybody, we got started and had another lovely evening with Spirit. After signing a few books, all I could think about was the lovely Italian meal we were going for. When we had put all the sound system and equipment in the back of the car, we made our way to Reception, only to see a poster that we hadn't taken down. And to my surprise and horror, the guy in the shirt was reading it. I put my head down and headed to the car. On returning to the hotel after a wonderful meal, securing a great parking spot just outside the main entrance – due to all our guests leaving – I said to Joanna "I'm going to have a good night's sleep." James made his way to the bar for a brandy night-cap, and we said our goodbyes. But yet again, fate played its hand, because the guy with the shirt from next door was walking down the corridor, directly toward me.

I couldn't do a thing except carry on, I felt really embarrassed, not knowing where to look, but to my surprise, as I got nearer to him, he just said "Hi, how did it go?" I replied "Very well thank you, and by the way, I didn't really mean to tell you a lie earlier, it's just sometimes easier to bend the truth when it comes to what I do. Everyone seems to ask the same questions and I just have to give the same old answers, 'Does it scare you?' 'How old were you when you first discovered it?' 'Are you like it all the time?' etc. etc."

He smiled and said "It must be nice to lead such an interesting life that people want to know all about it. Anyway, would you like a drink in the bar? I'm heading there now."

"Well, probably" I replied "I've got a few things to sort out in the room, but I might come down a bit later." Back in the room, I sat and thought, Should I? Shouldn't I? After all, it was only a drink, so after doing what I had to do, 20 minutes later I found myself sat at the bar, having an interesting conversation with the guy with the shirt, whose name turned out to be Rob, who worked for a national swimwear company. He was stopping in the hotel just for that one night, ready for a meeting the next day. We both remember the conversation to this day! He told me about his life, and I exchanged my life story with him. About 1.55am, I said "I'll have to get to bed now, we have an early breakfast, and we've planned a shopping spree to Gunwharf Quays. Great to meet you," and with that, I walked down the never-ending corridor at the Hilton, to my room.

Next morning whilst at breakfast, I looked up and saw Rob tucking into his cereal. I nodded sheepishly as he waved, as James and Jo had no idea I had returned to the bar the night before. Even though there was nothing to hide, I couldn't explain this feeling of secrecy. Anyway, off we went to the shopping mall and headed for a coffee. Most of the shops in the outlet weren't really my cup of tea, the likes of Edinburgh Woollen Mill and Millets, but needless to say, I had a good look round and passed a couple of hours. We were just leaving for the car park, and again, to my surprise, who should I see but Rob! This was getting ridiculous. A guy who I have never met before, and bumping into someone twice was unlikely, but three times was bizarre! I said hello and quickly marched past. I remember Jo saying at the time, "Do you know that guy?" but I brushed it off by saying "Yes, I think I saw him at the hotel last night."

Thankfully, nothing more was said. We returned back to the hotel shortly after lunch, and as I was negotiating the revolving doors (which incidentally I hate with a vengeance), I was to receive another shock. Who was sat there in reception, thankfully with his back toward me, but Rob?! I quickly went to my room, as were leaving shortly after for the Isle of Wight and, as I opened the door, I saw what I thought was a general note from reception laying on the floor, perhaps a survey or similar. However, it turned out to be a hand-written note, which read *'Hi, it's Rob. In a non-stalking, non-psychopathic way, I really enjoyed chatting with you last night, and if we are working in the same area again, it would be great to meet up, so just give me a ring.'*

Needless to say, I was fully committed for the rest of the year, and Rob managed to manipulate some of his work schedule to be in the areas where I was working. Our friendship developed, and now, 15 years down the line, we are still as happy together as when we met on the 29th April 2004. It is strange, looking back now on the situation, as the main problem was the fact we were both in relationships at the time. I had been with Caroline for 20 years, and Rob had been with his partner, Aidan, for 22 years. But, as everyone knows, any relationship, be it heterosexual, homosexual, or bisexual, doesn't always last forever. After we had both told our partners, which was by far the hardest thing we'd ever had to do, we knew we were in it for real. The worst case scenario for me was my children, who were at the vulnerable ages of ten, seven and five.

I had always done everything in my power to protect my children, but how on earth I was going to explain this situation? I didn't know! However, it was something I was going to have to face. So over the next few months, I arranged three meetings with three Headmasters/ Mistresses at three different schools, just to outline the situation that Caroline and I had separated, and to make it more complicated, I was now living with a man. In my eyes, this could cause so many issues with regard to schooling, i.e. bullying and name calling. My idea wasn't totally innocent: I thought that with the Heads of Year etc. being made aware of my new lifestyle, this would possibly help the kids get more protection if anything was to happen as a result of my actions. I suppose it was kind of selfish really, but only for the kids' sake, not mine.

All three Head Teachers were very understanding, and grateful that I had met with them. It was mainly a point of letting them know that our children would be getting the same support as they always had, if not more, and that Caroline and I couldn't love them or give them any more support than if we were still together. Our relationship had finished as Man and Wife, but we both agreed we were going to remain best friends. I remember thinking that if Caroline and I were truly best friends, after our 20 years of being together, that we would come through this and somehow become closer than we were before the marriage ended.

The next stop was to tell Aidan, Rob's partner, who again, I think, knew that things weren't all rosy in their relationship. I remember Rob telling Aidan, and knowing that Aidan was nine years older than Rob, I thought he would have the wisdom and strength to understand the situation. I recall going to meet him, and saying "It may be the last thing you want to hear now, but it would be nice, in an ideal world, if we could all remain friends and get along together." I don't think from his reaction that he seemed to be very enthusiastic in believing that scenario. After all, who could blame him?

Now, I must try and lighten this up a little, all this emotion flying round is very intense! A comical experience occurred about five weeks after meeting Rob. He rang and said "I'm free tonight, working in Cardiff tomorrow, and I see you're in Newport. If you don't mind, I could come over." I agreed, then about two hours later rang him and said "Jo and James are in the hotel with me, so it's probably not such a good idea." But sensing the rejection vibes I got back, I said "Oh go on then," even though I still had the sense of unease. He arrived just after 11pm, and I had already texted him the room number. After the demonstration, I had said goodnight to James and Jo, and gone to the room to watch TV. There was still that sense of unease that I couldn't shake or explain, and I felt distracted to say the least. When he arrived, we had a quick catch up and everything seemed ok. That was, until 3 am in the morning, when I heard loud knocks at the door, and none other than James' voice "Steve, wake up! I need to come in." Oh! My! God! What a scenario, what on earth was I going to do, and how could I explain this? I can honestly say, I have never felt panic like it!

"Just a minute" I replied. I quickly shoved Rob unceremoniously into the wardrobe, and made him promise not to make a single sound, took a deep breath, and opened the door. In walked a very sleepy James, who promptly sat on the bed and said "They've told me my car is parked in front of the fire doors, it's a hazard and needs to be moved ASAP, but I'm going to make them wait!"

No sooner had he said this, he lit up one of my cigarettes, and immediately launched into a lighter conversation. "At least I can have a cigarette in the early hours of the morning without Jo knowing!"

I can honestly say that what was actually five minutes, seemed like five hours! It only struck me afterwards, that there was no real reason for James to actually wake me up at that time, he could have just moved the car himself. I think it was because I was half asleep and in total shock that I only realised afterwards, it was because he'd run out of cigarettes and wanted one of mine, out of the sight of his disapproving wife. It just shows that that niggling thought about Rob coming to Newport was correct, I should have listened! But there again, I wouldn't be writing about this now. Needless to say, James left after about five minutes, and Rob crept out of the wardrobe, bent double and very stiff from being in one position. All I could think was thank God he didn't have to sneeze!

Shortly after we had told our partners, I was due to leave for a tour of the South West, starting with Plymouth Guildhall. Roger and Jill Prior were responsible for the running of these venues and Roger had called a couple of days before, saying that there was a lady called Charmian Evans who wanted to do an interview for a local radio station. I really didn't want to do an interview before my demonstration, but still, I agreed and she came along to the Guildhall with a mini-recorder. Trying to do my work as a Medium, and being responsible for all the emotional effect it had on my wife and children, I wasn't really in the mood, but she appeared at 5.30pm prompt.

After a brief introduction, she turned on her mic and started recording. I knew I wasn't in the right frame of mind, but I would try my best to cover it up. About three minutes in to the interview, she suddenly switched off the recorder, and said "This isn't working. You're not really with it, are you?"

I felt really embarrassed that I wasn't focusing on what I was meant to be doing and quickly apologised, wondering how to explain that I'd got a lot going on. Before I'd had chance to start talking, however, she interrupted and said "Everything will be perfect in the end, you won't see this right now but I assure you, it will. Your current partner, your wife, will always be your soulmate. She was brought into your life for a reason. You should have two, or is it three, children?"

"Three," I said, in total shock. She went on "These children are wonderful, they will all mature to be wonderful adults, with a widespread understanding of life. They will be understanding of your situation, and grow from their own knowledge and perception. They will all make you so proud. The male partner, who you have only just met - and no disrespect to you - is very intelligent, and your children will learn from him and his knowledge when it comes to study and homework. Trust me when I say his patience and understanding will totally inspire confidence where the children are concerned. You have reached a turning point in your life now, it's another stage you need to experience:

it will be very different and this second stage will allow you to discover different emotions within yourself. It's like a key has opened a new door, and you will grow within yourself, a growth that has needed to be activated by physical and mental changes. Living the second part of your life in this way will help you have a greater knowledge and spiritual understanding.

This year, bearing in mind it's only the beginning of March, you will all holiday together, with both your ex-partners, and children!"

To say I was stunned is an understatement! I was speechless. Where had all this information come from? I was perplexed to say the least: a holiday that year was simply impossible! As all this was taking place, tears were running down my face, in gratitude to this woman, who I now know had been used as a spiritual instrument at an incredibly desperate time in my life. A woman, who until 40 minutes before, I had never even met. She then said "You needed that! I knew I had to push to do this interview. I had no idea why, but I was sent."

To conclude what Charmian said that day, in August of that year, Rob, Aidan, my ex-wife Caroline, myself and the three kids, had a fantastic fortnight in Spain, and every year since that time, we always holiday together, depending on everyone's availability. This often includes Aidan, Rob's ex-partner, and we also all spend Christmas, Easter and New Year together. Caroline and Aidan have become best friends who often talk on the phone, and exchange presents and cards at Christmas and birthdays. Also, Aidan and I share the same wicked sense of humour and often, getting bored of being sat in the sun on holiday, we'll go off walking, leaving Caroline and Rob laying by the pool. So much so, that one day, Aidan and I returned from a long walk; the sun had gone in, and we found the pool area empty. The pool man shouted across to me "Oh, your brother and his wife left 15 minutes ago!" Aidan and I both laughed and thought it was hilarious, if only he knew!

We've had many laughs over the years, when we've been away with the kids, and when they meet up with new friends by the pool, their parents use their kids to find out who is with who, and what the relationship is between us.... No-one really gets it right! So, we have all moved on, and have become one big family, no jealousy or animosity, and above all, no secrets. We all move in the same direction, and again, to quote Charmian's words, my children HAVE grown up to be wonderful spiritual individuals, and it makes me so proud to say I am their Dad. They all have such individual personalities, but one thing they all share is they are all open-minded, compassionate people who do have a greater respect and understanding of life. And, more importantly, they all understand that no matter what happens in life, even if we think we know where we're going, in reality it is only a very vague picture. There may be many crossroads, pot-holes and unexpected turns in the road that we don't foresee on the way, but eventually we follow the path of life and make the very best of the journey. I always say, it's not about the destination, it's the journey that matters.

Despite all the emotions of opening up, and facing up to my real feelings, I had a sense of freedom like never before. I wasn't living behind a door, occasionally peeping out from behind it. Even though I knew there would be obstacles ahead, I felt a sense of peace-of-mind and strength that I knew would get me through it. And, to be quite honest, I made a decision a long time ago - although it was subconsciously hidden away under lots of debris - that if anyone could not accept me for what I was, he or she wasn't worthy of being part of my life, and I still stand by this, to this day.

After reading back over this chapter about meeting Rob, I felt that I had skipped a huge chunk of what I would have considered at one time to be no-one else's business. But I do feel that it is only fair to share some of my personal thoughts and feelings with you.

I have always been upfront and honest with people, and would hope that explaining my inner thoughts may give you, the reader, a better understanding of me. The question I was asked a million times about admitting my sexuality to my family and friends was "Do you think you have always been like that?" Well, to be honest, the answer is, obviously not. I have had a wonderful relationship with Caroline for 20 years, and together we have created three gorgeous kids, but admittedly, somewhere along the way, things changed. I had changed, people DO change. Everybody is unique. The trouble is, we all get tangled up with the rhythm of life, just going along with things and so often not assessing ourselves along the way... Never realising the changes that are happening within. And all of a sudden, you realise that what made you tick years ago, doesn't seem to have the same effect anymore. I don't gel with the idea "Oh you're a hairdresser, you must be gay" or "Oh you're a medium, and all male mediums are gay," I hate the idea of being put into a group and categorised. To this day I feel that sometimes you meet someone, and immediately there is a connection, whether it be spiritual, physical, emotional or mental, or a gentle feeling of "I like being around this person".

I can honestly say when I met Rob, it wasn't any of the above, it just felt like situations had arrived that I felt more comfortable with. So for the next 18 months, I fought a horrendous battle of emotions within myself, emotions that I never knew existed. I had a wonderful wife and children that I needed to protect, nurture and guide, but could I do that from standing outside the family unit? Would my world fall apart? Then, there were the thoughts of "What am I going to tell my Mum and Dad?" and then my friends, all the in-laws and out-laws. And then, even worse "What about the general public? What will they think?"

While I know I'm not Robbie Williams, I still have a wonderful army of people that had been attending my evenings for years. What on earth would they think of me? It was at that point I took a step back, and thought "Hang on a minute, do I have any prior knowledge of other peoples' lives? Do I know their intimate details and how they lead their lives?" And the answer to that, of course, is "No, I don't!"

I have already said that no two people are the same, and I'm very sure that if everyone had a birds-eye view of the lives of the person sat next to them, certain elements of that person's life could shock to the core. I am not a bad person, and I don't ever set out to intentionally hurt people, I just thought I'd have to be honest with myself, and now I know that being honest with myself meant being honest with others.

After dropping the devastating blow on Caroline and the children, my first port of call was my Mum's house, the wonderful three bedroom bungalow that I grew up in. I arranged for Mum, Dad and my two sisters to get together and explain the very difficult and sensitive situation. To my surprise, they were all just relieved that I hadn't got them there to tell them I had a terminal illness. It was at that point I remember thinking "Yes, the situation could have been much *much* worse."

After that, it was other family and friends, and then rapidly, the news spread through my small village, and probably lots of other places I knew nothing about. But in the midst of all this, I still felt a sense of freedom. I knew it was going to be a long journey, and not everyone would understand it, but I kept the thought in the back of mind that if anyone didn't understand or accept it, that was fine and I would have to respect that. But I also knew that there would be no place for them in my life.

Nobody knows unless they have been in this situation: the conflict, the massive mess of mixed up wires, the sleepless nights, having to put on a 'show' for everyone, the feeling that everyone is talking about you, the depression, insecurity, but most of all, the effect this has on other people around you. It was the 'knock-on' effect, and this is something that I would have no control over, however hard I might try. Again, the words my Mum said resounded in my head 'He who tries to please everybody, ends up pleasing no-one'.

So, together with the love and support from my wife, children, family and friends, we all moved forward. The thing to remember here is that although the situation may have changed, I hadn't. I am still a Dad, a Husband, a Friend, a Brother, Uncle and Son. I think that once the initial shock of telling everyone had settled, everyone realised I was, and still am, the same Steve. These days, sadly, we have too many labels that we attach to people. Boxes that we are all expected to fit in. I now realise that trying to fit into a box, while having a label attached to me, was simply no good. I feel now as though not only am I a better person, I can be of much more use to everyone around me. I really have had the experience of such a life-changing event and have 'come out' – forgive the pun – the other side, occasionally battered and bruised, emotionally, but stronger than ever before.

Why do some leaves fall of the trees before others? Why do some people have straight hair, while some have curly hair? Why, why, why? We will never have all the answers to all the questions! Why did I have to meet Caroline and have three children, only to realise after 20 years, that I wasn't where I needed to be? We often sit as a family now, and one of the children will say "I'm so glad that you're gay, Dad, we have the best life ever! With two Dads and a Mum, we have the best of both worlds."

They have all said that at different points in time. They are all, in their own way, totally unique, with a fantastic outlook on life. Never judging anyone, and they exercise both understanding and tolerance. They have all had to be understanding from the beginning of this journey, and I couldn't be more proud of them. Also, Caroline is now at her best, stronger than before, and I can see today how we have all changed. My being honest with myself, has had a huge bearing on everyone's lives, but we have all managed to be there for each other and, as a result of this, have created an openness that is hard to describe. I just wish it could be the same for all the families that encounter this massive interruption. Sadly, we all know this isn't often the case.

I need to talk about Caroline!

We all meet that someone in our life that turns it upside down, inside out, and round and round. And as far as I was concerned I'd found that person in Caroline. Yet again, synchronicity formed its own pattern: the prestigious Pussycatz Club in Wakefield (which sounds actually more like a pole-dancing club, but was in fact a newly opened club that had taken over from Wakefield Theatre Club) was where I first set eyes on her. I can honestly say this was not a spiritual attraction, this was purely physical. Her short, cropped white hair, cut in an elfin style, framing her beautiful lightly tanned features, mesmerised me. Moments like that, you never forget. It was the eye contact that brought us together, and by the end of the night, I knew this was going to be something special. Caroline and I were together for over 20 years, and I think you kind of morph into one another. At first we had nothing to think about but us, enjoying wonderful holidays, and experiencing everything that two 18-year olds should do.

Eventually we married and have had our trio of gorgeous children.

Looking back now, I can cherish all these memories. My own memories in the bank forever. Now, when Rob and I go round to my old family home for a BBQ or get-together, all the old photographs come out, which bring all those fond memories flooding back. Photos from holidays in Spain and Portugal, to ones in the caravan in Filey and Skegness.

If you were to ask me or Caroline "Who is your best friend?" we would both automatically say each other. That is where we are at as I write this. If 48 hours pass without speaking with her, it is very strange. And we both remain totally committed to the children, now 26, 23 and 21. What we have is truly special, and we are very lucky to have this relationship, because jealousy and anger only serve to break down many special relationships. We have mutual respect and, above all, I am grateful for her kindness, willingness to understand and having a greater knowledge of life itself, to be able to detach herself from the situation. Enough to be able to see that I am still the same person she married over 22 years ago – although with less hair! It took time, as all separations do, but Caroline has found her true self, and is now stronger, wiser and content with her life. We have a wonderful family unit that could so easily have shattered into a million pieces, but instead, as each year goes by, it gets stronger.

I always think the roots that we lay act as a foundation that supports us throughout the journey of life. These foundations are the network of hidden roots underground that keep my family together. I fully understand that many people find this unusual to say the least, but I would probably find it alien to come out of a marriage, of whatever sexuality, to hold animosity, anger, and negativity. We are all different, all individuals, with a totally different thumb-print. Saying that, in my own mind, I suppose, to this day, this is why I think there is still so much trouble out there in the world.

Changing the course of my life had been the biggest thing I had ever had to do. But thankfully, everything had turned out better than I could imagine. Everyone was moving forward. Once I had made sure that the children's teachers and Heads of years had been made aware of our unusual situation, I had a plan.

It wasn't a selfish plan, but it was a plan to benefit my children long-term. Children who I constantly worried about because of the implications of having a gay dad, which could so easily lead to bullying and name-calling, being teased etc. This was my biggest fear. Ellie at this point wasn't such an issue, as she was only four and the children in her year were too young to fully understand. But Bradley, seven, and Robbie, going on ten, were where the possible difficulties could arise.

My plan was to literally encourage them, every weekend (and I mean EVERY weekend!) to have different friends come over, on a rotation basis. We would go swimming, visit the cinema, go bowling, or go to Hemsworth Water Park, or Lightwaves Leisure Centre in Barnsley. Robbie was allowed two friends and so was Brad. Despite the difference in ages between my two boys, and their friends, this became a regular event. This way, I would get to know each one of their school pals and, again, they would get to know me and hopefully I would gain acceptance as Robbie and Brad's Dad, a fun, happy-go-lucky guy, a normal Dad who invited them over to have a good time. Obviously, after swimming, or bowling, we'd have a picnic (weather dependent!), or the most popular proved to be Frankie and Benny's.

I dread now to think of the cost of these weekends! But looking back, it was money well spent. I can honestly say this WAS every weekend of the year. I don't want to make it sound like a chore and that I didn't enjoy it – of course I did – but it wasn't an easy task. Keeping your own two entertained with different things every weekend was a challenge, never mind another two of Brad's friends, and another two of Robbie's!

I think now, looking back on things, I was just trying to gain acceptance from anyone who was to be around my children's lives. Just to make things run as smoothly as possible for them. The thing is, it worked! The odd time anyone from another group of friends happened to say "Your Dad's gay" or "Your Dad's a bender" the small group of allies would come to Robbie or Bradley's defence, saying things like "Hey, he's a top bloke", or "Hey, we have a brilliant time at the weekends, leave him alone." So, yes, my little plan had come to fruition; there had been method in my madness, and everyone came out winning – except the bullies.

As Ellie got older, this then went on to develop with her friends too as, by this time, the word had spread and Ellie had friends queueing up to come on these weekend outings, and even stopovers. Never once did any of them get confronted by anxious parents.

I must add at this point, that Rob had led a life that at no point included children in the slightest. So this, in itself, was a daunting task – not only being a step-dad to my three, but the constant streams of boisterous, over excited yells from other peoples' children. However, I must admit he passed every step with flying colours. Everyone loved Rob, he just blended in. And, as always, he came in exceptionally handy with his organisational skills: I would invite the kids over, and he would plan everything the night before, get the cool bags ready, pop, crisps, sandwiches galore, spare clothes etc. I have many wonderful memories of these times, and often bump into these now fully grown adults whilst I'm out in town. They always stop to chat and we laugh about the funny incidents and escapades we had when they were younger. I'm sure they knew, even as kids, that there was method in my madness. Well, perhaps even if they didn't, their parents certainly did.

Life got better and better as time went on, and considering the kind of work I do, and that my photograph was in the local papers virtually every week, and most people knew who I was, I still remained very open with people. Everyone was very supportive, they were either sympathetic, others would simply say nothing, or say words to the effect of "I hope everything works out for you". Again, I didn't hide anything but really didn't feel the need to have to explain my actions.

Amazingly enough, whether it was a result of what had happened, or just sheer coincidence, more and more parents of the children at Robbie and Bradley's school attended my evenings. Even one of the Headmasters, two of the Heads of Year, and Student Liaison Officers from different schools would attend. It was somehow as if this had made them become more curious about Spirit and what I did. Or there again, was it more about my personal life? Whatever it may have been, I was still pleased to see them all.

This has been a long but very important chapter, but before we end it, I feel the need to make a couple of comments. First, I've known Steve now for more than 20 years and can validate the veracity of his words... And they are words which we would all do well to consider when we think of the painful process of 'coming out'. Sometimes, if it involves a media celebrity, it may be done in a way designed to grab the headlines, and even with an element of flippancy, but as you will understand from Stephen's story, in truth there is very little flippancy in the process. I do not think that anyone in Stephen's position looks for sympathy, but despite these seemingly 'enlightened times' it would certainly be very good if we could offer people a greater degree of understanding!

Again, on the subject on Stephen's words... As I say, I've known him for a very long time, have written three earlier books about him and, in the early days, getting any information out of him was like squeezing blood out of a stone! Yet, with this book he is being very open and forthcoming, and I am presenting you with his own words with only the minimal amount of editing. Stephen is not what you might call a Literary Bunny and yet when I read what he has written it is both honest and concise, with what could be described as a developing style of his own.

Or is it his own? Steve gives Rob the longhand pages he has written with a clear and definite instruction... "type it out exactly as I've written it" which Rob dutifully does before sending it on to me. But I do find myself wondering if Steve is doing the writing, or if there is a Spiritual personality working through him, helping him get his jumble of thoughts into order, and directing his hand across the page. I sense that this *is* the case and, if I am write, (sorry, *right*), there will be much further evidence of this phenomena in the future.

Chapter Eight
Margaret

I met Stephen's mother Margaret at the beginning of 2000. She was an effervescent lady, full of fun and good humour, and I think it's fair to say she was the apple of Stephen's eye. Unlike many people of her age, she was totally in tune with the modern world and emanated an aura of total *joie de vivre*; she was a committed vegetarian and had a great affinity with animals, especially dogs. I was deeply saddened to learn of her death in 2018 after a long battle with dementia, and I cannot even begin to imagine how deeply this affected Stephen. Perhaps it might be a good idea if I allowed him to tell you in his own words...

Stephen:
Looking back now, I can see that Mum's health started to deteriorate shortly after she had a general anaesthetic, after having been bitten by our pet Yorkshire terrier. We would notice she would be asking the same thing within a matter of minutes. Things would be left in random places, items put in the washing machine and hidden away, cushions stacked up in random parts of the house, and forgetting names. All this became much more frequent until finally, on our third visit to the doctor, it was agreed that Mum was in the early stages of dementia. Apparently, the consultant said it was so mild, it was borderline as to whether they medicated or not.

Sadly, over the next six month period, Mum deteriorated rapidly. She was always very sensitive, and even though she wasn´t aware of everything that was happening to her, you could always tell she felt an underlying sense of embarrassment. She always said "I will

NEVER go in to a Home" and this was always something that stuck out in our minds. So, between myself and my two sisters, Joanne and Adele, and my Dad, we tried to manage a very difficult-to-judge situation.

Eventually, it became very clear that even with the help of Caroline and Ellie, and my two boys Robbie and Bradley, plus a massive support network of friends and medical experts, we were never going to beat the dementia. By this time, Joanne had given up her job to become a full-time carer, as it became increasingly apparent that Mum needed 24/7 supervision.

Looking back now, we were not professional carers and it was so difficult to manage the emotional side of things when it's happening to someone you love, someone who is rapidly deteriorating before your eyes. At this point it made me wonder how on earth people cope who don't have any family to give them support.

Mum was going downhill on a weekly basis. She had two bouts of delirium during this time, which is a frequent complication in the advanced stages of dementia. At times, she was walking round in constant circles, not knowing where she was, or who we were; in her distress she would become very agitated. On both occasions, she was admitted to Pinderfields Hospital in Wakefield and was found to be suffering from a urinary infection. This is commonplace with dementia patients. Once treated with anti-biotics, she became less confused, but, reading in to what we had come to learn about delirium and dementia, and also what we had been told, we knew Mum's life expectancy was getting shorter by the week! This was unbearable to know, and I suppose now it emphasised the fact that there was not going to be a happy ending to this horrendous disease!

It was on the second admittance to the hospital with delirium, that we had no other choice but to start looking for a permanent Care Home. After looking round several, and some of which, believe me, I would not keep an animal in, we were extremely lucky to find Oulton Manor in Rothwell, near Leeds. It was a stone's throw from where Joanne and Adele lived, and only a 10 minute drive for me. This is a beautiful Home, more reminiscent of a 4 Star hotel, with a lovely, peaceful atmosphere. The staff were simply 5 Star Plus. I don't think Mum knew where she was; she probably felt like she was on holiday somewhere. She never once mentioned her beautiful bungalow and her garden, where she used to love to feed the birds. This was a clear indication to me that she felt somehow settled.

It was at this time, my youngest sister, Adele, gave us the news that she was expecting her second child, already having a three year old little boy, who my Mum worshipped. This was amazing news for Adele and her partner, Steve. A couple of weeks later, around midday, I had a call from Joanne to say that Mum had been admitted to Pinderfields with suspected Sepsis. This was a shock to say the least because only the day before Mum and I had been walking round the grounds, and she seemed in good spirits. Unfortunately, however, we discovered it wasn't Sepsis, but even worse, Type 'A' Flu, which is lethal in older people, plus the added complications of Mum's overall health situation.

Over the next five days, she went downhill drastically. We would sit there with her at the bedside, taking it in turns to hold her hands. She felt reassured when you did this. I would go to work to do my demonstrations, travelling back to be with her, after gowning up and putting masks on. At this time, she was in an isolation ward with another 3 patients with the same strain of Flu.

Something that is worth mentioning here is the fact that all our lives we have had dogs, and right to the last stages of her dementia, Mum always said she would like a dog. She would mention this on a daily basis, but for obvious reasons, this could not happen. However, it was sheer good luck that myself and Rob had, a few months previously, bought her two matching heavyweight Beanie dogs, that she used as door-stops. Pretty little things, made from corduroy. Despite their weight, and Mum only weighing five stone, for the last three months she carried them round with her, under her arms, obviously thinking in her own mind that they were real. Even sometimes, asking if they needed changing. This was typical of Mum, always looking after something, or someone.

I realise now, looking back on life with Mum, how totally special she was. I know everyone thinks their Mum is special, but she really was. She was a vegetarian, loved animals and children, and probably the most giving, loving, patient and understanding person I have ever come into contact with. So to say I have been privileged beyond belief to have her as my Mum is an understatement. My sister, Joanne, had to stop Mum's charity donations because she had direct debits going out left, right and centre. In the end, we realised she was actually paying out more than was coming in! Again, typical of Mum's selflessness.

Sadly, on the 24th February, we knew that Mum was not long for this world. Joanne and I made the decision to call Adele. Poor Adele had not been able to see Mum under her Doctor's recommendations, with her being pregnant, and Mum having the highly contagious Type 'A' Flu. We promised her that we would let her know if Mum suddenly took a turn for the worse. Adele and her partner, Steve, said they would be there as soon as possible, as all Adele wanted was to tell Mum that she was pregnant. Even though Mum wouldn't be able to answer, it was just the fact that she could tell her.

Unfortunately, this wasn't meant to be, as what should have been an easy journey to the Hospital was hampered by the road being closed and having to take a detour, sadly missing Mum's passing by 10 minutes. Mum passed away with her loving family around her.

I'm a Medium, and proving that life continues after the spirit leaves the body is what I spend my life doing. However comfortable that knowledge was, it failed to protect me from being vulnerable at that moment, and the feeling and sense of weakness I felt was unbearable. This was something, I realised, that I *had* to feel and go through...

I consider myself lucky to have had such a lengthy period of time with my Mum. All 52 years!!! Some poor people don't get that, they lose their parents when they're young, often in tragic circumstances, not having the chance to say 'Goodbye,' or 'I love you', or even 'Sorry'. But, taking all this into account, I am only human, and like the rest of you out there, I too miss that physical contact that I had with Mum. It is one year and five months now since Mum has passed, and I am only now feeling that the grieving process has started.

At first, all I had in my mind were those memories of the hospital, Mum's irrational and agitated behaviour, and waif-like frail body, falling to five and a half stones. I was consumed with all the sadness that led up to her death. Only now, I can see that these recent memories were blocking my ability to remember all the lovely memories throughout my life with her. Gradually, the negative memories are falling away, they have no place in my mind, and have made way for the new memories, with a firm foundation of love, life and laughter - 'Happy Times'.

Just 3 days after Mum had passed, I had to go back to Pinderfields Hospital, something I didn't really want to do, but I knew I had to collect the death certificate. As I walked through the main entrance, my heart was thumping with anticipation. I briefly remember walking past a Tombola stall, manned by two nurses, and saw a sign which said that this was to raise money for the Newborn Baby Unit. Seeing this reminded me that Adele never got the chance to tell Mum that she was pregnant. Suddenly I found myself turning round and walking back to the stall. This time, taking in the sight of all the prizes, which included Champagne, vodka, glass vases with beautiful displays, and electrical items etc – I just felt I had to buy some, so I gave the lady £5 and she gave me a selection of different coloured tickets. I then carried on my journey to the Bereavement Office. After collecting the Certificate, I headed back through the Reception and handed my Tombola tickets in, still in a world of my own. The nurse turned away to see if I had won, and to my surprise, looked rather embarrassed and passed a prize to me, and said "Do you know anybody who likes Beanie Dogs?"

Wow! Tears rolled down my face, I knew at this time that this was a clear sign that Mum was watching over me. Only three days after her passing! I walked back to the car, and explained all this to Rob, who was equally dumbfounded, as he had just expected to see me with the death certificate. Within seconds of explaining what had happened to Rob, I said I needed to call Adele, so I pressed 'Dial' and she answered. It was a whispering voice, not one I was used to hearing from her, because like me, Adele is quite loud!

"Sorry love" she said, "I'm talking quietly as I've just come out of the loo at the Doctors, I've been asking Mum for a sign. The scan shows I'm having a baby boy."

"Well," I said, "I think you've got your sign that Mum *knows* you're pregnant love, and that it's a boy."

I explained the Tombola prize and that it was for the Newborn Baby Unit and, of course, all this took place while Adele was asking Mum for a sign. Of all the things in the world to win, I won a Beanie Dog! Like me, Adele was astounded, but not surprised, knowing Mum's strength and determination. After only 72 hours for this to happen was wonderful. Bearing in mind, Adele wanted so much to go in and see Mum. Not only did she miss saying goodbye by 10 minutes, she so much wanted to tell her she was pregnant. This was Mum's way of letting her know that she KNEW.

After I ended the call with Adele, Rob came out with a random sentence, "Wouldn't it be funny if Adele decided to call the baby Luke?"

I said "Why do you say that?"

To which he replied "Look at the label," and passed over the Beanie dog.

To my surprise, there in front of me was a label attached to the dog, so tiny I had to put my glasses on to read it, and the name was Luke.

"Yes," I replied, "but I don't think Adele would choose that name for a little boy." So I never mentioned this to Adele. From that moment on, I placed the little dog in the handle on the inside of the car that you hold on to when going round corners. It's still there to this day, and every so often, I like to touch it, I suppose that's my own comfort blanket.

Fast forward seven weeks, and we were at the caravan in Filey, waiting for Adele and my nephew, Ashton, to arrive. I'd put the kettle on and in they came. And after greeting them, ten minutes in to the conversation, I said...

"Adele, have you any ideas on names?"

She replied "Well, actually the only name we can think of is Luca, it's Italian for Luke."

Margaret Holbrook - Game, Set and Match!

Just to conclude this chapter in my life, I have always said that Mediumship changes; it goes in stages, similar to a child having growth spurts. To me, however, these changes are not physical shifts, but mental ones. Often, when a new Guide or Helper comes in to work with me, there is a period of imbalance. This can last anything from a couple of days up to a week, if not more. Each time, this is different, but eventually when I become more settled with my new Guide, everything appears much stronger and returns to that familiar feeling of stability.

You have to remember that everything about my mediumship is natural and, whereas many mediums sit in development circles for years, this isn't for me. Oh no, I choose the hard way! Which, to be honest, often felt like I was trying to find a bedroom in the middle of the night, in a pitch black house that I didn't know. Mum used to say, "Oh Stephen, you never do things the easy way! You always have to complicate things". Sadly, Mum, this wasn't the case here. I have let Spirit guide me this far, and I am pretty sure I can trust them to take me the rest of the journey. So, in effect, mental growth has altered my Mediumship over the years, but the physical loss of Mum had to change things also. And it has: for 37 years I have been delivering messages to sons and daughters from their parents, not knowing or really understanding, the full impact and deep sadness of losing a Mum really presented. Now I can say that I really do. Yet, in the same vein, each time I pass on another message to a sibling, it has a direct effect on me. It's unusual, it's sharing an empathy between the recipient and myself.

Is there anything I can add to this candid and heartfelt piece of writing from Stephen? No, there isn't, so I'll just go and put the kettle on and have a quiet little cry to myself, thinking of my own mother and wishing that things could have been different between us. Even in his deepest grief, Steve knows how lucky he was to have had Margaret as a Mum, and I wish that my relationship with my own mother could have been the same.

Chapter Nine
Alan

Stephen:

Shortly after Christmas, in my first year with Rob, I started to notice something, and it was happening far too frequently for me to ignore it. It seemed to be when we were away in hotels, which in our work can often be five or six nights a week. We obviously use them for a means of accommodation between venues, but so often we come across families having a well-earned break, especially during school holidays.

I can't really say at what point I noticed it. Normally I would be so pleased to see families being happy together, laughing and giggling with the kids getting over excited, but over recent months it had started to cause me a knot in the pit of my stomach, which in turn left me feeling tense and unhappy. What on earth was it all about?

I love kids, and always made a fuss of the little ones, and one morning we were in the Imperial Hotel in Blackpool. We had been working there the night before, and this particular stay had breakfast included. While we were eating, I looked across to another table and saw a man, probably late 30s, simply trying to coax his little girl to remain seated and eat her cereal. We all know that when a child is hungry they will eat, but if they're not, and there are other more interesting things going on around them, you've got no chance. But bless him, he wasn't giving up! Now ordinarily this would have made me smile, but there it was again, that knot in my stomach. I just couldn't understand this feeling, it was like two polar opposites inside me – one enjoying watching him interact with his beautiful little girl, and two, not wanting to watch because of that sinking feeling it gave me.

I still, however, tried to ignore this and push these strange feelings to one side, and get on with the rest of my life. Everything else seemed to be running smoothly, but I realised I had to address this problem. It wasn't just when I saw families together, doing the most mundane things, but also just simple things like seeing a father play footie with his son on the local field. So, me being me, got straight on with it and started to look for a Psychotherapist. I called about 3 or 4, none of which I felt any connection with. But just as Rob was looking for another that was recommended, Alan Kershaw popped up on his computer. "Stop," I said, "who's he?" Rob went on to read a short paragraph about Alan's work, and gave me his number. Five minutes later, I was dialling it, and Hey Presto, a voice on the other end of the line, a real person! After briefly explaining what my problem was, Alan agreed to see me. Much to my relief, I was working locally and only had two days to wait for the appointment.

Again, all my life my work has been involved around voice vibration and, hearing Alan's voice, I knew this was the person who could sort me out. As you always do, when you tell someone something that's bothering you, there was that instant lifting feeling, but at the same time, half of me felt silly because I couldn't analyse my own true feelings. The appointment came round and my judgment was 100% right – Alan was so personable and I instantly relaxed around him.

To be honest, I look back now and the answer as to why I felt so bad was glaringly obvious, but when you are living in the moment and feeling the anxiety that the situation creates, it is totally impossible to get a clear overview.

Alan took me back to some of my favourite memories, through his hypnosis techniques, making me bring them out in to the open, so he was able to analyse them. These memories varied from teaching all three children to swim; calling Caroline from the sports centre to say they had swum a length or dived in, whilst treating them to sausage and chips in the café; the wonderful family holidays we shared, from all-inclusive in Spain to cosy caravans in Skegness; taking the kids round the estate on their electric cars; Robbie helping me doing the gardening; watching Brad on the trampolines; and chasing Ellie on the inflatable tunnels. All wonderful, natural memories that, as a father, I could keep forever.

After this session, Alan said I would probably need to see him only twice. He just needed to make me see the reasons behind what was making me feel so bad, and learn how to disregard them. I now know that my reaction was a self-blame mechanism. It would be activated when I was around families enjoying themselves, because deep down, I knew I had created a split in my family. I was blaming myself and sub-consciously, looking at other families having fun together was a reminder of what I hadn't got around me anymore.

Alan helped me to see, over the following weeks, that I was looking in to the past. I had already explained to him all the wonderful scenarios that made me happy, all the things I had already done with my children. He pointed out that I could still do those things! My children were not babies anymore, they were growing fast, and I had to look forward to making many more happy memories in the future. Doing different things with them, together as a family, and there was no reason to torture myself with these guilt-trips.

I learned so many things from Alan: he taught me to value myself, to hold my head up high, and look towards the future with optimism. All this emotion could now be channelled into my evenings, and not be wasted trying to untangle wires that over the last year had got into a mess.

After treating me, Alan was quite open with me and said that he knew who I was as soon as we met, but felt it better just to treat me and get me back on track, rather than mention my work. He was utterly professional and therefore became a very good friend. He always said it amazed him how the contact from a loved one could bring the emotion to the surface so quickly, and he explained that what could take him, as a practitioner, weeks or months to unravel, could be done there and then from that instant contact from that special family member or friend. My work certainly fascinated him but, needless to say, we are all unique in our chosen field and Alan's work still fascinates me to this very day. He was a true master of his craft, and I am proud to call him my friend. I know he will still be giving me help and advice from the spirit world. Some people come into our lives and leave a massive impression, and Alan certainly did that with me!

I need to back track here to just after my Mum's passing... We had to go through the awful process of arranging the funeral and, as everyone who has had the daunting task of organising a funeral will know, it makes everything seem so final. I spoke to three different undertakers over the phone and, just to re-iterate, my life over the last 30 years has all been about the voice and voice vibration, and each one I spoke to went into a great sales pitch on why we should go with them. None of them seemed to feel like the right one, and I knew I would just instinctively know. A couple of days later I just remembered going to a funeral of a friend of mine's Dad.

The lady who did the service, Lesley Blessington, was absolutely amazing. She made you feel like she knew the deceased personally, so much so that after the service I briefly told her how I felt, and asked for her card. Based on this, I picked up the phone and rang, to see if she was available to do the eulogy at my Mum's funeral. Just as I was about to put the phone down, as if reading my mind, she said "I know a very good Funeral Director, John Bell. He lives local, and is a very genuine, lovely bloke." I phoned John within minutes, and Hey Presto! The voice was exactly what I was expecting. Cheerful without being over the top, and very friendly. Much to my relief, he didn't have the same sales patter as the other three. It was now my job to inform my Dad, Joanne and Adele, and I instinctively knew they would approve.

Meanwhile, behind the scenes, I knew that my friend Alan had been going through a very rough time with his health, and had deteriorated drastically over the last two months, finally to be diagnosed with Cancer, and had been admitted to Wakefield Hospice. Sadly, I had not had the opportunity to see him, being pre-occupied with my Mum being in and out of hospital. Even so, I was totally aware that his wife and children would be going through a horrendously emotional time, dealing with the situation. Alan was a wonderful husband and father, open and emotionally forthcoming, as I had always been with my children. Knowing that Alan's admittance to a hospice couldn't be a good sign, I prayed for the best but accepted the inevitability of the worst.

Now, to get on with arranging Mum's funeral... We met with John Bell at his office, in Stanley, near Wakefield. We went through the familiarities and, needless to say, as we did, I knew my intuition had not let me down. He was sincere in every way, and a man that made you feel at ease. When we came to discuss the song we wanted in the 'Time for Reflection' section in the middle of the service, I said "I know the song I want, but you may not have it on your playlist." When he asked me what it was I told him it was "The Hand That Leads Me".

To my surprise he said "Yes, I do have it and it's the very song I played at my own Mum's funeral last year. It was written by Jane McDonald for her own Mother." Wow, another sign!!! Of all the BILLIONS of songs in the world we could have chosen, not just me, but collectively as a family!

This was yet another clear indication that we were on the right track. Shortly afterwards, I rang Jane and asked her permission to play it. Her reply was "I would love more than anything for you to play that song darling, I'd feel honoured. Let me know the date of the funeral, and I'll be there." I agreed to let her know and an hour later, after discussions of all kinds (which was always the case with me and Jane), we ended the call.

Just as we had finished arranging Mum's funeral, and I was beginning to let everyone know the date, I received a call from my cousin, Claire, to say she wouldn't be in the country on the date, as she would be on holiday in Jamaica. I immediately called John Bell to re-arrange the date, and he came back with an earlier date (which incidentally suited us much better, as the initial date meant we would have to wait almost 4 weeks, which seemed to be such a long time). We then set about telling everyone of the *new* date. In the meantime, we all busied ourselves with the finer details, flowers, where to have the wake, who to have the donations collected for, etc.

A week later, I received some more very sad news: my friend Alan had passed away in Wakefield Hospice. Oh my God! February wasn't turning out to be such a good month. My heart went out to Gina, Alan's wife, and her family. I could honestly say, I could truly sympathise with them, but things then would turn out to even more complex. A week later, I received a call from Gina that she had arranged Alan's funeral, and wondered if I would be prepared to do the Eulogy, as in Gina's words "Alan thought the world of you, and held you in such high regard."

I hadn't even attempted to start writing my own Mum's Eulogy, and here I was, facing the daunting task of arranging my special friend's Eulogy too. Needless to say, I was still managing to do my demonstrations six nights a week. Trying times and emotionally exhausting!

I must admit, and it seems quite surreal now, but at the time, it didn't sink in. Gina relayed the date and time of Alan's funeral, which was Wednesday 28th March 2018, which was the very day that we had arranged for Mum's funeral before we'd had to change it. Not just that, but the exact time too and the exact same place! Could things have been synchronised any finer? There seemed to be forces out there that neither I, nor anyone else, could either explain, or predict.

I won't go through the whole funeral but, suffice to say, that collectively, as a family, we did my Mum proud. Both my sisters managed to get up and say some beautiful words that Mum would have been very proud of and, after a rocky start, I managed to do the Eulogy. I can quite honestly say I would rather stand up in front of 1200 people in a theatre, or on board a cruise ship, but to stand up in front of a congregation of 100 people in a Crematorium (many of which are your family and friends), is very difficult to say the least. I was way out of my comfort zone, but I knew I was doing it for my Mum. I had never foreseen that just that 10 days later, I would be behind the same lectern, in the same Crematorium, doing yet another Eulogy for my good friend Alan Kershaw. Just a note here - and some of you may find this strange - but we can't plan our own deaths, although it would make it a lot easier if we could!

On both Mum's, and Alan's funerals, I was committed to doing demonstrations which had been arranged a good year in previously, and there was no way on this earth I would let these people down. On both occasions, I fulfilled my obligation to my audience – not just on this side of the veil but also on the next. However, I won't pretend that it was easy.

From being a child, one thing Mum always instilled in me was the fact that we must never, ever, let anyone down. If you're going to do something, be true to your word and do it. Needless to say, both demonstrations went without a hitch. If she's listening, and I'm sure she is, I'd just like to say Mum, I made sure I did this, not for my audience, but for you! Both demonstrations finished at 9.50pm, and by

10pm I was in the car asleep whilst Rob was behind the wheel driving home.

Chapter Ten
Rob Green

I didn't meet Rob until some six weeks after Stephen's coming out. We were staging a demonstration in Southampton, and just before he went out on to the platform, he shyly confessed that Rob was waiting in the bar if I wanted to meet him. Despite all my earlier reassurances, he was still nervous about the whole situation, to the extent that he deliberately avoided the process of making formal introductions. It was a typical example of the old Taurean philosophy of 'I don't quite know how to handle this, so I'll let them sort it out for themselves.'

"Er, how will I recognise him?" I'd asked.

"Don't worry, you'll recognise him all right," Stephen had responded. "He looks a bit like me and, anyway, he knows who *you* are, so he's bound to give you a clue."

So, Stephen had walked out to face his eagerly waiting audience and I marched down to the bar, very eager to meet the guy who had turned Steve's life round on a sixpence. And he was quite right, I did recognise Rob Green straight away! It wasn't difficult, because apart from the guy behind the bar, he was the only man in the room, and he did look a lot like Stephen... Slim, fair hair, nicely balanced features...

As I walked towards him, he stood up and, smiling shyly, held out his hand. "Bugger this," I thought, and ignoring the hand, wrapped my arms around him in a huge bear hug. Whether it took him by surprise or not, I really don't know, but it broke a lot of ice very quickly; it was a totally spontaneous thing on my part, which was my way of saying "welcome to my world".

Over the weeks and months which followed, I spent a lot of time with Rob and, fair to say, got to know him very well. He is a modest man with a dry humour and a lovely sense of mischief. He is calm and practical, the perfect foil for Stephen's boisterous exuberance, and he very quickly became the lynch pin of all the boring and time consuming business aspects of Stephen's life. Just as importantly, he did all the driving! This is not to say that Stephen is a bad driver, only that Rob is a whole lot better! I remember numerous occasions in the early days of my association with Steve when we'd be belting up the A1 at 60 mph: Steve would be driving with one hand on the steering wheel, mobile phone jammed between his chin and his shoulder, trying to write a name in a notebook which was balanced precariously on his left knee. Needless to say, those days are long gone!

So, Rob is a good driver, a great manager, a caring partner and a very nice man to know. But who is he? Where does he come from? This next section, written by Rob, may give you some answers and insights...

From Rob Green:
You will, by now, have heard how Steve and I first met. It certainly was a bizarre set of coincidences that brought us together; you really couldn't make it up! I have heard many times over the years, the phrases 'It was meant to be' and 'Spirit moves in mysterious ways', and certainly in this case, Spirit totally worked overtime! I really can't pinpoint an exact, specific 'thing', but I really felt Steve and I really connected, it seemed like we had known each other for a lifetime already... we just gelled together. We had so much in common, although conversely, so many things were totally different. Steve was married, had three children, a huge family, whereas I was living with my partner, Aidan,

had never ever considered children in my life, and it was just me and my Mum, and a few aunties.

Of course, back in those days, I had never really considered the 'Spirit World', never even thought about it, I wasn't even religious in any shape or form. As regards death and dying etc, I simply thought that once you were gone, you were gone. I had certainly HEARD of Mediums etc., but just never looked into it.

That first night I met Steve, we talked about a lot of things, his work being one of them, and it actually totally fascinated me. I suppose I didn't really fully understand everything about it, but after that evening, I definitely had more of an understanding. Over the years, working and living with Steve, I have gained a lot more knowledge, and even though Steve NEVER* lets me in on his demonstrations, I know enough to answer any questions people have when I re-appear at the interval.

I tried as much as I could to arrange my busy work schedule around where Steve was working, and although this was often impossible to do, Steve and I met up several times over the next few months, and it became apparent that we were becoming more and more inseparable. I knew in my head though, that it could never work out, Steve had three kids and a wife, so how the hell COULD that work? He was never going to leave that behind and I just resigned myself to the fact that the relationship would die a natural death; we would just drift apart and it would become something that I would remember fondly for the rest of my life, and possibly shed a tear or two thinking 'what might have been'.

Months went by, and I had already met Steve's children, they were all delightful, and seemed to really take a shine to me. Steve didn't want me to meet them, he thought it would be a step too far and, anyway, if it didn't work out, why would it be important? I didn't know, but it just seemed the right thing to do, and I really loved being with them. I had also met Caroline and she was a really lovely warm person. One day, Steve told me that he had spoken to Caroline, and told her everything. Absolutely devastated doesn't come into how Caroline felt, and it was going to be very hard to come to terms with it. I made the decision to tell Aidan at the same time, and it was the hardest thing I have ever had to do.

There were then several months of discussions, and lots of tears. It was, as Steve likes to call his demonstrations, a real 'emotional rollercoaster'. We talked about several options, and decided to move into a house only two miles from the family home, so Steve could still take the kids to school every morning, and still be a huge part of their lives. It worked well, and still does, we live in the same house and even though the kids have grown up, we still see them all on a daily basis.

As I said, for almost all my life, children were never an option, and it scared the living daylights out of me having to be 'Daddy Two' as the kids called me. Apparently, according to Steve, I took to it like a duck to water, and I absolutely loved every minute being with the kids. Even at weekends when we were overtaken by the kid's friends too! It was certainly a non-stop whirlwind of meals out, bowling, watching kids' tv, fetching and carrying for them all, clearing up, trying to get them all to go to sleep (mega challenge!), ferrying them all back home etc. It was full-on but I loved it.

By this time, Caroline and I had become friends, and she knew she could trust me with her children, and it took a lot of time, but Aidan had also accepted what had happened and we all moved on together. I think we were all mature enough to accept that there was no point in being bitter and twisted, creating rifts; we should all work together and be strong for each other and the children. Aidan and Caroline are best friends – they probably both talk about me and Steve behind our backs! – and all the extended Holbrook family on both Steve's and Caroline's side have accepted both me and Aidan into their lives. So much so, that the first year, we all went away together on holiday. Some people don't understand, they just don't 'get it', but for us all, it works and it's amazing. We have had family holidays every year, weekends away with the kids, days out with the in-laws and out-laws, and it couldn't be better.

That being said, there is a running joke that I'm 'Not Part Of The Family!' It all started when we were shopping for presents for Ashton and Luca, his sister Adele's two children. I had a handful of gorgeous little outfits, and suddenly Steve said "Why are you buying pressies? You're not even their Uncle!" To which I replied "Huh! Throw me out of the family why don't you?!" Now everyone says it — in jest I hope! I often joke back that I'm not even part of my own family as I was adopted, and even went to the extreme of joining Ikea so I could at least be part of the Ikea Family!

It's funny how kids accept things at face value. Steve had explained the situation to the children, and it really did help that they had met me before, and knew who I was. They were all so young, and it didn't appear to faze them at all. There were a lot of questions from them, naturally, sometimes it was hard to try and find the right things to say in response, especially as they were so impressionable. Their concept of being gay was in its infancy I suppose, but they just knew they were in a happy home. There is an expression — 'out of the mouths of babes' — and you can't even make up some of the things the kids asked me, but I do recall one day when Brad absolutely floored me. We were in a fairly upmarket shop on a day out, Brad was holding my hand, and we were just looking round. Soft, gentle music was playing, a few well-to-do people were browsing, and it was very, very quiet. Quite out of the blue, Brad said "Rob, you know when you were younger, did you touch little boys' bottoms?" Oh my God, Earth, please swallow me up was all I could think about, as people turned around and stared at me, holding Brad's hand, totally red-faced and spluttering "Absolutely NOT!!" I have never walked out of a shop quicker in my life, I think I may have given Usain Bolt a run for his money that day!

At first, I was still working at my old job, travelling around the country, but it gradually dawned on me that it wasn't what I wanted any more, I wanted to work with, and for, Steve. He was adamant that there wouldn't be enough for me to do, and he'd say things like "don't be hasty!" etc. But I knew it would work. I handed in my notice to the firm where I had worked for almost 20 years, and took a deep breath! Steve had done all his own work for the best part of 25 years, so to let me actually DO anything was hard at first. He couldn't let go. Very set in his ways, but everything worked, there was a system, a procedure, and it didn't fail. He couldn't see how modernising things and using computers would be any help. How could anything be better than what was already in place? Well, it took a while, but I did manage to take over a lot of stuff, putting everything on spreadsheets, using emails for contracts, doing the accounts with all the formulas and VAT etc. Now, he says he has no idea how he actually did everything – and believe me, I don't know how either.

Steve is famously a technophobe – you've only got to see his phone to realise this! – and still to this day he believes computers are not totally infallible. I like to have things on either a paper-trail, or email, so I can see what has been said etc. If something needs chasing, I'll send another email to check. If then I still haven't had a reply, I'll say to Steve, "Oh I'm still waiting for a reply" and he'll be like "Oh for God's sake, just pick up the bloody phone and talk to them!" This is true, to be honest, you can become a bit reliant on automation. Of course, it wasn't just the office work, I had to be front of house for the demos too. It was nerve-wracking at first, as Steve's audiences were used to the door being run by Steve himself, or his friend Pat. I thought they'd all be thinking "Who the hell are you? Where is Steve, why isn't he here?" I really needn't have worried in hindsight, it was fun and I really enjoy doing it.

Over the years, as the Medium Charmian Evans mentioned when she interviewed Steve many years ago (as mentioned previously in this book), I have become an integral part of the Holbrook clan. In the earlier years, helping the kids with homework, answering questions about many facets in life, my opinions on any given matter, and as they have grown up, have become more valued and respected for my input. Obviously, the children are a product of Steve and Caroline, and they have had the most loving, caring and nurturing beginning to life that any child can have, and naturally their opinions and advice are the most important, but I think they also like to have another take on things, just to give a different view. I don't push obviously but, if they ask, I'll give my response. It is a good feeling to know my opinions count and to be thought of enough to be asked.

Living with Steve is an education, there's always something that makes me think about life. He is the main one-stop, go-to person if there is ever a crisis, a problem, or a falling out in the family. Steve has always said "there aren't such things as problems, it's simply a matter for things to be looked at and resolved, they are all lessons to be learned". This is true, and each time I listen to the advice he gives, it's a breath of fresh air. Each time you come out of a problem feeling lighter, and more positive. Everyone relies on the views and advice given by him and, to be honest, it sometimes can be too much for one person to take! Advice not just for the children, but for Caroline and the family too. We have joked that he should charge for his time – if he did, he'd be a millionaire by now!

Steve is a natural born comic too. As you may have seen in his demonstrations, his natural humour shines through, and he can make some of the hardest messages become softer and more palatable. He is also dyslexic, and comes out with some hilarious phrases and words. A laptop is a "labtop", he calls Lyonnaise potatoes "Lioness potatoes", and my favourite is "RoseMarie" sauce instead of "Marie Rose". He sees colours differently to how we see them, and gets mixed up on numbers. I am not taking the mickey here, it's simply how things are with his dyslexia, but we all do have a laugh about it. There's nothing you can do, so just go with the flow. It's a bit like my Mum, who is 85 now, getting her words muddled, Taylor Swift is Taylor Smith, and her piece-de-resistance is calling Tommy Hilfiger "that ruddy Tommy Higfrigger"!

Of course, living with Steve isn't always a bed of roses, he can be bloody irritating sometimes (as I guess I am to him of course; every person in every relationship does things that annoys the hell out of the other!). We're only talking about little things here, like never putting the lid down on the loo, ALWAYS leaving lights on, never rinsing his bowl out after having cereal, always getting a new spoon out rather than rinse and re-use one that's been used before. From his point of view, I know it annoys the life out of him when I leave my clothes in a heap at the end of the bed, and many many other things. It's all give and take, and if we can spend 24 hours a day, living and working together, and haven't yet strangled each other, we're doing bloody well!

On balance, I wouldn't change a thing. I love my life, and I love working with Steve, and, despite being 'Not Part Of The Family', I have gradually become part of a bigger entity, the Spirit Family who have given me a new outlook on life, learned to be more open and honest and, to use another well known phrase, 'grab life by the balls'. We've only got one physical life, live life to the full, do everything you can, enjoy it, have no regrets, look forward, and just simply relish everything you have.

*With regard to the demonstrations, it is a running joke that I'm never allowed in, which these days IS true and has been for the best part of 15 years, but there was ONE occasion he let me in, and that was the first time I had ever been to a demo. He wanted me to see how they worked. It was all very well knowing what he did, but if I didn't see it for myself, I would be hard pushed to believe it. I was a little nervous to be honest, sat on the back row in the Coachman Hotel in Darlington, sweating like I was waiting for a job interview. Steve ran through the introduction, putting people at ease with his usual panache, and I settled in and listened intently to the messages he gave. God help me if comes to me, I thought, I'd DIE! I had nothing to compare any of the messages to of course, but it was absolutely amazing, very very emotional at times, especially when he brought through a very young child who had died, but also full of laughter too. I really rather enjoyed it, and it's a pity I have never seen any more, just heard about them afterwards. Maybe one day, when we get older, I may just get to go back in! Steve has enriched my life in so many different ways, but the most important thing he has ever done for me is to awaken my own sense of spirituality.

Chapter Eleven
Mysteries

Spirit moves in mysterious ways, and sometimes those ways are not always obvious. It seems quite clear that if someone in spirit wants to make contact with a loved one down here on the earth plane, they'll bust a gut trying to do it. Sometimes, if the living recipient has some degree of spiritual atunement, it might come in the form of direct voice contact, such as the incident Stephen experienced with Eric Hatton, but sometimes it can be much more subtle. Furthermore, if a spirit has only recently passed over, it is believed that they might need some time on the 'other side' to adjust to their new situation and learn how to communicate. For example, Margaret Holbrook communicated with her son and daughter indirectly through a stuffed dog only a very short while after her passing, but who is to say that a year from now, or however long it might take, she might not be talking directly into Stephen's ear just as Eric Hatton did? The precedents are in place, for on a number of occasions Stephen has heard his Grandfather John's words passing on advice in this 'direct voice' mode.

There are numerous situations when spiritual intervention in our human lives can help us avoid disaster. In the heat of a blazing argument when anger and resentment rule the day and tempers have long since been lost, I could open my mouth to say something harsh and cruel. I am being hurt, and I want to lash out and retaliate. I open my mouth to launch a tirade of vitriol – and then I shut my mouth and say nothing. Is this me, consciously admitting defeat, backing off out of fear of making things worse than they already are, or is this a friendly voice from my long dead Grandmother saying "Whoa lad, you've said quite enough already. You've made your point, so just shut up and walk away." Common sense, based on previous experience, would suggest the former, but if you believe in the world of spirit, you cannot just ignore the latter, especially when there are other things to back it up.

Many years ago I had a friend called Trevor. He loved the sea, and would do anything he possibly could to get on board a ship, even to the extent of booking a return trip from Dover to Calais. He got on board at Dover, sailed to Calais, didn't disembark, and sailed straight back to Dover. He did this four times on the same day on the same ticket and no one was ever the wiser. He booked a ticket from Hull to Zebrugge in Holland, and yet when he came to get on the ship for the outbound trip, he couldn't do it. His feet felt as though they were glued to the jetty and he was overcome with feelings of breathlessness and nausea. He thought he was having a stroke or a heart attack, and ended up being transported to Hull Royal Infirmary in the back of an ambulance. He was fine, but a few hours later the ship overturned and capsized in Zebrugge harbour with a terrible loss of life. He does not know what happened on the quayside in Hull, and neither do I – but I could make a fairly accurate guess!

I have a very similar personal experience. In 1972 I was booked to fly on a Dan Air flight to The Canaries, and yet couldn't for the life of me bring myself to board the aircraft. I feigned illness and the plane took off without me – and three and a half hours later it crashed into the side of Mount Tiede on Tenerife, killing everyone on board.

You could, at a stretch, call this some kind of sixth sense, but what if any kind of sixth sense, gut feelings or hunches, are a mechanism used by spirit to intervene in our lives?

I suppose that one of the key questions that everyone asks (and probably more times than many might care to admit to) is what happens and where do we go when we die? There is no definitive answer to the question, but there are masses of theories and suppositions. The hard truth is that no one knows for certain! Some may say that they do, but they are hard pressed to prove it, and are simply offering their own visions based on either their own expectations or blind faith.

The Spiritualist Church offers a gentle guide line based on a comprehensive archive of research. It acknowledges that it is *just* a guide line and not a proven truth, but the opinion is based upon the testimony of many thousands of people who have had contact with the spirit world: some of these people have been mediums and clairvoyants, but testimony has also been taken from the recipients of messages, and religious theologians from a variety of different faith structures. As a personal observation, I have to say that this is more than you get from many other faiths. Anyway, the consensus of opinion is this...

When our body ceases to function, our spirit departs from the body and transcends to another sphere of existence. This first 'sphere' is the first of many other such spheres, and could be likened to the admissions ward of a busy hospital where there is some sort of triage system in operation. If you arrive in a traumatic state as a result of military combat or some catastrophic accident, psychic surgery is performed fairly immediately before you are passed on for recuperation. If you arrive gently as a result of a natural passing you nevertheless will feel some initial confusion, and will enjoy a rest period to become orientated with your new home. Some admissions are damn glad to get there, some are distressed and need to be calmed and healed, and some are in total denial, not believing that they are, in their own words, 'dead'. This latter group needs very special attention and, usually, once they have been persuaded to recognise the fact that they have actually passed over, they are the first to put in a request for a brief return trip to the earth plane to say a proper goodbye to those they have left behind.

A number of things are almost universally agreed upon, which is that when we arrive on the other side, all our wounds, be they mental or physical, are healed. There is a rest and reception period in which we become familiar within our new environment. We are presented with the opportunity to offer reparation to those we have hurt during our human lives, and that if we ask for forgiveness, we are given it. If there is anger and resentment in our hearts because of those things which have been done to us, these emotions are removed when we are encouraged to give them up and move on from them. Needless to say, this process will be easy for some and more difficult for others, depending on the contents and events experienced during our earthbound lives.

Inevitably our spirits transcend and become lighter and more enlightened, but love is the most enduringly powerful energy and it is only natural that in spirit form we still choose to look out for our loved ones left behind – still long to make contact with them, even if it is only to reassure them that death is not the end and is merely a portal of transition.

Stephen has a valid point when he says that if Ted wants to make contact with his wife Ethel, there is no point in Ted presenting himself as a new spirit full of sweetness and light, if while he was alive, he was a grumpy old codger who didn't have a kind word for anybody. Ethel might recognise the latter, but she'd have no terms of reference with the former. So, for the sake of contact, a spirit will retain its earth plane identity.

I think there is an allied point to be made here. Stephen says he is a 'natural' medium, but that doesn't mean he hasn't got to work hard to bring a message through. He likens himself to a telephone exchange that's only got one line working. Now, maybe there are 20 people wanting to make a phone call at the same time and they're all shouting their heads off to make their voices heard. He, as the telephonist, has got to pick out one voice at a time and try and figure out what the voice is telling him. He might make this look easy and 'natural' but in reality it is exhausting work! He also recognises that it is probably very hard work for the spirits to lower their vibrations to such an extent that they can descend to his level, connecting with his psychic beacon, wherever it might be emitting from, be it in Bournemouth, Brighton, Bridlington or Barbados.

As part of my research for an earlier book, I remember once asking Stephen if he believed in evil spirits. His answer was that he believed that there were many evil people, but he'd never come across an evil spirit.

This is interesting, because it made me wonder how the world of spirit would cope with an Adolf Hitler, a Josef Stalin, not to mention Pol Pot and a plethora of other international nasties from Jihadi terrorists to your local neighbourhood axe murderer or serial killer. This made Steve smile knowingly, and he commented that they might have to spend a *very* long time in spiritual rehab, and that it might take them a much *longer* time making those reparations I spoke about a few paragraphs ago.

Some might say that Stephen is letting these monsters off lightly, and that they should be locked in hell without the possibility of parole. This brings me nicely to the subject of heaven and hell. Until relatively recently, the Christian Church said that if you were good, you'd go *up* to heaven, but if you were bad, you'd go *down* to hell. Modern theological thought now dismisses this mediaeval notion (although there are still many who cling to the basic tenets of this concept) and a more enlightened view is loosely held by many spiritualists. Hell and Heaven *do* exist! But take note... Man has created Hell, while the Spirit World has created Heaven! This may sound very simplistic... but think about it and find your own truth.

Maybe the ultimate mystery revolves around the identity of God. Is there a God? Is He the God of The Bible or the God of the Quoran? Might he even be Jahweh, the God of the Jews? What is His name? Could it be Buddha or might it be Jesus or Mohammed? Where does He live and what does He look like? Is He even a "he" or might he/it be a She? (You might want to talk to the Wiccans and Pagans about that last one!)

These questions have divided men for millennia and have been the cause of many wars and conflicts. We search for the answers and the answers we find are based on the teachings of the faith structures of our various cultures. Everyone is convinced that they are right and, ergo, anyone who disagrees with them is wrong.

The Spiritualist Church is generally Christian in its outlook, although the Archbishops of Canterbury, York and Durham would argue strongly against that statement... or at least, this would have been their traditional position held for many many years. Thankfully, over the last decade or so, the Christian Church has opened its mind a little, and now at least there is some cordial communication between the two bodies. Having said that, there is still a long way to go.

I remember once asking Stephen if he believed in God, and I also remember that his answer, by no means evasive, was nevertheless quite a cautious one.

"I suppose I do," he admitted thoughtfully, "but if we're talking about a white haired old gentleman sitting on a throne on top of a fluffy white cloud, surrounded by chubby little angels playing golden harps... well no, I don't see God like that at all."

"So how *do* you see him?" I persisted.

"Oh James, I just don't know! All I *do* know is that there is a world of spirit waiting for us in the afterlife, and common sense dictates that someone has got to be in charge of it, sorting things out! I'm not sure it matters much what we call Him, and maybe it's only natural that people should have their own visions, and who is to say that their visions are wrong? All I know for certain is that there is a force of spirit that guides us and looks after us from another dimension, and maybe all of those spirits together go to make up the identity of what we think of as being God!"

This, I thought, was a fair and honest answer, but neither back then nor in this present day, does it do anything to assuage my own curiosity. So, along with a host of other things, the Face of God remains a mystery.

To me it seems quite obvious that there is a Higher Spiritual Authority abroad in this human world of ours, complete with a spiritual hierarchy and a route map of different pathways to spiritual enlightenment. But I do have a problem. If God is an omnipresent power, responsible for bringing love and light into this world of ours, how does one explain all the bloody conflicts of war, genocide and Man's bestial behaviour towards his fellow men?

"Ah," The Faithful will cry. "This is not the work of God, but the work of Man!"

When I respectfully point out that According to The Bible, God made Man in His own image, The Faithful fall disturbingly silent. When I ask that if God is this all-powerful being who "so loves this world", why does He allow famine and starvation, storms and tsunamis that claim thousands of lives, etc., I am told this has got nothing to do with God, but it is the force of nature. So, our all-powerful God, who created this world, has no power over nature... Ergo, He is not really *all*-powerful at all, is He?

Over the years I have spoken to various members of the clergy, who just like many of our politicians, seem incapable of giving any kind of straight answer, and so, with Stephen's permission, through these pages I appeal to you... If you've got the answer, please tell me what it is, because until you do, while I readily accept the concept of a Higher Spiritual Authority, I suspect there maybe is an element of truth in the claim that instead of God making Man in His own image, Man has made God in *his* own image!

Finally, let me make it crystal clear that these thoughts and questions are entirely my own, and do not necessarily represent Stephen Holbrook's beliefs or the teachings of The Spiritualist Church.

Chapter Twelve
Curry

Sometimes a message from Stephen can be clear and concise, and directed to a single member of the audience. The observer is privy to an exchange of words and, on the strength of the responses from the person receiving the message, they will form their own opinions. The lady in the blue hat gets a message from her late sister, and there is certainly enough evidence provided to indicate that post mortem communication has taken place. Amazing! Next message please!

What the observer, and indeed the rest of the audience, does not see are the subsequent ramifications and knock on effects that Stephen's message might have. It is not always quite so simple and straightforward as it might seem. To make this point, allow me to tell you the story of the Mitchell family, a natural death and a suicide, Stephen's unusual hair style, a dog called Bobby and a take-away curry.

From Julie Mitchell:
I have to go back a few years to tell my story which ended at Mill Hall in Rayleigh in October 2007.

My Dad was diagnosed with lung cancer on his birthday 10th September 2003 and was given six months to live. He died 10th March 2004, exactly six months to the day.

As my Dad took his last breath, his four children were by his bedside at home; myself, Carol, Allan and Lee. The loss was immense and seemed cruel; I was bereft with grief and was pointed in the direction of spiritualism. I found comfort through this but became a psychic addict, to the point I was spending up to £300 per week on psychic phone readings, getting Sky Plus to record everything supernatural, and reading until my eyes popped out – oh, and not to mention the seminars and spiritualist churches I attended! Anyway, my siblings, Allan and Carol, were concerned and felt I was not dealing with my grief but supported me, even when I got readings that might as well have come from Septic Peg!!! ("it could be a man or a woman who will have had a birthday this year." You get my drift)!

Anyway, Elaine, Allan's wife, had purchased tickets to see Stephen Holbrook at Middleton in 2005 and had roped Allan into going. This is where the story really begins.

Stephen, from what I now understand, was on form, and brought through messages with sincere clarity that it left Allan and Elaine with no doubt in their minds there was indeed an afterlife. Although they did not personally receive a message they were happy with the evidence.

At about ten thirty that evening I received a phone call from Allan who was on such a high, "Ju, you're not going to believe it! We have just seen this guy and he is amazing!" He went on to tell me about the evening with sheer enjoyment in his voice. Me never really getting any proof, scoffed and tried to pick holes in what he was saying. But Allan was so convinced that he said to me "well, I tell you what, if anything happens to me you go and find Stephen Holbrook and I'll come through because I believe in what he does!" My response, yeah, alright Al! The conversation turned humorous and Allan being the comedian completely ripped Stephen's hair to pieces, I was crying with laughter.

I took some comfort from Allan's story but still was on my own journey to find proof of the afterlife!

I came to terms with losing my dad and life seemed to resume to normal. We had down days and up days like anyone else but the bond I had with Allan and Carol really got me through and since Dad's passing we made a pact to go on holiday every New Year.

I received a phone call at four in the afternoon on 17th July 2007 from my sister Carol; her voice was subdued but not alarming. She quietly told me that Allan had died. I screamed like a banshee for over an hour and when my children wanted to know how it had happened, I didn't know, but assumed it must be a car crash and thought some bastard has killed my brother.

I phoned Carol back which felt like thirty seconds later which I now know to be over one hour later to ask how it had happened. I was not prepared for what she had to say, "Ju, he hung himself at home from the loft." I then went numb almost to the point of fainting, my Allan, the comedian, the happy one, the rock, the one who never gets depressed, why? What a waste! He was 35 years old, had a wife he loved, a daughter and stepson and a grandson who he doted on and who, in return, doted on him. Everything went on autopilot, arranging the funeral and dealing with the grief.

On the day of his funeral we were overwhelmed by the turn out; the largest crematorium in Blakely was still not big enough. People had to stand everywhere to pay their respects. The local paper shop closed until after the funeral as did the Labour Club. We found this a great comfort for it showed how much Allan was loved.

One night not long after the funeral I was crying in my bedroom when I remembered what Allan had said about Stephen Holbrook. I shot out of bed, got onto my laptop and found that he was appearing local to me in October at Mill Hall in Rayleigh. I booked two tickets for myself and Carol.

The day had come when I felt sure that Allan would keep his word and make contact. We arrived what we felt would be early to get good seats but on entering, the hall was packed. I found two seats about six rows from the back in the middle. I was holding Carol's hand praying we would receive a message. No doubt there were a lot of other prayers that night! Stephen came on stage and did his introduction. He made the whole crowd feel at ease and he was underway at a thousand miles an hour.

The first reading went to a lady sitting one row behind us. So straightaway I was gutted. I thought that we were doomed as he was bound to move to another part of the hall next. The reading was successful and the granddaughter of the lady who was coming through was in tears. As the reading was coming to a close he said "God bless and thank you" and as he turned to walkaway he said to the lady "have you just lost someone to suicide?" She responded with no, so he said thank you again and god bless.

My heart was in my mouth. I clung to Carol's hand cutting off all blood supply. Stephen turned to take a sip of water and then looking in our direction said – "Someone here has just lost a brother to suicide." Both our hands shot up, Stephen then said relax and we will get things through.

Stephen: "I've got a gentleman here, but this gentleman is telling me that he died of natural causes... Something to do with his chest... and he's telling me that January is significant for the family."

Julie: "Yes, we holiday together then."

Stephen: "He is now telling me July."

Julie: "He died in July."

Stephen: "He's telling me it was lung cancer and he's telling me there is something significant about 3 o'clock in the morning."

Julie: "We believe he died around that time and, yes, it was lung cancer."

Stephen: "Who keeps waking up at that time?"

Julie: "His wife and myself."

Stephen:	"He's around you but is there one of you missing? Another member of the family who didn't come tonight?"
Julie:	"Yes, my brother, Lee."
Stephen:	"He's telling me that he knows how much you miss him and he knows how low and unhappy you've all been feeling, but he wants me to say that he is very happy where he is right now and you've got to work hard at concentrating on all the happy memories, not the unhappy ones. Do you understand what I'm saying here?"
Julie/Carol:	"Yes."
Stephen:	"All right... Now I'm tuning in to a younger gentleman who took his own life, which happened out of the blue and was totally out of character. He's saying the pain and the agony that night was just too much, but he wants you to know he felt no pain in the passing over. It's important you know that. Now, am I right in thinking that a few places that should have been open, closed on the day of the funeral?"
Julie:	"Yes."
Stephen:	"He's really happy about that and he literally stopped traffic, didn't he?"
Julie:	"Yes, he did."
Stephen:	"He has just put a big letter 'J' and a love heart above your head. Whose name begins with a letter J? Is that you?"
Julie:	"Oh my God, yes that's me!"
Stephen:	"He's a bit cocky, isn't he? A bit of a comedian! Now he's making fun of my hair and you know why, don't you?"
Julie:	"Yes, I do. He saw you in Middleton a few years ago and said you had weird hair!"

Stephen:	"I know you said he passed in July but there will be a baby born *next* July."
Julie:	"Oh my God, no-one's pregnant yet!"
Stephen:	"Anyway, he's saying he's sorry he did what he did but he wants you to know he's okay now. Thank you."

Stephen then went on to tell us all that he had just lost someone really close to suicide by hanging. The funeral was to be held the following Monday and that, as far as he was concerned, it was no coincidence that we had received our reading that evening.

We were so amazed that he got Allan's character to a tee, to the point it felt at times, with his banter, that it was Allan on stage. The night proceeded and then there was an interval. I went outside to phone Elaine, Allan's wife, to give her the news that Allan had come through. Elaine was so excited for us but felt a little low as she was not there to witness it for herself. Elaine was convinced that Allan would mention his dog, Bobby, as within days of Allan's passing she clearly saw an image of Bobby in the clouds. Anyway, I ended the conversation and realised that the demonstration had begun again so I returned to my seat.

Stephen carried on with his readings making people laugh and cry with joy. He asked if there was a Pauline in the room and the lady in front of me put her hand up. Stephen went on to bring through her father and validate many things. Then he said God bless and thank you but then shot back to her and said 21st December? Pauline said no but my sister Carol shot her hand up as it was her stepfather's birthday.

Stephen said "I knew it, I've got your brother back. I don't feel that your stepfather wants to talk, it's not his kind of thing." To which Carol confirmed that he was quite right. Then Stephen added that her brother just wanted to let her know that her stepdad was OK.

Stephen was about to start wrapping up the evening when this happened.

Stephen: *Pointing right at me.* "Do you know where your brother died?"
Julie: "Yes."
Stephen: "He is telling me about a curry."
Julie: "I don't know what he had that last night."
Stephen: "No (I will, I will!)" *It looks like he's talking to someone just behind him. Then back to Julie...* "He's put curry in my mouth from an Indian."
Carol: "He lives opposite a chip shop."
Julie: "And his wife is a really good cook!"
Stephen: At this point, a bit frustrated... "No, get on the phone to his wife because she is where he died and she's just had a curry from an Indian."
Julie: "OK I'll phone her."

Stephen went on to say thank you for attending. Then he shot round and pointed to us yet again and said, "He's back. Who is Bobby?" Stephen did not need answers, my face said it all. I laughed and cried at the same time, it was the validation his wife had wanted.

Stephen did eventually wrap up the night and everyone, even those who never got messages, went home on a high. From Julie and Carol's point of view, there was one thing which needed validation, namely the curry.

Once the girls got into their car Julie phoned Elaine and told her that Bobby the dog had come through. Elaine was tearful but totally delighted. Then Julie asked Elaine where she was…

Elaine told her that she was at home. Julie wasn't sure what she meant by 'home' because since Allan's death she had been spending a lot of time with her mother because she couldn't stand being alone in the house that had once been such a happy place while her husband had been alive. Julie picks up the story...

Julie: "When you say at home, do you mean as in yours and Allan's home?"
Elaine: "Yes, that's where I am. Why?"
Julie: "Have you had a curry tonight?"
Elaine: "Oh my God, yes! Why?"
Julie: "From an Indian?"
Elaine: "Yes, The Bombay Spice."
Julie: *To Carol* – "My God, she's had an Indian!"
Elaine: "Julie, what's all this about?"
Julie: "Stephen said you were in the house where Allan died and that you'd had an Indian dinner tonight."

In conclusion, Stephen said that there would be a baby born the following July. Both Carol and I thought it couldn't possibly be us, but then a few weeks later I discovered that to my surprise, I was pregnant, and I gave birth to our new baby the following July! What is quite amazing is that when I first thought I might be pregnant, I was staying in Allan and Elaine's house, and went into the local Boots to get a pregnancy test kit. When I came out there was a big white van parked at the side of the road with the name ALLAN written in big letters down the side. Usually the name is spelt with a single letter L but Allan's name had two L's and here was this white van with Allan's name spelt with the double L. Obviously he knew what was going on and he wanted to let me know that he knew.

I have written the above section, quoting directly from an email sent through to Rob Green shortly after the demonstration. Curiously, the Rayleigh event was one which I had arranged and promoted, and I have a memory of a message such as the one I have narrated. On raking through my archives I have found an old notebook recording the events of the evening, and my scribbled shorthand pretty well confirms the story Julie has told. This is an interesting example of synchronicity because Rob only passed Julie's email over to me a couple of weeks ago in preparation for this new book and, prior to that, I had never seen the email or had been aware of the fact that such an email even existed. As it had been directed to Steve through Rob and not to me via Mage Publishing, this is not entirely surprising.

When you analyse it, this was a complicated and multi-faceted link from two spiritual personalities directed towards not just one individual but to a whole family. Health conditions are identified, as are times of death and the manner of death. A pregnancy is predicted, even down to the month of the confinement. The clinching evidence comes from Steve's hairstyle of a few years ago, the name of a dog, and an Indian take-away dinner. *(How on earth, I ask myself, could Stephen possibly have known about that?)* If you count up the salient points there are more than a dozen references that could, in isolation, be taken as 'evidence', but surely, when you put them all together, that has got to constitute a body of proof.

If you are a sceptic, you may disagree with my assessment, but you cannot argue against the fact that Stephen has bequeathed a grieving family with a healing quality of peace and calm that has given them the strength to carry on with their lives after having suffered the tragedy of a double bereavement. They are stronger for knowing that their father and their brother are still watching over them, and that there is no censure or judgement directed towards those who, for whatever reason, have chosen to take their own lives.

Chapter Thirteen
Ghosts

Over the years the demographic of Stephen's audiences has changed quite significantly. When I first met him in 1999 it's fair to say that there was an 80/20% split between ladies and gentlemen, with the men in the audience being there either under sufferance or as taxi drivers, or even as a result of bribery and blackmail. *"If you don't take me to see Stephen Holbrook tonight, you can forget about sex for the rest of the year!"* The Spanish concept of *La Ama de Casa* was alive and well and living in Otley, and just about every other town in the North of England to boot!

Of the 80% majority of women attending a demonstration, more than a good half were in the 50+ age group, although there were sprinklings of younger girls, usually attending in small groups. This was nothing like a hen night out, but there was safety in numbers, and a demonstration of clairvoyance certainly stimulates the sisterhood gene.

If we examine the imbalance between male and female attendees, the sceptic or the cynic would say it is because women are more gullible than men... Less scientific, less objective, less critical and less analytical... Which is an absolute load of old sexist rubbish! The bottom line here is that women are more sensitive than men, have a deeper connection with the spiritual side of their natures, have a stronger sense of family bonding and are more receptive to the idea that even if something is invisible and intangible, that doesn't mean it isn't there! It may be a sweeping generalisation, but women are more *emotional* than most men, and it is this emotion which provides the foundation stone of acceptance.

Still generalising, when a father loses a son or a daughter, then obviously it hurts, but I think that for the mother of the lost child, it hurts a damned sight more for, at the end of the day, was it not she who carried the child in her womb for nine long months and was it not she who went through the pain of confinement when the child made its entrance into the world? Faced with the loss of a parent the same emotional mechanisms apply, for it has been a long accepted and self-evident truth that when a parent passes over, the daughters always suffer more. Or at least, they *appear* to.

Yes, I know that this is not *always* the case, but please remember I am only generalising, and I mean no disrespect to the many men out there who have suffered just as much as their female counterparts, albeit in different ways.

Talking about men brings me back to Stephen's audiences.

By the mid Naughties, say 2004 and 2005, we were noticing a distinct shift in the balance of the audience demographic. For one thing, the audiences seemed to be getting noticeably younger and there were a lot more men attending. Not only that, men were either coming on their own, not with female partners or family groups, and on one occasion in Bournemouth, we even had a quartet of bikers! I wouldn't call them Hell's Angels, but with their leather jackets and helmets, not to mention their scuffed motor cycle boots, they looked as rough as old tree bark. I remember thinking "Oh hell, we're going to have some trouble here" but the fact of the matter was that these four lads were as good as gold, sat quietly at the back of the room, and one even got a message from his late brother!

The other thing which registered was the number of children attending the demonstrations. At that time

Jo and I were running the booking line for the tours, and on numerous occasions we would get asked "can I bring my son/daughter, they're only 12/13, so it won't be too scary will it?" Or as a variation on this theme... "can I bring my little girl/boy/baby, and are there any discounts for kids?" Our stock in trade reply to this last one was to ask the parents to bring along their children, for which there would be no charge, on condition that the kids were kept under control, and if the children did become noisy or restless, the parents would quietly take them out of the room or auditorium to avoid disturbing other people, especially if Stephen was mid-message. By and large this worked very well.

I remember an occasion at The Victoria Hotel in Lowestoft, which will indirectly bring me to the crux of this chapter. Stephen had just gone on stage to begin the evening, and I had left the room to check something out at the hotel reception. As I walked through the bar I noticed two children sitting at a table near the window overlooking the car park. The little girl, who was about eight, was reading a book, and the little boy, who was maybe five or six, was scribbling with crayons in a drawing book. There was no sign of a parent, or indeed, anybody else who might be looking after them.

Now it is no secret that children are not always my favourite people, but these two kids looked so out of place that I paused in my tracks and asked them what they were doing all on their own.

"We're not really on our own," the little girl said chirpily. "We've got a baby sitter with us called Sandra but she's just disappeared for a minute to talk to her boyfriend on the phone."

"Er, so where are your parents?" I asked.

The little boy pointed his pencil in the direction of the function room. "They're in there," he said, "listening to The Ghosty Man!"

Now I've heard Stephen called many things over the years but 'ghosty man' was a new one on me... And, of course, this brings me directly onto the subject of ghosts. I suppose that many people might assume that Stephen is talking to ghosts during his evenings of clairvoyance, but he is quite adamant that this is not the case. As far as he is concerned, he is communicating with *spirits* not ghosts, and he is clear that there is a definite and distinct difference between them.

From what he has told me and from what I know from first hand experience, Stephen has only come into a contact with a ghost three times in his life. The first incident occurred many many years ago when he was woken at two o'clock in the morning by a phone call from his sister's best friend's boyfriend, Paul.

"Steve, sorry to bother you mate," Paul said breathlessly, "but can you get over to our place as fast as you can. We've got a bloody ghost here who keeps appearing through a brick wall, then walks across the room before disappearing through the door!"

Steve was half asleep and assumed that Paul had either been on the cider, or was smoking something other than Golden Virginia in his cigarettes.

"I'll come over first thing in the morning," Steve muttered sleepily.

"No mate, you've got to come now!"

"In the morning, Paul. I'll see you in the morning."

Ten minutes later the phone rang again, and this time it was Stephen's sister's friend, Angie, on the line.

"Please Stephen," she pleaded. "Don't make us wait until the morning. There's this horrible little old man here and he's scaring us both to death!"

Stephen was more awake this time round, and as this was Angie crying for help and as he knew she wouldn't press the panic button without good cause, he pulled a pair of jeans over his pyjamas and drove across town to Paul's house where he found Paul and Angie cowering on the sofa staring at a patch of wall just to the left of the fireplace.

"He appears through the wall," Angie pointed out, "then walks across the room between the fire and the sofa, and disappears through the door."

"So what does he look like?" Stephen asked, stifling a yawn, and still half believing he was on a wild goose chase.

"Old and bent and smelly," was Angie's succinct reply, "and if it shows up again, just tell it to go away and leave us alone!"

Stephen sat down on the sofa next to them, and all three waited for something to happen. It was only then that Stephen realised that despite a roaring fire in the hearth, the temperature in the room seemed to be very cold; he was wearing an old cardigan over his pyjama tops, but he still found himself shivering. This reinforces the frequently noticed phenomenon that wherever there is paranormal activity, there is a marked drop in temperature, which, interestingly, does *not* occur when spirit makes contact with Stephen on stage.

It took about ten minutes and then, just as Paul and Angie had described, the figure of a man stepped out from the wall and started limping across the room. As far as Stephen was concerned, this was not a hazy apparition covered in mist or carrying an aura of soft focus blur. It was hard and tangible and real, and despite the crooked hat and old clothes associated with a long bygone age, it was as though a live flesh and blood human being had just entered the room. There was a foul smell of rotting cabbage and excreta, and when the figure passed in front of Stephen it was less than a foot away. It grinned balefully, reached over and lay a hand on Stephen's knee – causing Stephen to jerk back and cry out in alarm – then carried on with its journey across the room to walk through the door which led to the back garden.

Stephen remembers feeling shocked. He'd never experienced anything like this in his life before and, as well as being shocked, he felt physically sick. When he'd regained some composure, he quickly realised that whatever he had seen – and he was clear in his mind that he *had* seen it and, more than that, the bloody thing had actually *touched* him – was nothing like the spiritual beings that he came into contact with as part of his work as a clairaudient medium. With those entities there was always a tingling sensation of love and warmth, but the ghostlike apparition he encountered with Paul and Angie emanated an aura of baleful coldness.

Stephen didn't know what to do exactly. He may have been a medium but he wasn't a ghost hunter or any kind or psychic detective. If you'd mentioned the word 'exorcism' to him, he'd have thought of a couple of horrible Hollywood movies, and wouldn't have known where to begin. In the end he said a few ardent and heartfelt prayers, and thankfully the ghostly apparition put in no further appearances, which just goes to show one should never underestimate the power of prayer!

The second incident happened many years later in Stratford-upon-Avon. Partially through old friends and partially through their attendances at Stephen's demonstrations at The Falcon Hotel, we met a very unusual couple called Steve Devey and his wife, Kay Whittacker. Kay was (and still is) an extremely talented artist and I have a number of her wonderful pictures hanging round the house, while Steve (who we shall refer to as Devey to avoid confusion) was an entrepreneur with a flair for the flamboyant. In some ways they were an odd couple, for while Devey was a 'hail fellow and well met' character, full of life and always bubbling over with excitement and for his latest business venture: Kay was much quieter, frequently living in her own little world of artistic creativity. Their relationship was obviously based on the attraction of opposites, and their love and open affection for each other clearly indicated that it worked remarkably well.

We were invited to stay with them in their home, which was a building called The Shrieves House on Sheep Street. This house had been *renovated* in 1497, and then repaired and given a new roof after a fire in 1688 – thus it would have been standing long before Shakespeare and Anne Hathaway walked the streets of Stratford, and it was a building that they would have known well. Although it had a relatively small frontage on the street, once you got inside the house you soon realised that it stretched a long way back off the road and it was a veritable labyrinth of small rooms and narrow passages with low beams and slanting floors.

The floor of the room that my wife and I were allocated tilted at an alarming 20 degrees, and Devey had had the foresight to screw the bed to the floor boards, otherwise we'd have probably been up against the wall by the middle of the night. Stephen's room was one floor above us, tucked away in the rafters, and between the door and the bed there was a heavy wooden beam that you had to duck under to get into the room proper.

Now, this room was at the *top* of the house. It was mid-summer, and as we all know, hot air rises. Despite this fact, Stephen said that the room was uncomfortably cool, and it didn't take him too long to understand why this might be. He was unpacking his suitcase on the bed when a clear and distinct voice spoke from behind him...

"This is *my* room! You can't stay here!"

Stephen spun around expecting to see a child standing in the doorway, as it had been a child's voice that he heard. And yet there was no one there... What there *had* been, however, was a sudden drop in temperature, and although it had been a long time in the past, he was immediately reminded of the incident with the little old man that had caused Paul and Angie such a problem. Looking nervously around him, he made his exit, went down into the kitchen, had a cup of coffee with the rest of us, and made no mention of the discarnate voice he had just heard.

The demonstration at The Falcon went very well and, later, we all gathered around the table in the Shrieves House kitchen and tucked into a lavish Chinese takeaway. Inevitably it became time to go to bed, and not without some small degree of trepidation, Stephen went up to his room. Now the room seemed very warm and cosy and, lulled into a false sense of security, Stephen climbed into bed and was about to turn off the bedside lamp, when without warning the temperature dropped liked a stone and Stephen looked up to see a small figure staring at him angrily from the foot of the bed.

This was a young girl, seven years old, with curly blond hair. She was wearing a white mop cap and a garment which looked like an early Victorian nightdress. She stood with her legs slightly apart, her tight little fists digging into her waist. Bright blue eyes flashed with anger.

"This is *my* room, and that's *my* bed, now get out, get out, get out!"

Stephen sat bolt upright, experiencing a cavalcade of conflicting emotions. Initially there was an element of alarm, but this very quickly changed to bemusement, which transmuted into plain old fashioned Taurean stubbornness. For heaven's sake, he was a professional clairvoyant, and he refused to be spooked by the anger of his ghostly intruder.

"It might have been your room once," he said firmly, "but for tonight it's *my* room, so just clear off and leave me in peace or I'll have to speak to your mother and father, and I'll bet they won't be pleased by your rudeness and very naughty behaviour!"

He flicked off the light and lay back on his pillow. After counting to ten he flicked the light back on and the little girl had gone! The room temperature was back to normal and with a slight feeling of smug self-satisfaction, he turned the light off again and fell into a long and undisturbed sleep.

The third ghostly incident occurred in Stamford, Lincolnshire. We had just checked into our rooms at a rather exclusive hotel on the outskirts of the town and when we met in the reception area later, Stephen wore an ironic expression writ large upon his face.

"Are your rooms okay?" he asked.

"Yes, lovely thank you," Jo answered.

"What about yours, Rob?"

"Fine thanks," Rob answered. "Bit small, but very neat and cosy. It comes with a nice view of the gardens."

"So, I'm the only one out of the lot of us who's got a haunted flaming bedroom!" Stephen looked wryly amused. "Why does it always happen to me?"

"Well Steve," Jo pointed out in a matter-of-fact tone, "you are a medium, love, so what would you expect? If it's going to happen to anyone, it would have to happen to you!"

"So tell us about your ghost," I said eagerly.

"Not much to tell really, just a woman sitting in the corner, looking out of the window with a load of sewing on her knee, looking very sad and forlorn."

"Do you think she might still be there?" I asked, my eagerness increasing.

"Dunno, she was there when I left. Just hope she isn't there when I get back!"

"Can we go and check it out?"

Jo laughed and laid a restraining hand on my arm. "Darling, if you actually saw a ghost you'd probably be quite terrified and, in any case, even if it was still there you probably wouldn't be able to see it. You've got many talents, love, but clairvoyance isn't one of them! In any case," she looked at her watch pointedly, "we're running late as it is."

She had a point, so we headed out of the hotel and down the road to the Stamford Arts Centre, which was always one of my favourite venues on the circuit. After another successful evening, we returned to the hotel and sat out on the terrace overlooking the lawn. It was a hot oppressive night and although it had yet to start falling we could smell the rain in the air. In the distance there were occasional flashes of summer lightening and grumbles of thunder; paradoxically scudding clouds raced across a full moon and with the neo-Gothic hotel immediately behind us, it was a bit like a scene out of a Hammer horror movie.

At some point we were joined by the owner of the hotel who brought us another bottle of ice cold Pinot Grigio, this one on the house, and who sat down and joined us for a while. Quite casually, and with total innocence, I asked him if the hotel had any kind of ghostly history. He answered with great alacrity... No, there were no ghosts associated with his hotel and there was no ghostly history that might provide an interesting story for the book we were putting together at that time.

He said this with a bright cheerful smile, but I noticed that his teeth were clenched and, even if his hotel had been full of Harry Potter's mates, he would never have admitted to it in a million years. He left a few minutes later, giving me the distinct impression that we had upset him in some way. I glanced across the table at Stephen, with what might have been described as an enquiring look. Stephen said nothing, just shrugged his shoulders in acceptance of a denial he knew to be invalid because if Stephen Holbrook says he's seen a ghost, then you'd better believe that he's seen a ghost.

To prove the point, a few moments later, he got up from the table and walked briskly over towards the rear entrance of the hotel. The first drops of rain were just beginning to fall, so the remaining three of us drew our chairs more closely beneath the canopy of the large umbrella.

"Where's he off to in such a hurry?" Jo mused out loud.

"Knowing him and his weak bladder, probably just the loo," Rob retorted, not unkindly.

147

But Stephen had not dashed inside to visit the toilet. As he told us a short while later, he'd been aware of someone watching him from one of the hotel's downstairs windows and, when he'd turned to look, he'd seen the woman he'd encountered earlier, who had been doing her sewing in the corner of his bedroom. Entering the hotel, he'd taken the first door on the right which led to the room he thought he'd seen her in and, sure enough, as he entered the room the lady turned her gaze from the window and stared at him directly.

No words were spoken, but he was assuaged by a feeling of great sadness. Upon those waves of sadness he took a number of psychic impressions.

"She lived here about a hundred years ago and had a pretty awful life," he told us. "She was married to a man who regularly beat her and had a great many illicit love affairs. In the end he ended up making her pregnant, but at the same time passed on a virulent strain of venereal disease which caused her to lose her baby. She sank into depression and ended up hanging herself in the pantry."

"So, is she a spirit or a ghost?" I wanted to know.

"She's a bloody ghost," Stephen said emphatically. "Feel my flaming hand!"

I reached out and took his hand and it was like a block of ice.

"It might be a bit fanciful," he continued thoughtfully, "but I think she's still hanging round here hoping to find her dead child. I don't know if she's understood me, but I've told her that her baby has passed over and if she wants to see it again, she's got to let this place go and pass over herself."

There is an interesting epilogue to this story, because when we were checking out the following morning, it was the hotel owner's wife who was in charge behind the reception, and I happened to mention that I thought we might have upset her husband the previous evening with all our talk about ghostly goings on, and would she please apologise to him on our behalf.

She gave me a very old fashioned look. "And I suppose," she said, "he told you that there are no ghosts in this hotel?"

"Pretty much," I confirmed.

"Then can you tell me why he will never set foot in Room 13, which I believe was inhabited by Mr Holbrook last night, and why he will never go into the kitchen storeroom without all the kitchen lights being full on?"

"Is the kitchen store room where the old pantry used to be?" Stephen put in quietly.

"Yes..." she looked at him shrewdly. "Why do you ask?"

Stephen gave her his disarming little boy smile. "Oh no reason really. I just wondered..."

So what is a ghost? Stephen is adamant that it is not a spirit such as he encounters in his daily work. It is something different. His best guess coincides with the consensus of opinion which suggests that while in one sense, it *is* a spirit, it is one that has been unable to, or has chosen not to, 'pass over' into the realm of spirit and is still tied to the earth plane, for any one of a number of reasons.

Perhaps it is tied by trauma to the time and place of its human death. Perhaps it doesn't even know that it is dead. Perhaps it is unaware of the fact that there is another realm which it can transcend to. In the erudite words of the late Donald Fairhurst, philosopher and humanist of his time, a ghost is simply a spirit in the wrong place!

There is a theory which suggests that buildings and locations are impregnated with the psychic memory of dastardly deeds committed in the past – for example, Nearly Headless Nick who was almost (but not quite!) decapitated on the executioner's block for treason against Queen Elizabeth the First, or the Headless Horseman who lost his head at the battle of Sleepy Hollow in the American war of independence – but such examples do not allow for less dramatic, but still well documented hauntings. The Grey Lady who has on many occasions been seen in the York Theatre Royal was an elderly nun who died a peaceful death after many years or service as a nurse when the theatre was a hospital back in the 17th century. Stephen's visitor at the Shrieves House and the sad lady in Stamford were, to all intents and purposes, ordinary people who did not make any great mark on history, so it is easier to slip them into the former category rather than the latter. I suppose the absolute bottom line here is that, despite a plethora of different theories and opinions, no one actually *knows* what a ghost really is, and there are even some folk who don't believe they exist at all!

Certainly there are many places which connect with an individual's psyche, places which generate auras of atmosphere that can alarm and (sorry about this) spook different people in different ways. Think of walking through a graveyard at midnight, or being in an underground cellar beneath an infamous old castle, consider the way in which the mind could play tricks if you *knew* you were sleeping in a reputedly haunted house. In such cases, autosuggestion would mean a whole lot more than *"would you like to come for a ride in my car?"*

And yet there are other less tangible examples of the way in which any mind remotely susceptible to atmosphere can be affected. A relative of mine, when he was a young boy and later as a teenager, could not for the life of him, enter a church! He would be both terrified and almost petrified at the prospect of entering any kind of religious building – and yet he attended Sunday school quite happily which was held in the local village hall!

When I was in my late teens I was working in Basildon and living in Laindon, and my commute home was a complicated one. I could take a bus so far, but then had to choose between walking five miles along the narrow country lanes, or one mile if I took the short cut along the bridle path through the fields. Never one for the dubious joys of exercise, I chose the bridle path, which for most of the way led across three large open fields to my left and heavy trees to my right. It was the autumn of the year and I would be walking my route in the late twilight. I only did it about three times because by the time I got to the final stile I was a nervous wreck! The sound of the trees creaking above me, the long shadows which obscured my path, the sensation of being watched by something – not someone but *something!* – the wind blowing spits of rain in my face… Ah well, in the end, I walked the longer way round and was better off for it. I tell myself now as I told myself then, that my imagination was playing tricks on me, which was almost certainly true. The trouble is I can remember quite clearly, even after all these years, just how unnerved and frightened I felt at the time.

I am often asked if I have ever seen a ghost or a spirit. The answer is yes, but with a couple of very strong caveats. In my mind, and *only* in my mind, I get occasional glimpses of my late Grandmother. Sometimes, my early mentor Ossie Rae puts in an appearance and there are two dead friends who passed over in Spain. There is no verbal communication here, but I do take strength from their fleeting presences, and these visits always bring me a feeling of reassurance.

As for ghosts... Well, that is a slightly different matter. Although I have on occasion sensed the proximity of spiritual entities close to me, I've never seen a Headless Horseman or a Grey Lady. I do, however, see (albeit briefly and only ever out of the corner of my eye) dead cats. Not just any old dead cats, but animals that have been most precious to me and who have caused me to weep when their time has come to go and live a life of luxury in that Great Cattery in The Sky. In my mind I see Merlin leaping after butterflies in the long grass, Morgana suns herself on a warm tiled patio amid pots of flowers and verdant palms. Jaikie, my Red Manx, is stretched out along the branch of a tree keeping company with a pride of lions... And I could give you another dozen examples of this. Again, these visions are only ever in my mind, and they usually occur very soon after the pussy cat has passed over...

And yet, very frequently I see *real* cats winding their feline bodies round my feet and legs, intent on tripping me up, or sitting on the end of the sofa, or loitering in the corner of the kitchen staring intently at where their food bowls used to be. The cat called Morgana was the bane of my life, and used to love sitting snuggled up to the TV blotting out half the flaming screen. I'd see her for a millisecond, then she was gone, but for a good few seconds thereafter, the lower half of the TV screen was a good shade darker and dimmer than it should have been.

Despite the firm but gentle teachings of Saint Francis, the church's long held dogma is that animals don't have souls, so therefore they cannot transcend into Heaven. This is one of the biggest loads of old twaddle that I've ever heard and Stephen, through his work, provides the evidence to prove it. On so many occasions he has brought messages through which involve beloved pets. For example, at the Cochrane Theatre in London:-

Stephen: "I've got a big green parrot here, sitting on my shoulder, and telling me this should connect with you."

Lady: "Well, my late husband and I ran a pub in Plaistow called The Rat and Parrot. Could that be it?"

Stephen: "No, I don't think so… Who's Tony?"

Lady: "My late brother was Tony, and… Oh my God, he did actually have a pet parrot!"

Stephen: "So who's Monty?"

Lady: "Oh my God, that was the name of the bloody parrot! It used to go with Tony everywhere, sitting on his shoulder and pecking at his ear!"

In Stratford-upon-Avon:-

Stephen: "I've got a lady here, surrounded by at least a dozen cats. She's laughing her socks off and she's telling me that she used to be called The Mad Old Cat Lady…"

Gentleman: "Me over here! That was my Mum and she never had less than a dozen cats. Her all time record was 18!"

Stephen: "She's telling me that she's got Rusty with her and that he's well and happy and that she's looking after him for you. Who's Rusty?"

Gentleman: "Rusty is *my* cat, and I had to have him put to sleep only this morning!"

In Retford:-

Stephen: "Don't be upset m'love, but I've got your husband here with me and he's telling me that he's found Bernard and that he's looking after him, taking him for walks every morning and evening. So, can you tell me, is there a dog in the spirit world called Bernard?"

Lady: "Yes, we lost a wonderful dog three months before Jimmy died. It nearly broke Jimmy's heart! But it wasn't called Bernard…"

Stephen: "Okay, well who is Charlie?"

Lady: "That was the dog's name!"

Stephen: "Well, Charlie is with Jimmy now and Jimmy's just brought him onto the stage…" *Stephen looks at the lady in the audience with an expression of admonition…* "but tell me, m'love, what breed of dog was Charlie?"

Lady: "Oh heck! Of course! Charlie was a Saint Bernard!"

Now obviously animals can't give Stephen a direct message by barking or meowing, but their presence as evidence is undeniable, especially if the pet owner's relationship with the animal was as strong or even stronger than any relationship he or she might have had with a fellow human being. If a pet can be 'brought through' by someone in the spirit world, it stands to reason that both human spirits and the spirits of animals share the same habitat. I reckon Saint Francis of Assisi knew this very well, and we could all benefit from giving this possibility some thought and consideration.

Stephen cannot speak or understand *Canine Vulgaris* (everyday dog) let alone the more complex and complicated tongue of *Felinus Familiarus Humilis Cattus,* (every day cat) but with regard to the latter, I am pleased to report that I am making some progress!

Chapter Fourteen
Evidence II

In seeking to expand Stephen's sphere of influence and to find new audiences, I booked him into the Hilton Hotel in Liverpool. On paper this looked like a very good move to make; the function room was reasonably priced, the newspaper advertising rates were not exorbitant, and Liverpool was a major city with a broad demographic. And yet, somewhere down in the pit of my tummy, I had some vague feelings of unease. Liverpool had played an influential role in my own history – there had been some really good times, but also one or two fairly bad times – and now with Liverpool looming large in the diary, my thoughts kept returning to the bad times and I found myself wondering if I had done the right thing or had reached out to cross a bridge too far.

As the date for the demonstration drew ever closer, my jittery feeling increased. Advance bookings were not encouraging and I had lurid visions of Stephen demonstrating to fifty people in a room that was laid out for 200. My jitters were enhanced when, just one week prior to our visit, I was cheerfully informed that I needed a double heart by-pass operation... which was something I needed like a hole in the head!

Two hours before we were scheduled to leave, our departure was complicated by the arrival of my long lost son whom I had not seen for the better part of 30 years. This caused a flurry of very weird feelings, because when it came to being a father, I'd made a pretty good plumber. Nevertheless, despite the initial awkwardness, my son decided he was going to follow us over the border into Lancashire, would spend some more time with me, watch the demonstration and then head back to his home in Essex from there. Obviously, he had no idea what he was letting himself in for!

Cutting a long story short we arrived at the Liverpool Hilton with advance bookings of only 52 people. Frankly, I was anticipating a disaster! Steve, however, was quite sanguine about it. He told me not to worry because there would, he assured me, be a very strong walk-up with people wanting to pay on the door. I don't know how he knew this, because we'd never done a demonstration in Liverpool before and we had no idea of Liverpudlean habits. Maybe he was just being optimistic?

And yet, he was quite correct! Over 150 people turned up without tickets and we had to scramble round at the last minute looking for extra chairs. To say that the demonstration was a major success is something of an understatement. Stephen was on fire, shooting off messages at great speed and with his usual unnerving accuracy.

Now, I need to tell you about the lady who got the second message of the evening. Her name was Jennifer Lumsden and she had good cause to be there that night. One year previously her son, Peter, had been killed in a car accident and she had taken it very badly. Perhaps not quite as badly as her husband, Donald, who had been so overcome with grief that he had killed himself by linking a hose to the exhaust pipe of his car then ramming it through the back window of his vehicle. It had been a classic case of carbon monoxide poisoning.

Stephen opened the link by saying he needed to talk to a lady who had had to arrange two family funerals within the last twelve or thirteen months. Jenny Lumsden's was the only hand to go up and Stephen homed in on her straight away.

Stephen:	"Hello m'love. Don't be frightened and don't be shy. Can you just confirm that you have lost two people to the spirit world within the last year?"
Jenny:	"Yes, that's right."
Stephen:	"And am I right in thinking that both of these passings were connected in some way to cars?"
Jenny:	"Yes, the first was..."
Stephen:	"No, m'love, don't tell me anything. Let me get there on my own, okay... The two people who have passed over, they were very close to you, yes?"
Jenny:	"Yes, very!"
Stephen:	"Okay... I'm getting a picture here of a tall young man with fair hair. He always had a smile on his face and never took life too seriously. Can you recognise him from this description?"
Jenny:	"Yes, he's my..."
Stephen:	"No, don't tell me anything! Am I right in thinking that this young man was your son?"
Jenny:	"Yes!"
Stephen:	"Good! Who is Peter?"
Jenny:	"That was his name. My son's name is Peter!"
Stephen:	"I'm getting the impression that Peter was killed in some kind of road traffic accident... Is this right?"
Jenny:	"Yes."
Stephen:	"Late at night?"
Jenny:	"Yes."
Stephen:	"Around midnight?"

Jenny:	"The police logged it as having been five minutes past twelve."
Stephen:	"Right, well Peter just wants you to know that he didn't feel a thing. He didn't see the other car coming 'till it hit him. He's also telling me that it wasn't his fault. Do you understand that, m'love? He's saying it wasn't his fault and that he didn't have a chance to get out of the way. This is very important to him because he knows that you've been wondering if he made any kind of mistake behind the wheel, bearing in mind he was a very new driver. He's telling me quite emphatically that he didn't make any mistakes and that *it wasn't his fault!* Do you understand all that, m'love?"
Jenny:	"Yes, yes I do!"
Stephen:	"Now then, who is Don or Donald?"
Jenny:	"That's my husband's name."
Stephen:	"Well, Peter is telling me that he's got Donald with him and that they've both been watching over you, sending you all their love and protection, and they're telling me that although things have been very bad for you, they will start getting better soon, especially after tonight, and oh, hang on… Donald has just stepped forwards and he wants to say he's sorry he did what he did, but he couldn't live with the pain and he couldn't stand watching you suffer and go through what you were going through and, oh my goodness… am I right in thinking that Donald took his own life while he was sitting in a car?"

159

Jenny:	"Yes, he gassed himself with exhaust fumes."
Stephen:	"Well take heart… Who's Jennifer?"
Jenny:	"That's me. I'm Jenny."
Stephen:	"Well all right, Jenny, just be told that Peter and Donald are looking after you from the spirit world, and they're asking you to be brave and to hang on, and they promise you that things will start getting better for you soon. They know how you've been feeling and they know what you've been thinking of doing, and they're saying that you mustn't do it, because if you do, you'll be leaving Jackie all on her own. Who is Jackie, m'love?"
Jenny:	"Jackie is my daughter!"
Stephen:	"Right, well your job now is to look after Jackie and to allow yourself some time to heal from these horrible wounds. Do you understand what I'm saying, m'love?"
Jenny:	"Yes, I understand."
Stephen:	"Now then, have you just sold something for £1500?"
Jenny:	"Yes I have."
Stephen:	"And am I right in thinking that you advertised it for £1750, but accepted the £1500 just to get rid of it?"
Jenny:	"Yes, that's right!"
Stephen:	"And am I right in thinking that you sold your husband's old car, because you couldn't stand the sight of it anymore?"
Jenny:	"Yes, that's right."
Stephen:	"Was it a goldie yellow colour?"
Jenny:	"Yes it was."
Stephen:	"And am I right in thinking is was a Ford?"

Jenny:	"Yes, it was a Ford Mondeo!"
Stephen:	"Well, I've got Donald here, nodding in approval, and he's saying that this was something you should have done ages ago!"

Again, transcribing this from the cassette recording I made of the demonstration, it conveys nothing of the emotion or raw energy that passed between Stephen and Jennifer Lumsden. When I spoke to the lady at the end of the demonstration she quietly confessed that she had seriously been thinking of taking her own life. Her daughter, Jackie, was 17 and could have coped alone if she'd had to, but Stephen's message made it very clear that she could not sacrifice herself on the altar of her own anguish and that, while being 17, her daughter would not have coped very well on her own at all. She may have lost her father and her brother, but losing her mother as well would have been the last straw!

The first message of the second half of the evening went to an elderly gentleman who was sitting on the front row. His name was Johnny Marshall and, just like Jenny Lumsden, he had good reason to be there that night. When Stephen said he wanted to talk to someone near the front of the room who had lost his wife within the last six months, the gentleman's hand shot up in the air and Stephen went straight to him.

Stephen:	"I'm connecting with a lady who passed over in March, with some kind of lingering sickness which finally got the better of her. Can you tell me, sir, why March 17th is an important date?"
Johnny:	"My wife died on March 17th."

Stephen:	"And am I right in thinking you were there by her bedside up until the very last minute?"
Johnny:	"Yes I was."
Stephen:	"All right sir... she's telling me she wasn't conscious but she knew you were there, and she wants to thank you for staying with her even though there wasn't anything you could do. Why is the number 53 important?"
Johnny:	"This year would have been our 53rd wedding anniversary. We'd have been married for 53 years come this September."
Stephen:	"Well, she's wishing you a happy anniversary, and she's telling me she'll be having her own party up over on the other side with Ken and Pheobe... Do you know who she's talking about sir?"
Johnny:	"Ken was her brother and Phoebe was her sister-in-law. They died within a year of each other in 2001."
Stephen:	"And who are Fred and Maisie?"
Johnny:	"Fred was her father and her mother's name was Maisie. They passed over a long time ago..."
Stephen:	"Well, she's got them with her now and they're all okay over on the other side. Also, she's telling me that she sees... er... I'm not sure if it's Gary or Gavin, so do either of these names mean anything to you?"
Johnny:	"Our son was called Gavin!"
Stephen:	"... Ummm, and am I right in thinking that Gavin passed over a long way away from here, somewhere overseas?"

Johnny:	"Yes, he was…"
Stephen:	"No, don't tell me, sir. I'm supposed to do this on my own – *long pause* – Sir, I'm seeing military uniforms, so was Gavin a soldier and did he die in somewhere like Iraq or Afghanistan?"
Johnny:	"Yes, he was killed in Helmand Province."
Stephen:	"And the most upsetting thing about this is you were never able to recover his body?"
Johnny:	"That is quite correct. He was blown up by an IED and his regiment buried what was left of him by the roadside."
Stephen:	"Well, he wants you to know that he's all in one piece now, and although his body might still be buried in Iraq, his spirit is here where it belongs, with the rest of his family. He's also telling me that you were always the strong one within the family and you've got to carry on being strong, not just for yourself, but also for Mandy and Andrew… Who are Mandy and Andrew, sir?"
Johnny:	"Mandy is my daughter-in-law, Gavin's wife, and Andrew is my grandson."
Stephen:	"Is Mandy here with you tonight?"
Johnny:	"No. She doesn't believe in this sort of thing!"
Stephen:	"I bet she would now if she'd come with you this evening… So what you've got to do is tell her all about this message… Can you do that for me, sir?"
Johnny:	"You can rely on it!"
Stephen:	"Finally sir, who is Colonel John Marshall? Was that Gavin's commanding officer?"

Johnny:	"No. *I am* Colonel John Marshall, late of the Royal Household Cavalry, and now retired."
Stephen:	"Thank you very much, sir. Take this message with you and be sure to pass it on to Mandy and Andrew. Oh, just a minute... Who is June?"
Johnny:	"That's my wife's name."
Stephen:	"She's rubbing her tummy and she's telling me all the pain has gone now. Does this make any sense to you?"
Johnny:	"Yes, she died of stomach cancer."
Stephen:	"She's telling me about the wigs... Did she lose her hair and have to wear a wig?"
Johnny:	"Yes."
Stephen:	"And have you still got the wigs?"
Johnny:	"Yes."
Stephen:	"Well she's telling you to burn them because she doesn't need them anymore. She's got her own hair back now, so you're to burn the wigs. Do you understand?"
Johnny:	"Yes, perfectly."

Stephen moved on to the next message of the evening and the batteries on my cassette recorder conked out shortly afterwards, so I have no further hard information to draw on. To be sure, I have vague memories of other links, but a vague memory does not provide enough documented evidence upon which to write a report.

And yet, there is one memory of that night which stands out very clearly indeed, which does not relate to any messages given or received, but which does relate to the three rather oddly dressed people, who were among the last to arrive and found the last three vacant seats right at the back of the room. There were two men and one woman. One of the men was very elderly, as was his rather portly lady companion. The third man looked to be in his mid-twenties with bright blue eyes and corn blond hair. Their dress was unusual inasmuch that they wore long coats, almost buttoned to the throat, and despite the rising temperature within the function room, those coats remained firmly buttoned up and draped around them throughout the evening.

Now, there is a hackneyed old cliché associated with every crime movie you've ever seen, where the villain sneers at the policeman and says something like "I know who you are! I can smell a copper from 20 yards away!" Well, I certainly can't smell a policeman, but I do get twitchy when I'm in the company of a priest, and I would have bet half the book sale takings on the certainty that these three odd bods were members of the church, and almost certainly the Catholic Church.

Playing a game with myself (albeit a very serious game) I drew up a chair behind them and tried to eavesdrop their occasional mutterings. The old woman was the most vociferous.

"It's just as I told you, Father O'Brian, that man up there is either a demon sent by the devil or he's a personification of the devil himself!" She hissed in a broad Irish brogue and the older man inclined his head away from her angry whisper.

"Hush now, Sister Mary," he retorted in a low voice. "We must not judge too quickly. Remember Saint Paul's letter to the Corinthians!"

The younger man seemed totally oblivious to this exchange of words. He was staring at Stephen with a look of rapt attention on his handsome face, a huge grin crinkling the corners of his mouth.

Later on, at the end of the evening when our audience was filing out, the religious trio was among the first to leave. The devil may have been a million miles away from Stephen Holbrook, but for a brief moment he was perched happily upon my shoulder.

"Good night Father O'Brian," I said quietly as he passed me by the door. "I hope you had an interesting evening."

He glanced at me with a small smile, looking for all the world like our wonderful actor Mark Williams in his role as G.K. Chesterton's Father Brown.

"Most interesting, thank you," he replied. And then, "God *does* work in mysterious ways, doesn't he?"

Tamworth is a small town in the East Midlands and it has been on Stephen's venue list for more years than he can recall. Despite some very poor nights of clairvoyance provided by *other* visiting mediums, Stephen has always enjoyed full houses, and in the immortal words of one of his fans: *"Nah, we never bothered going to see Thingy or Wassisname, 'cos we knew you were coming in September, so we were hanging on for your visit!"* It was on a recent visit to this friendly little town that Stephen brought through not one but two incredible messages, although at the time of passing them on, he had no idea how important they were.

It was coming towards the end of the evening and Stephen was getting tired. He'd been on stage for more than two hours and knew that his energy levels were rapidly draining. Glancing surreptitiously at his watch he reckoned that, spirits willing, he had time to connect one more message, then he could wrap up the presentation and start the long motorway slog back to Castleford.

Tuning in to the spiritual energy which began to surround him, he began tentatively.

Steve: "I have a lady here in the Spirit World, who would have passed away on the 8th May, or the 8th May is her birthday."

A lady put her hand up on the front row immediately.

Lady: "My Grandad passed away on that day!"
Steve: "No, sorry my love, it's not your Grandad – unless he wore a dress!" The crowd laughed at Steve's cheek and humour, "but thank you for your response. I think the lady I've got here was probably 86 or 87… certainly in the latter part of her 80s."

At this point, a hand shot up at the back of the room and a gentleman's voice called out quite clearly.

Man: "Yes, that's my Mum, she passed on the 8th May. She wasn't 87, but she passed over in 1987."
Steve: "The lady I have here," Stephen said, "says I have to tell you that you knew she would come looking for you, and you felt a reason you had to be here tonight, something just told you."
Man: "Yes, that is absolutely right."
Steve: "She says she has your brother with her!"
Man: "Fantastic! All she ever wanted to do was see him again!"
Steve: "She is telling me that the painkillers you're taking are giving you side effects, and that

167

	you have been backwards and forwards to the hospital."
Man:	"Correct, I've been there most of today, having some kind of drugs review, but I knew I had to be here tonight."
Steve:	"Your Mum is mentioning nursing?"
Man:	"Well, she *was* a nurse…"
Steve:	"She tells me she has seen her Dad, but she says he actually visited her after he had passed away."
Man:	"Yes, he did, that's what made her believe in the afterlife."
Steve:	"She's mentioning Australia, and also Grantham."
Man:	"Yes, she was born in Grantham, but visited Australia a lot of times over the years."
Steve:	"She says she has seen John."
Man:	"That's my Dad!"
Steve:	"Does your birthday fall on the 24th?"
Man:	"No, but my mother was 24 when she met him."
Stephen:	"She's telling me about having a stroke, or maybe even more than one…"
Man:	"Yes, she had two strokes before she finally passed."
Steve:	"She is also mentioning the word *'Sutton'*, is this a place?"
Man:	"No, that was her maiden name before she was married."
Steve:	"She's now showing me an RAF badge, but it's not your Dad holding it, it's her."
Man:	"Yes, that is where she met my Dad, in the RAF."
Steve:	"Are you Michael? And she's also mentioning John again?"

Man: "I'm Terry, but my brother was John Michael, he was the one who died as a baby."

Steve: *Choosing his words carefully* "She needs you to look toward the future, and promises that she will help you, from the other side of life. But, you need to get the correct help and treatment down here, so don't avoid the hospital, and keep your appointments!"

This turned out to be the penultimate message of the night, but the *next* message was to blow Stephen away. He delivered this message to a very well-spoken lady, three rows from the front, who had lost her husband 18 months previously. Steve had said that there had been problems with the will, and also a younger son. The lady looked gob-smacked. Steve mentioned the name of 'Trudy' to her and she acknowledged that this had been the name of her sister who'd only been 61 years old when she had passed over suddenly.

Unlike many recipients of messages, this lady handled the information Stephen passed on with a quiet calm, without showing any emotion. After Stephen had established that she lived at house number 18 and that her birthday was the 22nd of November, he said the usual "Goodnight my love" and turned away, to move into his last few words of the evening.

But, as he did so, a young male presence said to him, *"I'm Robert and I died in a road traffic accident. Please tell her I am here!"* so Steve did as he'd been instructed and told her exactly what he'd heard Robert say. To his surprise, the lady's calm reserve suddenly evaporated and she broke down into tears! This was a shock for Steve, because during delivering the messages from her husband and her 61 year old sister, she had remained perfectly composed. But the mention of Robert clearly made her buckle.

Stephen realised that this must have been a very sensitive issue, so he decided it was probably best just to say "Goodnight, but please know Rob is happy in his new life, and despite the road traffic accident, he didn't know anything about it, and felt no pain." But as Steve turned, again trying to move on, Robert quite clearly said *"I didn't know her. We'd never met!"*

This almost floored Steve, as he had seen her reaction, but even though the lady still had her head down wiping away tears, he had to try and satisfy his curiosity. So, with great sensitivity and as diplomatically as he could, Stephen asked her outright...

"Excuse me, my love, but Robert has just said something to confuse me. You're visibly very upset, and you clearly know who this gentleman is, but he's clearly just told me that he doesn't know you and that he's never met you!"

The lady lifted her head and looked directly up at Stephen. "No, he didn't know me, and I never met him, but he's my donor, and I have his kidney." From the audience there came a mixed reaction of gasps of amazement, and shrieks of "Oh my God!" Stephen stood there, for once, speechless, trying to take in the enormity of what had just happened, not yet capable of exploring the spiritual links which might have facilitated such a contact.

This was the last message of the night, and the evening came to a close.

The theatre had cleared, and work commenced packing up. In some ways this is the most tiring part of the evening. All the adrenalin has gone and you're left with feelings of anti-climax. The exhaustion kicks in, but you know the night is not yet over. You've got to load all your gear into the back of the car, and then you've got a two and a half hour drive to look forward to before you can even think of having a nice cup of tea and maybe some beans on toast.

It's bad enough for a jobbing musician, but I would imagine it's ten times worse for a medium. As a musician you walk onto the stage hoping that you've got your PA set up correctly; certainly, you checked it earlier, but then the room was two thirds empty, and now it's full to the brim. Past experience tells you that the acoustics will now be very different. You've got other things on your mind as well... Has your guitar stayed in tune, is it in pitch with the organ that is going to be played by the organist who is employed by the club? You've never met this man before other than to hand over your dots and you wonder how good this guy is at reading music? Can he even *read* music, or is he just a busker? Other questions plague the mind, along the lines of what will the audience be like, what kind of music do they like, will they like your choice of songs, and will they even like *you*?

Despite all of these concerns, within certain parameters you know what to expect. You know the songs you're going to be singing (you've been singing them for years, so you flaming well should!) You know the chords and riffs you'll be playing on your old guitar, and you're reasonably confident that unless you drop a couple of major clangers, you're going to pick up your eighty quid fee at the end of the evening and then start your drive back through the late hours of the night to your version of beans on toast.

For a medium like Steve Holbrook, he walks out onto the stage with absolutely no idea of what he is going to say or what is going to happen. He takes it as an article of faith that the spirit people will be with him, filtering the messages through to their loved ones in the audience. Frankly, I cannot imagine how totally nerve wracking this must be, but Stephen does this night after night in town after town and, despite the bright smile he flashes to the audience at the end of the night, I've seen him come off stage looking totally drawn and haggard. He'll have been in the public's eye for the better part of two hours, looking cheerful and enthusiastic about what he's doing, but believe me, his work exacts a terrible toll, both emotionally and physically. This, of course, is something which the audience does *not* see!

In 2002, Stephen had an old Marshall Amplifier that was on wheels; it was his pride and joy and, as he set off out of the theatre with it, he said his farewell to the ushers and the theatre staff, who always enjoyed the show. As he approached the doorway, he saw it was still raining and was just about to make a mad dash for the car, but a hand touched his shoulder. He jumped a foot in the air, and said "Oh bloody hell! You scared the living daylights out of me!"

Stephen thought everyone had gone, however the gentleman who had stepped out of the shadows and had accosted him looked to be in poor health and was leaning heavily on a walking stick. Stephen put his things down, after getting over the shock, and asked if he was waiting to talk to him.

"Yes, I am. I was about to leave and I thought you may have gone out the main entrance. But then I remembered there was this side entrance and following a hunch I came and waited for you because I just needed to thank you for the wonderful message you gave me tonight."

Stephen hadn't the faintest idea which message he had given to the gentleman, but he was obviously going to tell him! Stephen's thoughts were still pre-occupied with the guy who had come through who had donated his kidney!

"My Mum came through" the man said. "It was the second message before the end of the night. She said the 8th May was her birthday."

"Oh yes," Steve replied, "I remember now. The Nurse!"

"Yes that's right. I understood everything you said. I was in the hospital today, trying to sort out the correct medication. Whilst I was waiting, I was reading the Tamworth Times newspaper that someone had left lying round. Three pages in I came across your advert, and my Mother's voice said: 'You *must* go Terry, and I will be waiting.' Towards the end of the evening, I was beginning to think I'd misheard her, but she managed it at the last minute and it may surprise you to know, my Mother was Doris Stokes!"

Stephen thought he'd misheard this, and said "What? You mean *the* Doris Stokes?"

"Yes," the gentleman replied with a wry and somewhat gratifying smile.

What a night this had turned out to be! First, a message from Doris Stokes to her son Terry, and we're talking here about a woman who at the height of her celebrity was regarded as one of the top clairvoyants in Europe: she demonstrated to packed theatres all across the land, was the subject of many TV shows and was the author of a whole series of best-selling books! Then a message to a lady from her kidney donor who, to all intents and purposes, was a total stranger!

However, it all goes to prove something important was going on here!

Although obviously Stephen had *heard* of the great Doris Stokes, he had never actually met her in this world, and therefore wasn't familiar with her, and wouldn't recognise her in any capacity. As far as the demonstration was concerned, she was just another lady wanting to pass a message to her son. Steve always says he has stopped questioning the Spirit People, because as soon as you think you have all the answers, even more questions seem to surface. One thing for sure is that were two very happy people in the audience that night, and probably another 250 that were left speechless!

I am not entirely speechless and mulling over this scenario in the quietness of the afternoon, tapping away at the PC keyboard and watching the rain dribble miserably down the office window, I am both frustrated and irritated. Probably the greatest medium of *her* time passes on a message through someone who, in my opinion, is the greatest medium of *his* time. For Heaven's sake, couldn't they have had a chat about the two different worlds? Couldn't they have made a date to have such a chat at a later time? Couldn't Doris have fed Stephen some hard information with regard to what it was actually like over on the other side? To be sure, she was there to pass on a message of support to her son, and in part I have to accept that this is the sum total of the encounter, but there is another part of me which thinks what a wasted opportunity! I know I like a lot, but am I really being too greedy about all of this? I suppose, in Steve's defence, he didn't know that he'd been communicating with Doris Stokes until her son told him about it afterwards, but, even so, hey come on!

My final thought on this subject is something I've ranted on about for years. When you think of the billions of pounds which are spent each year on guns and bombs, unnecessary railway lines, extra runways at airports and a plethora of other vanity extravaganzas which waste the taxpayer's money, couldn't someone just allocate the odd billion quid to do some serious psychic research to investigate the possibility of creating some provable scientific contact with the other world? The Russians tried it in the 70s and 80s, but they only got as far as some rudimentary tests in telekinesis while, at the same time, the Americans wasted millions of dollars trying to teach dolphins to attach mines to the hulls of Russian battleships. If some serious work could be done to normalise the paranormal, the need for bombs and battleships would become immediately redundant.

Chapter Fifteen

Blackburn

If I'd had a jittery feeling about our visit to Liverpool then it could be said that Stephen had the same kind of jittery feeling about a forthcoming demonstration in Blackburn. In Liverpool's case, all went well and my nervousness was proved to be groundless. Unfortunately the same could not be said for the event in Blackburn!

Although Steve and Rob set off in good time, the traffic on the M62 was totally horrendous. There were speed restrictions all over the place and the traffic was nose to tail for most of the way. The rain fell in absolute torrents, and there were times when even the most efficient of windscreen wipers simply could not cope with the deluge.

Stephen became ever more anxious and, watching the minutes tick away, he knew there was a good chance that he was going to be late: at best, he might just be able to walk through the doors at 7.30, but that would give him no time to catch his breath or prepare himself mentally or spiritually for the evening ahead.

As I've said before, Stephen is a Taurean and Taureans hate to be late for anything. We'd rather get there half an hour early, even if it means sitting in the car and reading a paper or just listening to the radio until the appointed time. Furthermore, he didn't know *exactly* where the venue was, or what it might be like when he got there. It was a Council run hall, and although he had asked for 200 seats to be laid out theatre style, past experience told him that his request might, or might *not*, have filtered its way down to the hall management. Many times in the past he had arrived at a venue to find the seats stacked up at the back of the room, and had had to set them out himself. Under normal circumstances he could have coped with this, but with time running out, he just hoped that the hall staff were on the ball.

After driving round the streets of Blackburn for the better part of fifteen minutes in search of the venue, they finally found it on a street corner they must have passed at least half a dozen times without recognising it for what it was. Stephen jumped out of the car and dashed into the building while Rob went to find somewhere to park. It was 7.35 and some of the audience had been in place for more than half an hour and the natives, as they say, were restless!

Thankfully there was no problem with the seating, so still in his damp clothes, Stephen just swung himself onto the stage from the floor and went straight into his opening preamble. The microphone and amplifier were still in the back of the car, so he did it 'free voice' croaking through the remnants of a bad cold which had been complicated by occasional bouts of laryngitis. In Stephen's own words, it was not the best start to an evening of clairvoyance!

While not exactly hostile, the audience was flat and unreceptive. People sat with their legs crossed and their arms folded across their chests, body language which could be interpreted as saying "Right mate, we've paid our ten quid, so get on with it and show us what you can do!"

By his own admission, Stephen struggled with the first couple of messages, the second message in particular was somewhat disjointed because Steve kept being distracted by some sort of kerfuffle that was happening at the back of the hall. It was difficult to see exactly what was happening. The hall was dimly lit with the only light available coming from three big chandeliers high in the ceiling and a dozen wall sconces. The walls were a uniform taupe brown with a few faded cream highlights, and he had to struggle to see what was happening.

There appeared to be an altercation taking place between two late arrivals who were demanding seats when there were none available. Rob was trying to placate them while one of the ushers was scurrying around trying to find a pair of extra chairs, managing to set them up at the back of the hall. This didn't seem to satisfy the late-coming couple, who insisted that they should be in the middle of the room somewhere near the front. They'd ordered their tickets over the phone and, all right, so they were a bit late but that had been through no fault of their own, so they wanted to sit where *they* wanted to sit. This was their right!

With some cajoling and brilliant diplomacy on Rob's part, the couple were finally settled, and Steve attempted to carry on. I say attempted, because half way through the fourth message, a loud voice yelled out from the back of the room. As I say, it was a *loud* voice, but it was also slurred by alcohol.

"Rubbish!" the voice bellowed. "Yer've got plants in the audience!"

Stephen chose to ignore the accusation, greatly reassured by the hisses of "hush" and "shut up" which emanated from the people sitting close to the man who had shouted out. Stephen didn't need to be psychic to recognise that it was the late-comer who had caused so much fuss ten minutes previously.

Steve carried on, but 15 minutes later, the late-coming man was on his feet in the side aisle, waving a bottle round in the air. "You're a load of sh**e!" he called out venomously. 'Just another f*****g fraud like the rest of your friggin' lot. I want my friggin' money back!"

Now Stephen did stop.

"I'm very sorry ladies and gentleman," he said quite formally. "This sort of thing does happen very occasionally, so forgive me for a moment while I sort this situation out." Then he raised his voice slightly and looked down the length of the room. "Rob, can you and maybe a couple of ushers show this gentleman to the door, give him a full refund, and tell him not to come back." Then he spoke directly to the trouble maker. "Obviously, sir, you're not enjoying the evening, but I'll not have you spoiling this demonstration for everyone else who is here tonight. As you've just heard, I've instructed my manager to give you your money back, so I hope you go and have a pleasant evening, only please go and have it somewhere else!"

"You ain't throwing me out of anywhere, you poncy little fake!" the man yelled back at the top of his voice, pausing only to swig from the neck of the bottle. "I know my f*****g rights!"

By then, Rob and two of the ushers were by his side, and were judicially manhandling him towards the door. His peroxide blond partner scuttled after him, the clickety clack of her outrageously high heeled shoes drowned out by the huge cheer of approval which went up from the rest of the crowd.

After that Stephen settled down a bit and brought through three rather better and more detailed messages than he had managed to get across thus far. During a short interval, Rob set up the PA and told Steve what had happened.

"Drunk as a skunk," he said flatly. "Said he'd booked tickets over the phone, and had been told to pick them up on the door. He couldn't remember the date he booked them or the phone number he'd rung, but I let him in anyway. Obviously, now I realise that was a big mistake. I should've twigged that there was going to be trouble when he started swigging whisky straight out of the bottle!"

"Never mind," Stephen consoled. "Hopefully that will be the last we see of him and, in the meantime, I'm going to keep my fingers crossed that the second half of the demonstration will be a lot better than the first. That was hard work out there tonight."

In part two of the demonstration Stephen returned to his usual form and brought through half a dozen detailed messages. Glancing at his watch he saw that it was a few minutes to ten, so went into the wrap up speech, said goodnight to the audience, then plonked himself down on the edge of the stage to sign copies of his book. As is always the case, other people milled around, some just wanting to say thank you for his efforts, others wanting to ask the usual questions which a demonstration of clairvoyance always precipitates, while a third group of interested parties wanted to tell him their life stories and their own involvement with the spirit world.

Finally the crowd thinned out, leaving perhaps half a dozen people who simply did not want to go home until they'd had 'their' personal slice of Stephen's time. He was in the process of talking to an elderly lady about her departed sister (she'd had a message in the second half and needed to tell Steve all about it!) but then Stephen was distracted by movement further back in the hall, and was alarmed to see the big man who'd been thrown out during the first half of the evening, marching purposefully towards him with a furious scowl on his florid face and a three quarters empty bottle of scotch in his hand. The other hand, Steve noticed, was clenched into an angry fist. *Oh Lord, here comes trouble,* he thought, experiencing a small pang of fear.

Barging past the elderly lady and shoving her out of the way, Mr Whisky shoved his face up close to Stephen's. "I don't like being thrown out of places," he snarled, "especially a dump like this."

"Sorry," Steve answered quietly, "but you were well out of order, just as you are now. I think you'd better go home now and sleep it off."

"Sleep what off?"

Stephen shrugged. "Well, you're obviously very drunk, otherwise you wouldn't be behaving like this…"

"Drunk am I? You cheeky little git! You need teaching a f*****g lesson!"

Two things happened at the same time. Mr Whisky drew the bottle back, clearly intending to bring it down on Stephen's head, and Archie May, Steve's principle spirit guide, spoke firmly in his ear… *You'd better do something lad, otherwise he's going to crack your skull!*

Even as the bottle was descending towards him, Stephen acted on pure instinct. He ducked to the left and jabbed out with his right fist. The fist connected directly with the end of Mr Whisky's nose and there was an audible crack. Mr Whisky took one step backwards, dropped the bottle, and then with blood pouring out of his nose, tripped over his own feet, and fell down flat on his bottom at Stephen's feet.

One hour later Stephen found himself closeted in an interview room down at the Nick, being interviewed under caution by a portly police sergeant accompanied by a pimply constable. Neither of the officers seemed in the least bit sympathetic and the sergeant was openly hostile.

"So, let's get this right," the sergeant said. "You threw Mr Whisky out of your show and when he came back later to complain, you lashed out and hit him, and broke his nose?"

"No," Steve replied indignantly, "that's not the right story at all." He went on to explain the events of the evening with as much detail as he could while the sergeant twiddled with a pencil, making the occasional note on a pad.

When he'd finished, the sergeant stared at him balefully. "None of what you've told me alters the fact that you're facing a charge of actual bodily harm. You don't deny that you hit Mr Whisky, do you?"

"No, of course I don't deny it," Stephen snapped back, "but if I hadn't, he'd have fractured my flaming skull with his bottle."

"You don't know that for sure, though do you? It might just have been an angry gesture, evening a *threatening* gesture, but you don't actually know that he was going to hit you with the bottle, do you?"

"Of course I do," Stephen retaliated. "The bottle was already falling towards my head when I lashed out at him and, if I hadn't, you'd be interviewing me down at the nearest hospital. This is all a clear case of self-defence and I've got a dozen witnesses who will prove it, if you ever get round to talking to them rather than raking me over the coals!"

"Ooh, quite the little expert, aren't you," the sergeant narrowed his piggy eyes, smiling sarcastically. "Either way, I can either charge you with actual bodily harm or public affray, but for the time being, you are being formally cautioned. Now, sign this document which says you accept the caution, then you can get out of here and go home."

Not thinking of the implications and just wanting to be on his way, Stephen signed the sheet of paper with an angry flourish, and headed for the door.

"Says here that you're clairvoyant?" The sergeant called after him with an undisguised note of glee in his voice. "Tell you what, Mr Holbrook, I bet you didn't see this one coming!"

A few minutes later Steve was out of the police station and climbing into the car. With Rob at the wheel, they headed out of Blackburn and started their journey home. Obviously Rob wanted to know what had happened, and Steve did his best to tell him. He was deeply upset and it was a tight lipped and terse conversation.

"The flaming police were behaving as if I was the guilty party, when all I was doing was saving myself from a head bashing," he complained bitterly. "Now, through no fault of my own, I've been cautioned, and I've probably got a police record."

"The other bloke has," Rob said reassuringly. "I was talking to one of the desk staff and they said that he was a regular visitor with a load of history involving drunken and aggressive behaviour, so if it ever comes to a court case, I reckon you'll be in the clear in five minutes flat."

"A court case?" Stephen echoed. "Do you really think it might come to that?"

"I honestly don't know," Rob said truthfully, "but I honestly don't think it would. Mr Whisky isn't likely to press charges, not with his record, and even if he does, we've got a couple of hundred witnesses who will confirm that he was drunk and out of order throughout the first half of the demonstration, and a dozen witnesses, including Council employees, who saw what happened at the end of the night. Also, on the bright side, I suppose you could sue him for attempted murder..."

"No, no, no," Stephen answered quickly. "I just want to forget this whole business as quickly as I can and put it behind me!"

...Which is what he did.

I knew all about this event very soon after it had happened and was eager to include it in 'Survival' which was the book we were working on at the time. Stephen immediately vetoed this idea on the strength of his determination to forget all about it. Maybe he was also a bit worried about what his loyal band of fans and supporters might think, knowing that he had received a formal caution. With *this* book, which is being written a number of years later, Stephen is more sanguine and relaxed and, in the spirit of openness, has 'green lighted' this incident.

I have to tell you that Steve Holbrook is not an angry man, and there isn't an ounce of aggression in his DNA. In 20 years, I've actually *seen* him lose his temper only once, and it was an incident which lasted for no more than a couple of seconds. I've *heard* him lose his temper once, when he was being interviewed on a local radio station by a very ignorant presenter who was trying to extract the urine at every opportunity just to get a cheap laugh. But that's it. Stephen is pathologically polite, and 'happy' and 'helpful' are his middle names. If they were giving out medals for compassion, he'd have a long row of ribbons sewn to his jacket.

Therefore, I've always been curious about this incident in Blackburn and I am even more so now. So,

I have done just a little bit of research, and thanks to a widely advertised law firm, this is what I have discovered.

Before a caution can be officially given, the interviewee is entitled to ask for the presence of a duty solicitor. If he doesn't ask for one, then he must be offered the services of one. In Blackburn that night, neither of these things occurred. Steve didn't ask for one because he honestly didn't think he needed one, and at no time was he advised by the police that the services of a duty solicitor were at his disposal.

The interviewee must be made aware of the fact that accepting a caution is an admission of guilt and will form part of the recipient's criminal record. Stephen was not made aware of this, either at the time or at any time thereinafter. Despite the fact that Stephen didn't have a criminal record, that caution is on file and could be used against him in the future.

If the recipient of the caution offers any kind of defence, even if they accept guilt, a caution is not appropriate. The interviewee must be allowed time to consider the implications of accepting a caution – in other words, they can go away and think about it for a while. No such explanation or opportunity was offered to Stephen.

Any infringement of the above conditions renders the caution potentially invalid and subject to legal challenge... but there is a time limit on this, which in Stephen's case has long since elapsed.

After having lived in a number of different countries over the years and travelling quite extensively to others, I firmly believe that our British police are without doubt the best in the world, but that doesn't mean that every individual copper is a saintly paragon of virtue or that they are not influenced by their own agendas and prejudices. I suspect that Stephen was just plain unlucky that night in Blackburn, and had there been other officers on duty, the outcome of that cautionary interview might have been very different indeed.

There is a delightful epilogue to this chapter. Three days later Stephen was demonstrating in the lovely little town of Axminster. He'd put the Blackburn incident behind him and was looking forwards to working with a new crowd of people in a different part of the country. As he and Rob were unloading the car one of the Axminster organisers came up and asked if they needed any help... and then dropped into the conversation the fact that Steve had been mentioned on Radio Two by no less a personage than Terry Wogan on his morning show. The Blackburn fracas had been reported in one of the Red Banner tabloids, Terry had picked up on the story and was having a good old chortle at Stephen's expense.

"Some clairvoyant!" Terry had said mischievously. "I bet he didn't see that coming!"

Stephen had smiled sadly. He loved Terry Wogan – in fact he was Steve's favourite broadcaster – but he thought to himself "If I hear that statement one more time I'll flaming well scream!" Like many clairvoyants and mediums, he'd heard the jibe many times before! It was both annoying and irritating but, as they say, all publicity is good publicity, and Mr Wogan's anecdote guaranteed Stephen a full house for the Axminster demonstration.

Chapter Sixteen
Stratford

It was late March and Steve and Rob had been for an early Sunday lunch with Caroline and the kids, and Steve's dad, Eric. It was now time for Rob to face the three hour drive to Stratford-Upon-Avon and, equally, time for Steve to get his old faithful pillow out and have a nap on the back seat.

Stephen had been demonstrating in Stratford for many years, the venue had always been the Falcon Hotel, but this was going to be the last time, as the hotel was under new management and re-developing the hotel, converting the Function room that had always been used for the demonstrations into a restaurant. This wouldn't pose a problem as there were a multitude of hotels that would be grateful to get 100 or so guests through the doors on a Sunday evening in March. As usual, 10 minutes into the journey, Steve was sound asleep, allowing Rob to play his 'music with no words' CDs, as Steve likes to call them (banging house and disco drums!)

Meanwhile, on the other side of Shottery, near Stratford, two of the girls from the newspaper that Steve advertised with, had been given a pair of complimentary tickets and were both excited about attending the evening. Helen and Liz had seen Steve demonstrate before at Leamington Spa Royal Spa Centre, which is where they were based. As Stephen had stopped doing that venue, their nearest venue was Stratford. Liz was having her sister-in-law staying with her, but knowing she had only two tickets posed a problem. That afternoon she rang through to see if there were any tickets left, and after being informed by the box office that there were only 11 spare, she reserved an extra seat and was told to collect it on the door. This was before she had even mentioned it to her sister-in-law, Carol.

At around 2.30pm, when Carol arrived, Liz said "I've got a little surprise later! Me, you and Helen have somewhere to go for the evening!"

Carol's immediate thoughts were "Ooh, lovely, a night out on the town, or a meal?" But she insisted on Liz sharing her secret so she could decide what to wear!

Eventually Liz said "It's an evening with a Medium!"

"Oh God" replied Carol, "I'm not sure that's something I'm really into!"

James, Carol's husband and Liz's brother, had been for a reading with someone in Milton Keynes, which wasn't very good, and this had obviously put Carol off, and to say she was dubious was an understatement. When Liz explained it was a group thing, she seemed to relax a bit.

Helen said "We've seen him before and we've got three free tickets!" This was bending the truth slightly, because she knew that Liz had only booked the extra ticket that afternoon.

"Okay," Carol finally agreed, "but he would have to say something only I knew, for me to believe him."

"Well, you never know" replied Liz, at which point Carol had a coffee and then went up for a shower.

Fast forward four and a half hours to 7pm and Steve was finishing his bookwork in a little back room that he had found, out of the way of the main function room. Meanwhile, all three girls had arrived and got seats, about half way back on the right hand side of the room. Both Liz and Helen had had a white wine spritzer, and Carol settled for Soda and Lime. It was time for Steve to start the evening.

The first part of the evening was a roller-coaster session of tears and laughter, varying from people losing their husbands, to one lady losing her daughter who was only three and a half years old. Stratford was a place where Steve has fond memories from over 14 years ago, when he brought through a wonderful message to a lady called Hayley Clarke, from her son who had died as a baby.

Hayley's story is an important one and, although I told it in Stephen's first book 'The Light In The Darkness', it is definitely worth telling again, albeit in an abridged form, so please, if you've already read 'Light' forgive the repetition.

When, in the late summer of 1998, Hayley Clarke discovered that she was pregnant she was both surprised and delighted. The year before, she'd given birth to her first child, a son called Brad, and now this new pregnancy provided her and her partner Sean with the icing on the cake!

It was a remarkably straight forward pregnancy leading up to what must be one of the easiest confinements in medical history. It was all over in forty five minutes – two gentle pushes and baby Callum popped into the world in the evening of April 24th 1999, weighing in at a healthy six pounds twelve and a half ounces.

Unlike some babies that look like a squashed up version of Winston Churchill, baby Callum was of the new breed – fine elfin features, thick black hair and enormous eyes with lashes that might make a budding starlet go green with envy. In short, the kind of baby that one might look at and muse "well, he's been here before, hasn't he!"

Callum passed the usual post-natal health checks with flying colours and the bonding energy between

Callum and his parents was both ardent and profound: here was a good baby who took his food with little fuss, rarely needed winding and for the better part, slept soundly through the night without waking or wanting. Hayley would frequently find herself singing to her new born son, humbled and at the same time overjoyed by his presence in her life. For his part Callum would follow Hayley around the room with a pair of bright blue eyes that shone with awareness and intelligence. Everything in the Clarke garden was rosy – in fact it was more than rosy – it was absolutely perfect.

The first note of disquiet sounded on Wednesday 26th of May. While playing with the baby and tickling his feet Hayley noticed that the middle toe of Callum's left foot seemed disproportionately longer than the rest of his tiny digits. To say that this caused her any undue alarm would be an exaggeration, but it was something she was *aware* of. It certainly didn't seem to be causing Callum any problems, but it was something she resolved to keep an eye on, nevertheless.

On the following day, Thursday 27th May, Callum developed a small problem that obviously did cause him some distress. Sobbing quietly and waving his hand in the air brought Hayley's attention to the fact that the index finger of his left hand was swollen with some sort of infection. Remembering that she was already uneasy about the elongated toe, she didn't think twice and immediately booked the baby in for an appointment with the doctor.

On Friday 28th May Hayley's GP gave Callum a close inspection and could find nothing intrinsically wrong: the infected finger had already begun to heal itself and because there was no obvious discomfort from the toe, it was left on a 'let's wait and see' basis. Reassured that there was nothing too much to worry about, Hayley and her family got on with the business of enjoying the forthcoming weekend.

Tuesday 1st June ended like any normal day. Callum fell asleep in his crib next to Sean and Hayley's bed, and a little while later Brad was settled down for the night in his own bedroom. Hayley and Sean enjoyed an evening meal, watched some TV and went to bed themselves around eleven o'clock. Callum seemed to be sleeping easily enough at that time – but both Hayley and Sean were woken a couple of hours later around 1.30am on Wednesday 2nd June. Callum was restless and uncharacteristically fretful and nothing that the parents could do seemed to ease his distress. In the end, after some considerable time of soothing and cuddling, the baby finally dozed off cradled in his father's arms. Sean gently laid Callum back in his crib, and the couple tried to catch up on the first night of lost sleep their new baby had caused them.

Neither parent slept well.

Sean struggled out of bed and left for work around six o'clock, at which time Hayley, Brad and Callum were sleeping peacefully. But when, at 7.45am Hayley climbed out of bed to check on her son she immediately knew that something was dreadfully wrong. The baby's skin colour was ashen grey, every part of his tiny body was pain sensitive to her touch and, most alarming of all, the baby's eyes had rolled up into its head, showing nothing but the whites.

Thus began one of the most intensely distressing and suspenseful three days that any family might fear to experience in their darkest nightmares.

An ambulance was called for and baby Callum was duly admitted to the special care baby unit at Warwick hospital. The day progressed agonisingly slowly as a number of prescribed tests and examinations were undertaken.

Hayley and Sean sat in the waiting room, holding hands in mute disbelief at this sudden turn of events. Various members of the hospital staff would occasionally smile encouragingly and they were never less than supportive, but the suspense of not knowing what was wrong and what the prognosis might be was excruciating in the extreme.

At five o'clock in the afternoon and after nine hours of unendurable tension, the medical team at Warwick Hospital advised Hayley and Sean that Callum was "very poorly" and that he was being immediately transferred to Leicester Royal Infirmary.

Once Callum had been admitted to Leicester Royal Infirmary his parents were allowed to see him, which in itself was a shocking experience. Wired up to a life support machine, his tiny body, so frail and defenceless, seemed to be a pin cushion for a dozen different lines and drips, but on a more positive note the emergency care team told Sean and Hayley that meningitis was low on their list of probabilities.

Knowing that their eldest son was safely being looked after by Sean's sister Siobhan, the couple settled in for an all-night vigil at the Leicester Hospital. Hayley's mother and Father, Sandra and Tony, sat with them, but there was little anyone could do other than sit and wait for any kind of news from the medical team.

Through these long hours there was little change in Callum's condition, but at seven o'clock in the morning of Thursday 3rd June baby Callum went into cardiac arrest and a team of seven doctors fought for many tense minutes to save his life. To their credit they were able to pull the little boy back from the brink but the prognosis was grave – so grave, in fact, that Hayley and

Sean called a priest and their baby was baptised even as he battled for his life.

At three o'clock that afternoon Callum had a second major heart attack and, for a second time, the dedicated team of doctors and nurses at The Leicester Royal Infirmary helped him hang on to a flickering spark of life. This time, however, it took well over an hour to resuscitate him and there were now serious worries about brain damage having been caused by oxygen starvation.

In truth, both parents were now having to face the fact that the chances of their baby pulling through this ordeal were extremely slim.

At four o'clock that afternoon the blood tests came through from Warwick indicating that Callum had acute septicaemia and (confirming all of Hayley's fears) the rare streptococcal B strain of the meningitis virus.

Callum remained critical but stable throughout Thursday night and there was little that Hayley and Sean could do other than to settle down and spend another exhausting night at their infant's bedside. Neither of them slept very much and Hayley's eyes were constantly drawn to the screen that was measuring Callum's erratic heartbeat. Even the most minute change of nuance in rhythm had her leaning forwards with her own heart in her mouth.

On the morning of Friday 4th June, LRI conducted a full brain scan, leading to more interminable hours of dread and suspense. The results of the scan came through at three o'clock in the afternoon indicating that baby Callum was 100% brain dead. They were told that whatever happened this was irreversible, and that it was only a matter of time, to be measured in hours rather than days, before the baby would have another, and this time inevitably fatal, cardiac arrest.

There then followed what was the worst time in their lives. Arguably the worst time imaginable in any parent's life.

After much prayer, soul searching and counselling, and following the advice of the doctors, Callum was disconnected from the life support system. At four forty five on the afternoon of June 4th, one day short of being six weeks old, the little boy quietly died.

At Callum's funeral, while Hayley managed to get through the day without collapsing into an emotional wreck, other members of the family were constantly near to tears.

One specific incident occurred that demands narration, which concerns Hayley's brother and sister-in-law, Rob and Barbara.

While still in the chapel of rest, a photograph of Callum, Sean and Brad had been placed in Callum's tiny coffin. Rob also enclosed his silver crucifix, which he lovingly placed around Callum's neck. Unfortunately, unbeknown to anyone, Barbara had gone out and bought a small gold crucifix expressly for this purpose and, now, being pipped to the post as it were, she became very upset indeed.

Sean quietly resolved this the next day by taking Barbara back into the chapel and moving Rob's cross from Callum's neck to his feet, replacing it with the gold cross that Barbara had bought. Thus both relatives were appeased and the coffin was finally sealed containing the family photograph and two crucifixes.

Hayley and Sean buried their baby and got on with the task of living their lives: Sean had his work to get back to and they both had Brad to think about and look after. Steadily, and in their different ways, they began to work through the grieving process that comes with bereavement. It didn't happen quickly and it wasn't easy. One thing that Hayley did do was plant a rose tree – a Calluna Rose – in her garden of remembrance.

Hayley's baby had been snatched from her and she was desperate to discover some meaning as to how and why this could have happened. Now she needed some proof and reassurance that there was life beyond death, for no matter who she talked to, be it friend, relative or counsellor, no answers seemed to be forthcoming. Try as hard as she might, whatever she did, wherever she went, she carried a cloud of dark misery with her that nothing seemed to be able to alleviate.

When she learned that Stephen Holbrook was to visit Stratford-upon-Avon in November of 1999 she immediately booked tickets. She'd never heard of this particular medium, but that hardly mattered. Any port in a storm and any chance was better than no chance at all.

On the evening of November 14th Hayley and her Mum were among the first to arrive at Stratford's prestigious Falcon Hotel. They took their seats, and sat through the first half of Stephen's demonstration, much impressed by his evidence and, as far as Hayley was concerned, willing his attention over to their part of the room in the hope that there might be something in the ether concerning Callum. When the interval break came without Stephen having so much as even looked their way once, Hayley was quite convinced that she would be returning home empty handed.

However, half way through the second half, the medium's attention did swing over to Hayley's corner of the room, and Hayley takes up the story from there.

From Hayley:

He said he had a connection with someone who'd passed over with brain damage – and then he changed it from brain damage to brain disease – he said that he thought that this might be somebody's son who had passed over some time in the last year, and that this would have been a little boy who was very very young. He wanted to know if anyone could take this information, so I waved my hand and said yes, and he came to me immediately with the number six, and said that he felt this number was very important for some reason, which obviously it was because Callum was just six weeks old when he died. Then he told me he was getting the letter 'C' very strongly, which was when I started getting very emotional. I told him that Callum had died when he was only six weeks old, and then Stephen said "well, he isn't dead now because he's right here next to me, and he's telling me to tell you that the photograph you put in the coffin is still with him, and he's also saying that there was some trouble about what else went into the coffin. He's also telling me that you planted a tree in the garden, and I think it must have been a rose tree, and that he's grown since he's been on the other side and right now he's as tall as that tree. He's pointing to his left foot and telling me that there was something odd about one of his toes – that it was longer than it should have been and that you were worried about it. He's sending you all his love, but says that he can't hang around to talk now because he wants to be off playing with his mates..."

Stephen wanted to know if any of this made sense to me and of course it all made sense to me, every last little bit of it. The only thing that was a bit confusing was the way Callum talked through Stephen... I mean you'd have thought he was six years old, not just six weeks, so obviously something has happened to him since he crossed to the other side, but I don't have any answers for that and I don't think it matters. As far as I'm concerned Stephen

Holbrook has given me absolute proof that my son is still alive, even though he may be gone from me down here. He talked about things that nobody but me and my family could know about, and to be so specific about the photograph and the trouble with what went into the coffin, the rose tree in the garden, the business with his toe, the number six and that big letter 'C', the brain disease tying in with someone who had passed over while they were still very very young... I mean, how much evidence does a person need?

Three months after Stephen's demonstration in Stratford-upon-Avon Hayley Clarke kindly consented to meet me at The Falcon Hotel. It is on the strength of that interview that I have drawn the source material for this chapter, and I take this opportunity to thank her most sincerely for opening her heart to me and telling me the story of Callum from her own unique point of view. Towards the end of what, in many ways, was quite a harrowing morning, I asked her how she felt about things twelve weeks down the road from her experience with Stephen.

She smiled, and the smile was filled with a gentle radiance. "Stephen changed my life," she said candidly. "Oh, I still miss Callum every hour of every day, but since that evening when Stephen spoke to me, the dark cloud that had been hanging over me ever since Callum died, well, it just evaporated. Now I'm able to get on with my life secure in the knowledge that Callum is having a great time somewhere else, and that one day we'll be together again. I don't have all the answers, I don't suppose anyone does, but Stephen Holbrook gave me the strength to tackle life again. That night, after his demonstration, I went home on wings of light and air – I couldn't wait to tell Sean what had happened, and when I did, we both just sat at the kitchen table and cried and cried and cried... But it marked a turning point in my life, and now I can get on with living and looking to the future, knowing that there is a future, and not just for me, but for all of us."

Now, fast forward back to Liz, Helen and Carol.

After the interval, Steve did another brief intro, and off he went. Three messages into the second half, he said he wanted to be over in the middle rows on the right hand side, and needed to speak with someone about 17th December, and a lady called Marjorie. No hands went up, but Carol whispered to Liz, "I think that's me!"

Liz didn't know, but Carol had previously worked in a shop with a lady called Marjorie, and it was Carol's Grandma's birthday on 17th December. Liz volunteered Carol's hand, and although Carol was hesitant, she didn't resist.

"Can I hear your voice please?" asked Steve.

"Yes" she replied.

"The lady, Marjorie, is surprised to see you here and even more surprised to be communicating with you. She's telling me she was very confused towards the end."

"Yes, she had Dementia."

"She's talking about Sooty."

"That's the poodle she kept as a pet because she couldn't sell him."

Steve looked confused. "Er, what do you mean, she couldn't *sell* him?"

"She owned a pet shop!" *The audience roared with laughter.* "He passed away a month after she did."

Stephen regained his credulity... "I also have a lady here called Molly, she is sending her love to you.

She says it's been a rough ride for you these last four years."

"Yes, that's my Grandma Molly, she died four and a half years ago."

"She is showing me a ring, and the initial 'D'."

"Oh my God, yes! It's her Mum's ring, my Great Grandma. She was called Dot, her initials DM were on it, but the 'M' wore off. I've got it in my purse."

"Is the 5th August significant?"

"Yes, that's my Uncle Jack's birthday, her son, but we don't get on."

"Your Grandma Molly says she believed in this sort of thing when she was here, but overheard you saying this afternoon 'He would have to tell me something I know, before *I'd* believe in it'."

At this point, all three girls burst into fits of giggles, and Carol's face was a picture.

"Oh my God, I did say that this afternoon, about 3pm!"

"Your Gran is just letting you know she overheard it. Just a minute, Julian is here, he wants to say something."

"No, Julian is still alive," Carol interrupted.

"He is telling me Thursday."

"No, Julian *is* still alive, I'm meant to be seeing him on Thursday."

"No love, this Julian has passed away."

"Well, it's the first I know about it. I only spoke with him last week." Again, the audience laughed, although Stephen wondered quite what they were laughing at.

"Okay m'love, does 17A mean anything to you?"

"No, sorry."

"Ok my love, goodnight and God bless from your Grandma Molly and Marjorie from the pet shop, and thank you!"

As so often happens after Steve's evenings, we are flooded with emails or calls to say "My mind went blank, I couldn't think at the time, but I've remembered now" but sadly by then it's too late.

Mid-morning on the Monday, no more than 12 hours after the evening at The Falcon, Steve had an email to say that all three girls were delighted to have received a contact, but Carol felt the need to explain something. She had intended meeting Julian the following Thursday, after speaking to him to arrange it on the previous Monday. However, over the last few days she had left two messages on his mobile checking the time of their rendezvous, as she needed to get to the dentist after their meeting; she'd had no reply, but thought nothing of it, since they weren't meeting until the Thursday, and she felt no great urgency. But a call at 9.45am from her husband James changed everything.

She had only been up half an hour, as the girls had been chatting about the messages 'til the early hours. Helen hadn't left until 1.15am and Carol and Liz had enjoyed a couple of extra nightcaps after that.

Unfortunately James' telephone call brought some bad news. Julian had been found dead in his flat, he was only 37 years old and, as far as Carol knew, had no serious health problems. Julian's flat was number 17A and according to the information available, he had been dead for at least 48 hours. Needless to say, this was a horrendous shock for Carol, but her thoughts immediately went back to the evening when Steve had said "Julian" and "17A". Now the message made sense!

From what we can gather, there is no concept of time in the spirit world. Spirits, it seems, have no reason to measure it, therefore once a spirit has left the body, it is quite often possible for the contact with a medium to be relatively immediate. This has been something which has happened on a regular basis throughout Stephen's career. People so often come up afterwards to explain to Steve that the person he's had contact with has yet to have their funeral. Also, so many people say the same thing... "When you are in the spotlight and you're actually receiving that message, it's a shock and your mind just goes blank". Carol certainly did not expect to get a message from her friend Julian, as she didn't even know he'd passed away.

Amazingly enough, after Carol took in the enormity of what happened, and relayed everything that had happened to her husband James, they both turned up to another of Stephen's evenings, this time in Warwick. I think that with Carol explaining things to James, and with both Liz and Helen on hand to back up the story, he wanted to give Stephen the benefit of the doubt and try again to find some satisfying evidence of his own. What he saw and heard that night made him completely dismiss the experience with the so-called medium in Milton Keynes and he was able to look at spiritualism and the idea of post mortem survival with fresh eyes.

Chapter Seventeen
Mickey Mouse

Thirty or more years ago at a time when I believed in my own publicity and thought I knew a whole lot more than I actually did, I had some very flashy and expensive business cards printed. 'James Christie' they proclaimed, 'International Psychic and Tarotmaster'. I was very pleased with those cards and gave them out to all and sundry, even to people who I knew would never in a million years call the telephone number on the bottom of the card. I was particularly proud of that word 'international' because I reckoned I'd earned the title, having worked in the USA, the (then) Soviet Union, Israel, Egypt and a dozen other countries on two continents. It was with some ironic bemusement that for some while afterwards I noticed that other psychics had also started using the international word in their publicity, and half out of pique and half out of curiosity, I did a bit of checking.

One medium, who I knew quite well, claimed to have done work in Italy, when in fact the nearest she'd ever got to Italy, was Ilford. Many people had done an odd reading by the poolside or in an airport departure lounge while on holiday in Spain, Greece, or Portugal, then claimed this as international status. From what I could gather, very few had actually been invited by, or had specifically travelled to another country for the express purpose of doing professional readings in the host nation.

Thirty or more years ago this meant a lot to me, but now, thirty or more years later, it doesn't mean a damned thing, and I cringe at my own superficiality and overinflated sense of self-importance.

Stephen can genuinely claim some elements of an international reputation, after all he's cruised the Caribbean and the Mediterranean, doing shipboard demonstrations in some of the most spectacular locations in the world. My wife and I were with him during a hectic week demonstrating in Tenerife and, yet, his globetrotting has never gone to his head, and as far as he is concerned a demonstration is a demonstration, be it in Bournemouth or Barbados. Half the time he is so busy he's not always sure where he is and I remember an occasion on the Isle of Wight when he walked on stage and said "Good evening ladies and gentlemen, it's lovely to be back on the Isle of Man!" As for business cards, I don't think he's ever had one, certainly not in the last 20 years, anyway.

One of Steve's favourite off-shore locations is Jersey, and he has been flying over to the Channel Islands once or twice a year ever since his first visit back in 2006. On his last visit, in January 2019, he was responsible for bringing through one of the most poignant messages of his career, which went to a lady called Sarah and her mother Jean, who had come to see him at Jersey's prestigious Mayfair Hotel.

It was fast approaching Christmas, and despite Sarah trying to be brave for her two sons, Marcus and Luke, she was dreading the arrival of the festive season. It marked the painful anniversary of losing her beautiful daughter, Leah, who had passed away on the 22nd December 2014, after losing a long battle with a rare form of cancer. She would have been 10 on her next birthday, the double figure, the true sign of a 'big girl', but she never got to that birthday which would have fallen in February 2015. Sadly, her young life became too fragile and, despite numerous rounds of chemotherapy and various types of other life-saving drugs, she developed respiratory problems and slipped away quietly in her sleep.

Sarah had explained everything as best she could to Marcus and Luke, but children are resilient, with that pure innocence that surrounds them like a protective bubble. This is not to say they didn't miss their big sister 'Leelee', as they affectionately called her. She had always been the Mother Hen, and when her 'real' brothers had come into the world, Leah had ditched her dolls, and had suddenly become a real-life second mummy to the boys.

Christmas of 2018 came and went and, as any parent who has lost a child but has other children will know, the show must go on. It can almost be robotic, all the excitement of the children's faces on Christmas Day, carols in the street, people going about their daily lives totally unaware of what Sarah was going through. She lived with that constant feeling of emptiness, that shallow feeling, ever-present in the pit of her stomach. Was life *ever* going to be the same? Was *this* it? Going to bed night after night with the tears and the sickly feeling when she opened her eyes in the morning. The constant clouds of oppression and depression hanging over her, almost making her feel as if she could physically collapse at any given moment.

There were, however, many *many* beautiful memories: the family trip to Disneyland Paris the summer before Leah had fallen sick, and Leah being a beautiful bridesmaid at her Auntie Sue's wedding. Nevertheless, all those wonderful memories were painful to recall, and just seemed to amplify the enormity of Sarah's loss.

Sarah had a part-time job in a Newsagents, not particularly because she needed the money, but because the job gave her something to focus on while Marcus and Luke were at school. Even with this part time occupation, the days seemed to be never-ending. Sarah's husband, Craig, worked ridiculously long hours, but they seemed longer now than they had before. Perhaps this was something of Craig's own creation... his way of dealing with the loss of his daughter.

There was always a heavy oppressive atmosphere within the home when he returned from work; this was something you couldn't ignore and even a number of years after Leah's passing, the situation had little improved. In fact, it had become the status quo. Sarah didn't have the strength to lift him up when he was feeling low, and neither did he have the strength to lift Sarah up when she was feeling depressed. To their credit, they both put on a brave show for the sake of their two sons, but after the boys had gone to bed, there was very little communication between them, other than to pass comment on a TV show or to discuss the shopping list for the weekend.

At the very best of times, Craig had never been a brilliant conversationalist, and now with the loss of his daughter he closed down even more. Like many men, he was not good at expressing his emotions and thus his pain and anguish were supressed and pushed under the carpet, festering away quietly deep within his soul. It would have been so much better if Sarah and Craig could have opened up, shared their grief and supplied each other with that much needed emotional support... but in some ways Sarah and Craig were a typical family and it was not to be. Not then, anyway.

It was Thursday morning, around 11.45am, when Sarah took a call from her Mum. She was on her own that day in the newsagents so she was free to answer, which wasn't always the case, as she wasn't really allowed personal calls. Jean was merely checking to see how Sarah was, and casually asked her if she'd be interested in going to see a medium, who was due to appear at The Mayfair Hotel in St Helier, Jersey, on the second Saturday in January. Jean had been recommended by two friends who went there every year, and both gave rave reviews of the visiting clairvoyant, a chap called Stephen Holbrook from the North of England.

After a brief chat, Sarah agreed to consider it, but it had only just been the fourth anniversary of Leah's death, and each time it came round it left her desolate for weeks afterwards. She would have to check the date and arrange baby-sitters if Craig was working; in short, far too many things to think about right now. She turned back to file the newspapers.

It wasn't until the following Tuesday (when Sarah met her Mother in Voisins Cafe for an early lunch) that the conversation turned to the clairvoyance evening.

"Yes, I have given it some thought" Sarah said. "I suppose it's worth a try, even if we don't receive a message personally, it may just hit the spot and give us a bit of a lift." Sarah was thinking that she would do just about anything to help herself feel better.

Jean and Sarah had always had a close relationship, and Jean had also been very close to Leah. She had been totally crushed by the loss of her grand-daughter. They'd had an amazing bond and although she loved the boys dearly, nothing would ever replace her beautiful princess. Jean was really pleased that Sarah had agreed to attend the evening, and as Craig was off that Saturday night, she didn't even need to arrange a babysitter.

In the week leading up to the evening, Sarah's emotions were mixed, she suddenly felt a rush of excitement that she may receive a message, only for it to be very short-lived as there followed the opposing thought of 'there will be an awful lot of other people there, all thinking the same thing'. The thought crossed her mind that perhaps she should see someone on a one-to-one basis, but then again, she thought, if her Mum hadn't mentioned the evening in the first place, she'd never even have contemplated seeing a medium! Her last thought was 'Oh well, what will be, will be. At least it's an excuse for a night out.'

Sarah had fed the children and even had time for a long soak in the bath and was waiting, ready for Jean to pick her up. She quickly went back upstairs and picked up her tiny silver locket, with a lock of Leah's hair in it, quickly pushing it to the bottom of her bag. Before leaving the bedroom, she gave yet another spray of her Chanel Mademoiselle perfume. Why not? She never went out these days, so she might as well use it!

The horn of a car sounded and Sarah said goodbye to the children and Craig, and went with a nervous excitement to get into the car. On the journey there, Sarah was making Jean laugh, explaining that earlier in the day, she had found lots of squishy bits under the settee. She couldn't work out at first what they were, but realised that they were soggy tomato pips. Luke had had a chicken salad sandwich at lunchtime and scraped the tomato pips out and rather than put them in the bin, tried to hide them under the settee! Sarah would never have noticed this, but she had picked an odd slipper up off the floor, and felt something wet on her hand. Jean laughed at this and said it was typical of Luke!

They pulled up into the car park, near to the hotel, and strolled the short distance to the The Mayfair. As Jean walked through the foyer, a lady handed her a leaflet. Jean just assumed it was a leaflet about the evening, but soon realised this was a church group, protesting about the use of mediums to connect with the spirit world. She quickly scanned over it and the last line at the bottom of the leaflet said "Look at Lady Diana, she consulted a medium, and see what happened to her!*"

The leaflet immediately went on to list the church service times, and details of how to get there. Jean was dismayed to say the least, thinking to herself angrily 'How could any church have the cheek to stand in a hotel foyer, handing out leaflets promoting a service that they wanted people to attend, using Lady Diana and her tragic passing as a selling point?' She quickly threw the leaflet in a nearby bin, not even bothering to show Sarah.

After getting drinks from the bar, they handed their tickets in and took some seats at the back of the room. That night there were approximately 200 people at the Mayfair, and Sarah could feel the disappointment coming over her in waves. With that number of people present, the chances of her receiving a message would be very slim indeed.

Steve bounced onto the stage in his usual style, and one thing with Stephen, which anyone will tell you who has ever attended one of his evenings, is that he has that undeniable ability to relax the audience within minutes. Sarah felt comfortable and almost relaxed for once, and ready to enjoy this rare evening out.

Stephen's first message went a lady who had lost her husband and he explained that she had had to cancel a three week holiday as he had passed over suddenly, only nine days before they were due to depart. Then he reunited a lady with her sister, whose birthday would have been that very day. The sister was only 48 and had been severely handicapped, but Steve insisted that she was now a free spirit and was in no way compromised. It was straight after this message that Stephen slowed right down, as if he was in deep thought. He said…

"I have a young girl here, and she says to tell me that the 22nd December is significant."

Instantly, Sarah's hand shot up.

"Yes, that's me, over here!"

"She says she was going to be a 'big girl' but didn't quite make it."

Sarah broke down instantly, and her Jean gave her a tissue, whilst also trying to compose herself. Jean took hold of Sarah's arm and held on tight.

"She says she is missing the boys," Stephen continued.

"Yes, her brothers!"

"She was like a little Mum herself, wasn't she?"

"Yes, yes, yes!" Sarah found she could hardly breathe.

"She is showing me a photograph and I am aware of big ears, this photo was taken somewhere abroad?"

"Yes!"

"Believe it or not, what I'm seeing here is Mickey Mouse."

"Oh My God! It's on my phone, it's Disneyland Paris!"

"You looked at this photograph today?"

"I did, just before I left tonight."

"Is the 22nd December her birthday?"

"No, it's the day she died."

"Sorry my love, but anniversaries are like a never ending circle. Death out of this world is like a birth into the next, I can't tell the difference."

"I understand, thank you."

"She is showing me a heart shaped silver locket with her hair in it."

"Yes! It's in my purse!"

Jean almost shrieked, she didn't even know Sarah had put it in there!

"Your daughter says you don't usually keep it in there, but you decided at the last minute to put it in."

"I did!" Sarah's voice was shaking with supressed sobs.

"She says you put extra perfume on before you came out tonight."

"Aaah! Yes I did, I did, I put more on just before I left the house."

"She likes the smell sweetheart. She says you smell gorgeous."

By this time, many members of the audience were reduced to tears and the room was so silent you could have heard the proverbial pin drop.

"I know this sounds strange, but she is talking about tomatoes and pips – did she not eat the pips?"

"No, that's my son. I was speaking to my Mum about it in the car. Oh my God!"

"It looks like she was listening then, my love. She is also mentioning Mark."

"No, it's my son, Marcus."

"Who is Craig?"

"That's my husband, her Dad."

"She sends lots of love to her Dad, and she says he has found it incredibly difficult to talk about what happened. But she wants you to know he's been suffering just as badly as you have, only he's had to deal with it in a very different way. Now, she's also talking about someone called Joan or Jean…"

"That's me, I'm her Grandma" Jean shouted out triumphantly.

"She is trying to tell me about a passage, or something you perhaps wrote out for her, something about a staircase or a lane – does that make any sense to you?"

Jean caught her breath "Oh goodness, it's a plaque I have near her special garden, it's from Wales and it says 'If tears could build a stairway and memories build a lane, I'd walk right up to Heaven and bring you back again.'" She recited from memory and, by now, the entire audience had their heads down, all dabbing at their eyes.

"She says she was your favourite!"

"Oh well, yes! She was very special" Jean admitted, looking a little embarrassed. Steve returned to Sarah now and said, in a proud way:

"She's just said February was her birthday, and she was really looking forwards to being to being ten."

Sarah: "Yes, she nearly was. She died two months before her 10th birthday."

"She says that now she's over there she can look after you and can be like a little guardian angel to you. She is showing me something pink in her hand, and it's soft."

"Yes, it's a pink Minnie Mouse, I put it in her hand in the coffin."

"She wants you to know that she's in perfect health again and enjoys coming back to visit you. And one day, she promises she will see you again, and she's saying 'please Mum, don't forget to give my love to my brothers'."

Steve finished – and even had to wipe his own tears away – and then went on to deliver another two messages before the break. But it's important to mention here that Sarah got up straight after the message and went outside, leaving Jean on her own to listen to the other messages that Steve was relaying. Sarah needed to catch her breath and get some air. Steve noticed her go, but just assumed she may need a cigarette or something, which he totally understood. Once outside, Sarah turned her phone on, hands still trembling, and still in deep shock. She flicked straight to the Mickey Mouse photo of Leah in Paris, and she quickly forwarded it to her Mum, knowing that her Mum's phone was in her bag and on silent, so wouldn't disturb the evening. As a memento of the night, she thought it would be a nice gesture, knowing Jean hadn't got the photograph and it was her Mum's wonderful idea in the first place to come to the evening. It was really down to her Mum that she had received the message. Sarah then sneaked quietly back to her chair hoping no-one would notice. It was fortunate that they were at the back of the room, but to her surprise Steve spoke directly to her, and said:-

"Excuse me my love, I need to come back to you."

"Oh yes, I'm so sorry, I needed some air."

"Oh no love, that's no problem, it's just your daughter has forgotten to tell you something. She says she knows about the text with three kisses on, and the photograph you sent with it."

"Oh no, I don't believe this!" tears poured down Sarah's cheeks. "I've just this very second sent my Mum a text from outside, saying 'thank you Mum for booking the tickets for tonight' with three kisses on it, and with the Mickey Mouse photo attached!"

"Well love, she really does want to let you know that she doesn't miss a trick, what a wonderful young girl! Thank you my love, and goodnight."

Sarah and Jean were once more left wide-mouthed and speechless. This was a seminal moment in both of their lives, possibly more so for Sarah than for Jean, for on the strength of Stephen's message she was able to go home with a new lightness in her step. She had been grieving for four years, and only now had the healing process truly begun. As she began to heal, so was she able to reach out to her husband and lift him up from the dark place into which he had fallen.

Stephen remembers the message he gave to Sarah with great clarity, and it has prompted him to write the following few words:

From Stephen:
One thing that has always fascinated me is the undeniable talent of toddlers and children to make a sad, depressing mood lift with their raw innocence. I say this because when my Mum was poorly and had to go into a home, my little nephew, Ashton, who Mum worshipped, was only four and a half at the time. He was passing by the care home with his mother Adele, my sister. From his seat in the back of the car, he just suddenly said "Are we not going to the Big House today to see Grandma?"

This was just a couple of months after Mum passed away, and Adele said "Grandma is in Heaven now, sweetheart" to which Ashton replied "Well, when is she coming back?"

Any parent who has had to answer a child's quick cross-examination will know their questions come from an inability to totally understand a situation. How can someone suddenly disappear out of your life? Someone you love, never to be seen again? It can often reduce you to tears, but it can often at times be the one-liner of a stand-up comedian.

One day, Adele and Steve, her partner, were having a discussion about the scattering of Mum's ashes and they weren't aware of 'little ears' listening in the lounge. Ashton was on his iPad, but it appears that children can also do two things at once and he was obviously ear-wigging into the conversation. Adele was explaining that Mum wanted her ashes digging into the grave of my Grandma and Grandad. Obviously over-hearing this, it went in, but as children do, it was put on a shelf to be used later. It wasn't until bedtime later that evening, when Adele had finished his night-time story, that he jumped out from under the sheets and said "Mum, if I had one wish, I would wish for Grandma to be magicked back to us."

Adele said "Well darling, you know she can watch over us, and see what we're doing all the time." Ashton came straight back with "But how she can see through the roof? It's IMPOSSIBLE! I miss her." The tears were rolling down his face and then, in an emotional and exasperating way, he said: "Anyway, if you dare dig her in that hole, I will just dig her right back out again!"

I am pretty sure that little ones find it equally hard to vent their frustration, being obstructed with an inability to fully understand. Even, bless him, when Adele had been in tears over Mum, he had the sensitivity to come across, put his arms around her, and say "Don't worry Mum, she's still there, she can still see us," repeating back the adult theory.

It's too easy to change the subject, and we do need to find an honest way of explaining the process of passing over in a very simplistic way. Thankfully, my three children have grown up steeped in conversations about the afterlife and spiritual revelations, so it has definitely helped them to see things in the natural way they are. What also made me laugh was when Ashton started one day to chat about Mum and at that point Adele, feeling very emotional anyway, just tried to divert around the question and change the subject, but from the car seat in the back, Ashton wasn't accepting this. "I know..." Adele had said, "let's practice the alphabet", and his reply was "Oh Mummy, let's not! You just concentrate on your driving!"

Mum always said "You wait and see, Ashton will make something of himself, he's very special" and I know she is right because I can already start to see the mind of a spiritually aware child opening up in front of me.

*On the 16th of August 1997 Princess Diana and Dodi Fayed consulted Derbyshire medium Rita Rogers. Rogers warned Fayed to avoid France, for there was danger waiting for him in that place. She also warned Diana of an accident in a tunnel caused by a car which had had its breaks tampered with. However, she went on to say that Diana and Dodi would be happy together for the rest of their lives. It could be said that her prophesies were correct, but what she did not mention was the fact that the 'rest of their lives' meant little more than a fortnight. In the ongoing argument as to whether did Diana fall or was she pushed, it is the considered opinion of the international psychic community that she was most definitely pushed. So many people in power had so much to gain if she died and even more to lose if she had lived.

Chapter Eighteen
Synchronicity

Synchronicity is one of those weird things which occurs in everyone's life from time to time and after talking about it the other day, Steve and I both came to the conclusion that it is noticeably prevalent in all matters appertaining to spirit and spiritualism. It is definitely a significant energy for anyone working in other branches of psychism and any astrologers and astronomers out there will be well aware of its recurring influence in their studies and research.

The dictionary definition of synchronicity is, and I quote, 'the simultaneous occurrence of events which appear significantly related but have no discernible causal connection'. This is a true statement as far as it goes, but it falls a long way short of telling the whole story. Carl Jung, who invented the word, was a little more forthcoming when he described it as being 'meaningful coincidences with no causal relationship, yet which seem to be meaningfully related'. When pushed into explaining how it might relate to the individual on a personal level, he went on to say 'for someone on a spiritual path, it is the moment in the frame of time when we suddenly and briefly become consciously aware that we have made a deeper connection with the universe or something which is greater than our individual selves'.

Many people I have spoken to over the years confuse synchronicity with coincidence, and while there is some connection between them, it's a bit like saying that all vacuum cleaners are Hoovers. Keeping it very simple, it might be said that while 'coincidence' has something to do with chance and luck, 'synchronicity' implies the presence of a deeper (or higher) intelligence at work within the framework of our human affairs.

Whether you want to call it synchronicity, coincidence or lucky chance, there are patterns within synchronicity which are not always present within the framework of the other two concepts, and the pattern I refer to here is that of cause and effect. A basic example might be in connection with a lottery ticket... John and Janet buy a lottery ticket and they win £10,000. They have bought the ticket in the hope that they might win and, hey presto, they have won, so, lucky old John and Janet! Ten grand is very nice, thank you very much, but to be brutally honest, they don't really *need* this money. Nevertheless, it gives them a wonderful foreign holiday that they didn't expect to have, and Janet gets her nice new conservatory.

It is, however, a different scenario if John and Janet just *happen to find* a lottery ticket that's got lodged under the front tyre of their clapped out old car which they can barely afford to keep on the road. They win the ten grand and that pays for an extra round of the expensive treatment which is keeping their disabled son alive, and during that treatment a medical breakthrough occurs which enables their son to *remain* alive. Their son may continue to be disabled, but the imminent death threat has been removed.

As I think you might agree, there is a huge difference between the two scenarios. The first represents coincidence or luck, while the second represents the power of synchronicity. I have painted this picture in broad brush strokes from within my own imagination, while in reality synchronicity can be much more subtle and obtuse. Let me, then, bend your ear with a few examples and ask you to draw your own conclusions.

In the mid-summer of 1999 Stephen had just finished a successful demonstration at the Guild Hall in York and was heading back home towards Castleford along the A64. About three miles out of York, just as they were passing the small garage and service area at Colton Lane End, he turned to his friend and passenger and said something like:

"Do you know, Pat, I've just had the strangest feeling that there's going to be a man who's going to come into my life and help me with my work."

Pat, also known affectionately as The Rottweiler, frequently travelled with Stephen and helped him with the box office at his various venues. She now cast a possessive and protective glance at him across the car.

"What," she asked, "you mean something like an agent or a manager?"

"Dunno," Steve shrugged in the darkness, "but maybe something like that but, well, not *quite* like that."

"And when do you think this might happen?" It was obvious from her tone of voice that Pat's feathers were very slightly ruffled.

"Not sure..." Stephen answered. "Maybe sooner rather than later. Possibly within the next month or so."

Now, at pretty well the same time and less than half a mile away as the crow flies, I was sitting in my little cottage in Colton village, reading the local weekly paper and checking to see if they'd got my advert in properly. They had, bless them, and then when I absently turned the page, I noticed the advert for Stephen's demonstration of clairvoyance at the Guild Hall. I was miffed to realise that it had been that same night and that I'd missed it. My wife, Jo, tactfully reminded me that we didn't read the local papers on a regular basis, so it was hardly surprising that we'd missed something we might want to go to. It was not the first time something like this had happened!

Anyway, the upshot of all this was that five weeks later I found myself talking to Stephen Holbrook in the Queens Hotel in Leeds at which time I propositioned him with the idea of arranging some venues for him and acting as an occasional *tour* manager, and also hitting him with the idea of writing a book about him which he could sell at the end of his demonstrations.

Now, you could describe this sequence of events as being synchronistic, but it becomes even more interwoven when you place it in a broader context.

A few weeks earlier in that same year I had become involved with a man called Leonard Bardy who was interested in starting a promotions company and was prepared to finance it if I was prepared to front it. He had the money and I knew the business, so it seemed like a match made in heaven and quite frankly I very eagerly bit his hand off.

Far too eagerly, as it turned out, because unbeknown to me, this gentleman was an undischarged bankrupt and, when his cheques started bouncing, it was me who caught the flack and carried the can. This caused me profound anger and embarrassment, it cost me a couple of good friendships and one very promising professional relationship with a musician I very much admired – and it also cost me a lot of money! And yet, it also brought me into contact with Stephen and opened a door of opportunity which was destined to fulfil my ambitions as an author and publisher.

When I first approached Stephen, I was able to offer him a booking at the Palace Theatre in Newark. Between the initial offer and the date of the demonstration I had already begun to feel very dubious and alarmed by my association with Mr Bardy, so when Stephen phoned me from his dressing room immediately after his show in Newark and told me that Mr Bardy wanted him to send in an invoice for his services, and then he would dispatch a cheque by return, I emphatically told Stephen to say no, and demand the cash he was owed there and then, in accordance with the contract I had issued and Mr Bardy had signed off on. Stephen did as I suggested and I'm glad that he did, because if he hadn't, God knows when he might have got paid, if indeed he ever got paid at all!

At a later meeting with Stephen he told me that he had a very bad feeling about my business partner, and by then so had I. Thus it was agreed that anything Steve and I did together would be on a one to one basis, and that's the way it has been ever since – and now we're 20 years down the road.

Elsewhere in this book there are other examples of synchronicity, for example the dovetailing of events which led to Stephen's first meeting with Rob at the Portsmouth Hilton and the raffle dogs that Steve won in the hospital tombola in aid of the baby care unit. One of the most potent examples of synchronicity (and indeed potentially lifesaving) involves Stephen's friends in the South-west, Jill and Roger Prior.

This couple had lost their lovely daughter, Lisa, a number of years previously when she had been taking a bath and had been overcome by carbon monoxide poisoning. It was, as you can imagine, a devastating experience for them, and it was through this that they made their initial contact with Stephen. This led to them promoting Stephen down in the West Country, doing something similar to what I was later to do in the North and the South-east.

One day, and quite out of the blue, Roger picked up the phone and gave Stephen a call. There was no reason for this, he simply had the compunction to make contact and say hello. When he asked how Stephen was, Stephen had a bit of a moan. Caroline, his then wife, was feeling sick and ill and had taken herself off to her bed, and there was something wrong with their gas fire. There were sooty black streaks above the fireplace and, indeed, even as Roger phoned, Stephen was standing in front of the fireplace with a tin of white paint and a brush, trying to brush the soot streaks away. Needless to say, this didn't work, as anyone other than a Taurean might have expected.

Roger felt quite alarmed by this news and told Steve to remember what had happened to Lisa. This resonated with Stephen and as soon as the phone call with Roger was over, he called the British Gas helpline. Cutting a long story short, the service engineer called round the following morning, did some twiddling and fiddling, and then told Stephen that he'd been very lucky because there was a fracture in the gas supply pipe and that it had been emitting carbon monoxide fumes for a number of days. Had the fault not been sorted out when it had been, there could have been serious consequences – very *serious* consequences – within a matter of hours. In short, Roger's phone call had averted a nasty disaster and in all probability had saved Steve's life and also the lives of his family.

Synchronicity works on a number of different levels. Roger Prior's story falls into the 'in your face' category, but there are other examples which are much more subtle.

In an earlier chapter on the subject of ghosts, you may recall that I mentioned two friends, Kay and

Devey, who took Steve under their wing and provided wonderful hospitality at their Shrieves House home in Stratford-upon-Avon.

This was, as I have said, quite an extensive property and Devey came up with the bright idea of creating a small museum in the furthermost wing of the house. It was a cross between a chamber of horrors, a wax museum and a haunted house film set from any one of a dozen Hammer movies from the 1960s and 70s. Two quid to get in and have a look around, six quid if you wanted the conducted tour and a mandatory stop in the gift shop before you were allowed back into the light of day. It was supposed to be haunted, but when Devey took us around the place, I didn't get any vibes at all and neither did Jo, or Steve. Frankly, the atmosphere was as dead as Marley's ghost.

However, the opening of this new 'attraction' did come to the attention of an independent production company that was filming shows about haunted locations, featuring the services of a well-known TV medium. Devey was delighted to make them welcome, because the TV exposure would be great publicity.

The production company duly arrived at Shrieves House with their cameras and lights, camera crew, sound crew, runners, producer and star medium. They spent the whole day filming and left feeling happy and well pleased with themselves. Devey was also pleased, because they'd paid him very well for providing the perfect location for their show.

Unfortunately, they did leave the place in a bit of a mess. Sweet papers, polystyrene cups, fag packets littered many of the surfaces, and in that part of the museum which contained a tableaux called The Plague Cottage, Kay also found a lady's shoe and a pair of gentleman's Y front underpants. That was not all she found, for tucked under the bed of a long suffering waxworks dummy depicting a young girl almost at the point of death, she found a slim pink folder with typewritten sheets and lots of notes and addendums written in biro pen.

When she took this back to Devey and they had a close look at it, it was identified as being the producer's shooting script for the show, and it turned out to be very revealing. On page 10 there is a typewritten section which states: 'Scene nine – Medium enters plague cottage and describes (a) brief history of the plague in Stratford, and (b) the oppressive atmosphere prevalent within the cottage. Suggest some sort of communication with the plague girl who will describe the horrors of the disease.' Then, handwritten in the column next to this text, *'Great idea! Medium should be seized by a fit and collapse on floor, foaming at mouth, and deliver plague girl's message in this way. Note: get corn flour and water standing by for mouth foam and get smoke machine rigged for SFX. Brief M and brief recording tex!'*

The synchronicity works like this. Devey meets Steve and is so impressed that he gets the idea of promoting a ghost tour around his house. The ghost tour angle attracts the production company. The production comes and does its filming, then buggers off, carelessly leaving a copy of the producer's shooting script behind. The shooting script indicates beyond all shadow of doubt that the whole programme is an absolute con, proving to Devey and anyone else he might show the script to that spirit has a wonderful way of getting its own back on anyone trying to make a dishonest buck on its back.

Devey did show the script to a few people, myself included, but he never went public with it. He'd signed a confidentiality clause in the contract with the production company and was worried about possible legal proceedings and potential loss of revenue caused by negative publicity.

The next example of synchronicity involves me directly. In the winter of 1988 I was wandering round Israel and ended up staying in the only hotel in the small resort of Ein Bokek on the shores of The Dead Sea. I was feeling far from well because two days earlier I'd been caught up in a riot outside the Damascus Gate in Jerusalem and had inhaled quite a lot of tear gas. I checked into the hotel, slept for the better part of the afternoon, then went down to the hotel dining room which was completely empty apart from a single woman eating on her own about three tables away. We exchanged a few words across the void, but had a proper conversation after the meal, sitting in the bar and drinking coffee.

We swapped names and stories (in my own case a very much edited version) and it turned out that this lady was called Ann Flowers who was going through a separation and divorce from her husband, Herbie Flowers.

I had never heard of Ann flowers, but I had certainly heard of her husband, Herbie, and had even met him once at the Marquee Club in London. I also knew many of his friends, because for a while in the late 1960s and early 1970s we had all moved in the same circles. Herbie was a bass player, regarded by many as being one of the best bass players of his generation. He'd been a founder member of Blue Mink, had been the bass player with T. Rex, and had the reputation of being one of the best session men in the business, laying down tracks for Elton John, David

Bowie and Paul McCartney, to name but a few. He also played the double bass, and somewhat bizarrely, the tuba.

His profession meant that he was always away from home, leaving his wife in a vacuum of solitude. They started having some marital difficulties and talked about trial separations. This was something which Herbie didn't want and he promised to reform, which for a while he was able to do.

Ann finished off the story with a sad little laugh. "It was all going reasonably well until he discovered Morris Dancing, and so if he wasn't off playing on stage or in the studio, he was off dancing around any one of a hundred village squares with rings on his fingers and bells on his toes, wearing straw leggings and a silly hat. I saw even less of him than ever and it finally dawned on me that there really wasn't room for me in his life – so I left."

So there was Ann Flowers sitting in a hotel dining room beneath the towering edifice of Masada, feeling miserable because she was going through a divorce, and there was me sitting in the same hotel dining room beneath the same mountain, feeling miserable because I was going through my own divorce... and yet we came from the same world, knew many of the same people, and were more or less in exactly the same boat... and what, I wonder, were the chances of that?

The bottom line here is that the meeting with Ann helped me in some small way to carry on with my journey, and I think I might have helped her on hers. The question here is, was it just a chance meeting, or did spirit have some influence in bringing us together for that very short time, to help us *both* on our journeys? I never met Ann again or ever heard from her, and I can only hope that she has found some happiness somewhere and with someone a bit more attentive than Herbie. She has probably forgotten me, but although I can't really remember what she looked like, I have never forgotten her.

A very up-to-date incident concerning synchronicity has happened just in the last few days. My desk calendar tells me that it is now Saturday 8th February, 2020. Earlier this week on Tuesday the 4th I met Steve in Wetherby to discuss the progress of this book and to chuck around a few ideas with regard to future content. Stephen asked me to email a few questions over to him and promised to give them some thought and attention.

Over the course of Wednesday and Thursday I drafted out some vague questions, but then on the evening of Thursday the 6th, I received a phone call from an old friend and colleague who wanted to know if I knew anything about automatic writing. I did know a bit, although not a lot, and gave my friend as much information as I could.

On the morning of Friday the 7th, I fired off an email to Stephen asking if he had had any experiences with automatic writing, working on the premise that if he did, it could make an interesting chapter. Literally, no more than five minutes later, my wife, Jo, came in from her own converted office on the first floor of our house, waving a batch of very tatty and faded A5 typewritten pages.

"Hey, look what I've just found in the bottom of the old cupboard!" she said with an element of supressed excitement.

"What have you got?" I asked, not entirely pleased by the interruption, not knowing that within the next few seconds my attitude was to change completely.

"It's the transcripts of a lot of automatic writing that my Mother did back in the 1970s!"

I know it's a cliché but the hair on the back of my head literally stood on end.

Let me say here that Jo's office is completely separate to my own. The walls are thick and there is no way she could have heard or seen anything that I'd been working on. Furthermore, she had not been privy to the phone call I had received the previous evening.

For my sins, I had forgotten that Jo's late mother had regularly attended local spiritualist churches and been interested in all spiritual matters when her first husband became ill and subsequently died. She'd sat in spiritual development circles with two other friends, Norman and Edith, who also were on their own spiritual pathway. Years ago Jo had told me that they had experimented with automatic writing which, to my shame, I had completely forgotten about.

For those of you who don't know what automatic writing is, let me give you a brief explanation of the concept, which is based on the premise that if we are calm and still it is much easier for a spirit to reach out and make contact with us, either directly or subconsciously.

Back in the 1880s and 1890s (particularly in the United States of America) it became fashionable to sit with a sheet of paper in front of you with a pen or pencil in your hand, and write whatever came into your mind. Frequently, the writers would write with their eyes closed and would have no idea what they were writing – many people were not even aware that they were writing anything at all until they opened their eyes and saw the lines of script upon the page! It was, and still is, assumed that these words are words directly from spirit, and contain messages of love and support from the other realms of spiritual reality. Frequently the handwriting is not in the usual hand of the writer and, sometimes, it must be admitted, many of the words are illegible. However, in the majority of cases, the words are crystal clear, even though the handwriting style might be unfamiliar.

To give you an idea of the kind of information that comes through in these messages, allow me to quote directly from two of Jo's Mum's pages:

'Pat Steers, June 20th 1976: communication.

Soul to soul, heartbeat to heartbeat, this is how close we are to you. In your lives we take the greatest interest. We love you and try to shelter you, as a mother hen with her chicks.

Down the silvery threads come the links, the words like beads on a necklace. To you we can send messages of hope and consolation, guidance in all aspects of your life, to allow you to fulfil yourselves and live your life to its full potential. We can, through you, reach others who have no means of developing spiritual communication.

By communication the knowledge of natural law is becoming widespread. Try to live by the guidance you are receiving. Try to be an example to influence others, for by their deeds you shall know them.'

'December 23rd 1976:

There is a silver stream of love cascading down from the spheres to the earth. A glittering stream of sparkling droplets, each one a word or thought to penetrate the denser atmosphere.

Love, like a kind and gentle hand, surrounds you, tries to protect and help you, even when it is unacknowledged or even rejected.

Those from spirit are not rebuffed. They go on caring and loving despite all. At Christmas time, the earth's atmosphere has a greater feeling of love and caring for others, and it is at this time that spirit can draw even closer as the vibrations are purer.* Then much valuable work can be done; peoples' hearts and minds be touched, and spirit rejoices in this good fellowship. If only it were possible to maintain these vibrations and purify them further for all time! A total amnesty from war and evil for ever!'

Now, I cannot attest to the fact that this was written in Pat's own hand, because I am quoting from a typescript. However, I am assured that Pat *did* write it. But let me add this... I knew Pat Steers very well and had my own special relationship with her. While I accept that the words may be hers, the presentation of those same words is not in keeping either with her character or modes of speech. One small example... Remembering that the lady was an experienced school teacher with a deep and profound love of the English language, she would never have said *'*purer*' choosing instead to say '*more pure*'.

This morning, February 8th, I received an email from Steve with the following information. Apparently he has never done any formal experiments with automatic writing, but a few years ago when he was profoundly upset and distressed by a situation which could potentially have caused him deep and lasting harm, he felt compelled to put a sheet of paper and a pen on his bedside table. He woke the following morning to find the pen and paper still in place on the table, but now there were words on the paper which read '*Stephen, we love you and we're looking out for you*'. It was neatly written, but most definitely not in Stephen's hand.

That weekend Rob had been with his mother in Lancashire, no one else could have entered the house, let alone his bedroom, without him knowing about it, and he's absolutely certain that he didn't write the message himself. He has promised me more on this subject later, so needless to say, when it comes through, I'll keep you in the loop.

...And we don't have very long to wait, because less than two hours later (I'm writing this in 'real' time, by the way) I had Steve on the phone with a very interesting addition to the story he'd already told me, which involves what might be described as automatic writing and certainly is another weird example of coincidence or synchronicity.

In the August of 2012 he was facing a crisis of confidence, caused by that professional situation over which he had absolutely no control. He was extremely low and profoundly worried by the unfolding events, and after a demonstration in Plymouth found himself driving aimlessly around the town. He was both mentally and physically tired out, but the idea of trying to sleep was a million miles away. He knew that he would just lay in the bed, staring at the ceiling, fretting about what his future might hold. He had a sick feeling in the pit of his stomach which made him think that he was being told by spirit that this might be the time to give up being a medium and return to the world of hairdressing, which was something he most ardently did not want to do.

At one point he parked the car and walked along Plymouth Hoe, hands thrust deep in his pockets and totally oblivious to the warm summer breeze and spits of rain. Towards the end of the Hoe he found a small shelter with a wooden bench, and sat there for quite some time. He's not sure, but he thinks he might have dozed off for a few minutes. Either way, he was gradually overcome by a sense of clarity and a whole sequence of unbidden thoughts began flowing through his mind. Frantically, he scrabbled in his pocket for a bit of paper and a leaky biro, and tried as best he could to get the words down before he lost them. Basically, this is what he wrote:

'Lessons to be learned'

Valuable instruction introduced in a way that is unprepared. Mocking and taunting is rife in a world where little is known – who says what, where and when, can all be disputed. But justification will shine through. We will walk with you and take all the torment and pain you will endure. Tonight will show your strength, and we will match it from the other world. Anticipate movement, we are breaking boundaries up here to severely dampen this intrusive ignorance. Worlds will never unite, but when your flame flickers, ours will ignite and take the strength from our endless devotion to you and your co-workers who aim to bring a little of our peace to your world.

Now it may well be Stephen's handwriting on the back of a rather damp and doggy A5 envelope, but anyone who has only ever had half a conversation with the man will clearly recognise the fact that these are not Stephen's words. Whose words they might be we'll never know, but they're definitely not Steve Holbrook's.

Where the element of synchronicity comes into play is that 44 years earlier in the August of 1968 I also found myself at the end of Plymouth Hoe, sitting in a car (you could drive right to the end of the Hoe in those days) and wondering whether or not is was worth driving all the way back to Torquay, or if it might be a better idea just to shove the old Vauxhall Victor into gear and drive it into the sea. Obviously I didn't, but at least you can understand how easy it is for me to empathise with Stephen and to know how he was feeling on that particular night. Also, both in astrology and numerology, four and eight are my key numbers, and 4+4=8.

Many of you who have read Steve's first book 'The Light in the Darkness' – which was first published 20 years ago – will know that Steve once received a spiritual message from the one and only Marti Caine, whilst driving to work in an old Austin Maestro. She simply said she was going to help both Steve and Jane McDonald and to read her book, but Steve didn't even know she'd written a book! Her communication made little sense at the time but now, more than 20 years later, it all makes perfect sense. Steve had told Jane at the time about this very personal message from spirit and, whilst Jane listened with interest, neither she nor Steve were able to make much sense of the connection.

Upon reflection it was glaringly obvious that Marti Caine could help Jane from the other side, and it was equally obvious as to why she would want to. Just like Marti, Jane was an excellent vocalist who used her personality with great power to communicate her talent. Just like Marti she had learned her trade in the cut and thrust world of the Northern club circuits. Jane even went on to host 'Star for a Night', a version of the older talent show 'New Faces' which Marti had hosted some years earlier, and had actually won it herself in 1975. The Jane McDonald version of the show was received with great enthusiasm, and it was the kind of show that had launched Marti Caine and brought her into the public eye all those years ago…

There have been common threads that have engaged both Steve and Jane's lives ever since they met. Even while this book was being written, Steve was on holiday in Spain, finally having the time to read Jane's new book 'Riding the Waves: My Story' – which hit the Top 10 Best Seller List – and Jane said of herself that she sees herself as a modern Marti Caine! This really brought everything together for Steve. It shows that the spirit world really do seem to have the ability to see round corners – even with a 20 year gap!

He loved reading the book, as he knew a lot of the back stories, and found it enthralling. When Steve is away, he tries his best not to text anyone other than Caroline and the kids, and immediate family, but even though he knew Jane was filming in Cuba, and didn't want to disturb her (and totally unaware of the time difference!), he felt compelled to send her a text saying that he thoroughly enjoyed the book. He even put "Hi darling, it's me, I have just spent three days in bed with my best mate Jane McDonald!" I must explain that he always reads in bed at night! He then, in one of those occasional moments of psychic precognition, went on to say that there were so many new things on the horizon, things that she would never imagine and that Jean, her Mum, was pushing her from the other side to think out of the box, and it was time to introduce changes!

Jane's mother, Jean, was a truly wonderful lady whom Steve held in high regard and found her a font of spiritual knowledge. There were many times when Steve and his Mum had chatted to Jean at shows and concerts etc, and often Jean and Margaret had bumped into each other whilst shopping in Wakefield, and ended up having a coffee and putting the world to rights. Never in a million years did Steve and Jane think that they would both be losing both their Mums within nine months of each other. Another thread to link them, as they both adored their mothers and both shared that unbearable sense of pain and loss.

Jane texted back three hours later, and sent a photo. Now, just like me, Steve has a mobile phone that would probably have been made before the war and runs on gas, so he couldn't even see the photo, just a message which popped up saying 'photo unavailable'. So he texted back to ask if she could send the photo to Rob, which she promptly did, with the words "Can you believe this?"

Earlier that same day, Ed, Jane's partner, had rung Jane to say that he was sorry but that whilst putting away the Christmas decorations, he had knocked over a framed picture of her, and it had smashed to bits. Jane said not to bother, just get a new frame, but the strange thing was that when the frame hit the floor and broke, another photo came out from behind the original picture of Jane. Ed saw that it was a photo of a much younger Steve, hair pulled back in a ponytail, Jean and Peter (Jane's parents), and another lady he didn't recognise. That person was Steve's Mum, Margaret. So, both Mums together, in a photograph Steve and Jane never knew existed.

This had all happened within a few hours of Steve's first text to Jane. That photo must have been behind Jane's portrait for over 18 years. Even in December of the previous year when Ed and Jane had invited Steve and Rob over for a meal, and the conversation had revolved around the two mums and their respective passings, the two ladies had been there, quite literally, hiding of sight, and listening in a spiritual and physical way to the conversations of their children! Ironically, neither Steve nor Jane know what the photograph was doing there, who had put it there, or even who had taken it!

Again, there are many many more incidents over the years that have bonded them together, but one thing is for sure – the bond between them is unbreakable.

A final word on the subject of synchronicity is something so obvious that I almost forgot to mention it. When Stephen is delivering a message from spirit to a member of the audience, this is a glaring example of what we've been talking about. There is a three way link here insofar as the spirit has got to be in the right place at the right time, the member of the audience has got to be in the same place at the right time, and Stephen has got to be in the same place at the same time to facilitate the communication. This is something which would be impossible to arrange without a powerful element of spiritual involvement, so ladies and gentlemen of the jury, I rest my case!

Chapter Nineteen
"Weeee..."

Yes, okay, I admit it's an odd title for a chapter heading, but stay with me because all will be revealed! First, however, for the sake of context, I must make mention of Stephen's collaboration with other mediums.

Basically Steve prefers to work alone, but there have been times when he has collaborated with other clairvoyants, notably with psychic artist Sandy Ingham, and earlier in his career with Sue Cunningham, the well-known psychic from South Yorkshire.

Steve and Sue had an interesting relationship, always light with banter and laughter, although there were occasional undercurrents of tension when it came to deciding who took the platform first to warm the crowd up for the other. Steve liked to go on first, leaving the second half of the evening to Sue, and while in one sense Sue was happy enough with this arrangement, it created a subliminal tension within her because she full well knew that anything she did after Steve's half of the demonstration would be an anti-climax. On the other hand, she didn't like the idea of going on first to a cold audience, or seeing herself as a 'warm up' act for the main event. They tried the combination in a number of different ways, and although Steve was sometimes frustrated by Sue's constantly changing mind, the pathologically helpful side of his nature inevitably ruled the day and he usually ended up allowing Sue to have her own way.

Almost without fail they presented their demonstrations to receptive and enthusiastic audiences, despite some glaring cock-ups by the newspapers which carried their adverts. On one occasion they were called 'International Physics, Stephen Alcock and Sue Cumminem' – it didn't keep the audience away, but Stephen was rightfully indignant and complained to the newspaper in question, demanding either a partial refund or a credit for a future advertising campaign. The newspaper declined and drew his attention to the small print in the advertising contract (the *very* small print) which stated quite categorically that, while every effort would be made to carry the advert as placed, they could not *guarantee* that this would be so and that no refunds would or could be made.

Hey, look, you're reading this, so you tell me... Do you think that's fair? Because I certainly don't! So, a word of warning here – if you're dealing with a newspaper's advertising department, always read the small print. The other thing worth mentioning here is the dreaded VAT. It is a matter of policy that the advertising departments of most newspapers quote you a price for your advert *without* the VAT and it doesn't matter if you say "exactly how much is it going to cost me to put this 3x5 advert in your entertainments column?" they still pull the same trick. I got very fed up of this once, and actually challenged a newspaper on this count, and the matter ended up in the small claims court. I am pleased to say that I won the case in less than 10 minutes, but regrettably it has had no effect on the advertising policy of most newspapers. So, in short, always get your quote inclusive of VAT to avoid a nasty surprise when the bill pops through the letter box.

However, I digress, and so must now get back to the business of 'Weeee'.

When I first saw Steve demonstrate back in 1999 I was slightly disconcerted by the fact that he did not work with a microphone. With a clear ringing tone of voice, he was able to project to the back of most of the venues he was working in, but when occasionally his voice dropped, frequently key elements of the messages were lost. We didn't fall out over this matter, but with some constant chipping away on my part, he did finally start using a mic. For one thing, he suffered from chronic sore throats and frequent bouts of laryngitis, which in the circumstances was hardly surprising. You can only demand so much of a voice before it starts kicking back, saying enough is enough, now give me a rest! Using a microphone took the pressure off, and gradually he came to accept the new routine.

Nevertheless, he found it difficult at first because he could never hold anything in his left hand... *(when Steve's principal spirit guide, Archie May, makes his presence felt, Steve's left arm constricts into a frozen rictus to reflect the physical damage Archie himself had sustained in the trenches during the first world war)...* and as he was wont to wave his right hand about in a windmill of enthusiasm, some microphone technique disciplines needed to be learned. It took him a long time to embrace working through a PA system, and it took me even longer to discover why his aversion to microphones went so deep.

We need to turn the clock back to the previous year when Stephen and Sue Cunningham had been doing a demonstration in a particularly large venue: there were more than 500 people present, and fortunately (or unfortunately, depending on how you look at it) the venue was manned by a team of very professional staff who were experienced in presenting everything from big band concerts to pop gigs. A very efficient stage manager rigged Sue and Steve up with throat mikes, and Steve was happy to go along with this because it left him with his hands free. The stage manager clipped transmitters to Steve's trouser belt and the back of Sue's dress, they did a quick sound check, and then the audience started piling in.

It was one of those nights when Sue had decided she wanted to go on first – the fact that she had a lot of personal friends in the audience might have been influential in this choice – and while she was on, Steve whiled away his time by sneaking a sly smoke by the slightly open stage door. He glanced at a local newspaper to make sure the advertising for the event was okay and then, still with plenty of time to spare, wandered through to the public loos which were off to one side of the main hall and could be accessed by a back entrance.

They were nice loos, probably scoring nine out of ten on the James Christie good loo guide, but what caught Steve's eye was some of the graffiti. Normally graffiti is carved into toilet doors or etched onto walls, but in this instance the management had made a fashion statement by framing some of the comments and annotations and Stephen got a fit of the giggles when he read some of the stuff that had been highlighted. 'Eat Poo!' one message said, 'Fifty zillion flies cannot be wrong!' He guffawed with schoolboy laughter when he read a short poem which proclaimed *This flaming toilet is no good at all, the seat is too big and the hole is too small. To this I must make the most obvious retort, your bum is too big and your legs are too short!'*

His eye came to rest on a reproduction Victorian print which showed a well-endowed lady in a flurry of petticoats, showing rather an indecent amount of leg and an extremely ample bosom. "Umm, you're quite nice aren't you? Very sexy!" Stephen mused – and then catching sight of his own reflection in the mirror, added... "And Mr Holbrook, even if you say so yourself, you're not half bad either!" Stephen had had his hair done that morning and was sporting a new shirt tucked into his favourite trousers. In his defence, Stephen is not a vain man, but on that particular evening he was quite pleased with his own appearance.

He flushed the toilet, washed his hands and whistling cheerfully to himself made his exit from the bathroom – *through the wrong door!*

He only realised his mistake when he emerged into the crowded hall to be met with a huge cheer and a thunderous round of applause. Sue, he saw, was stood on the stage, convulsed with laughter. There was a table, which was there for a carafe of water and a couple of glasses. Sue clung to the edge of the table for support while tears of laughter caused her make-up to run.

Stephen, bless him, had no idea what was going on.

"Could you," Sue finally spluttered, "hear us all right in the loo?"

"Er, no…. Er, why?" Steve called back.

"Because we could hear you. Every damn thing you did and everything you said. You silly bugger! You left your throat mic on!"

Stephen was horrified, and even more so when he later came to realise that he hadn't just been reading the graffiti, he been reading it out loud! To this day, he has never lived that incident down and Sue Cunningham, Lord love her, went to her grave still laughing about it… And if nothing else, it explains Stephen's deep abiding suspicion of microphones!

As I have already mentioned, in the early days of his career as a clairvoyant, he would travel all over the North of England in a very rickety Austin Maestro. The journeys were frequently exhausting, and even though he often travelled with a friend who would help him with the box office, he still had to do all the driving himself. Therefore when I came along and he was able to relax, either curled up asleep on the back seat or stretched out in the front with his eyes closed, a happy precedent was set. One of the main reasons for taking on a full time manager was the fact that Rob could do all the driving while Stephen did all the relaxing.

This was a very successful system because he would arrive at the given venue feeling relatively fresh and rested, with all of his energy conserved for the demonstration ahead. With increasing regularity, especially where long journeys were encountered, Steve would spend the outbound trip fast asleep in the back while Rob negotiated the slings and arrows of the British motorway grid. However, no system is ever totally infallible, and when things go wrong in Steve's life, they always go wrong in a big way.

On a particular November evening when the rain was raining and the sleet was sleeting and 60% of the M1 and M42 was coned off because of accidents caused by unattended roadworks and pockets of flooding, they arrived late at the venue. Rob brought the car to a halt by the stage door, and turned to Steve who was fast asleep on the back seat.

"You stay here," he said, "and I'll go and get someone to open the doors."

Steve muttered something like "Ogglewakurt" – which was what Rob said it sounded like to him, anyway – and as he disappeared into the night, Steve began the slow process of starting to wake up. He'd been in the deepest of deep sleeps and now felt very confused and disorientated.

Where had Rob gone? *Where* exactly were they? *Why* were all the lights out and why was it so dark? *Where* had the sun-kissed beach disappeared to that

241

he'd been basking on only a few moments before...? Slowly it dawned on him that the beach had only been in his dreams, but now he was beginning to return to wakefulness and he managed to get a grip on reality – but only up to a point. Where was Rob, where was he and why was it so dark?

The other thing which impinged upon his consciousness was the fact that he was desperately thirsty. He'd eaten a bacon sandwich just before leaving home and had washed it down with half a mouthful of cold tea, but that had been almost three hours previously and now he needed a pint of cold sparkling water or, if nothing else, a generous glass of his favourite white wine.

Wondering if there might be anything in the car, he rummaged around and finally retrieved a Starbucks takeaway coffee cup from the left hand foot well. It was half full and still relatively warm. Tepid coffee wasn't sparkling water or Pinot Grigio, but it was better than nothing and would have to do. He flipped away the plastic lid, and took a long gurgling swig from the cup... a long gurgling and very *generous* swig... and of course, you're way ahead of me here, it wasn't coffee. *It wasn't anything like coffee!* With dawning and horrified realisation, he identified the mysterious liquid as pee and, by default, it had to be Rob's pee.

He was quite correct in this assessment. Rob had been driving against the clock and, caught in one traffic snarl up after another, had come to the conclusion that he desperately – and then *very* desperately – needed a loo. Already running late, he knew he couldn't afford to stop at one of the service stations, the hard shoulders were either cordoned off or were being used as an extra traffic lane and, faced with the choice between wetting his pants or using an old coffee cup from a previous journey, Rob chose to use the cup, balancing it precariously between his legs with one hand while steering the car with the other.

Stephen thrust open the back door of the car, leaned out and gagging with disgust, vomited all over the car park. His timing was impeccable, because at that precise moment the car park lights came on with a blaze of amber tungsten, revealing a crowd of people who were strolling round the corner of the building, heading towards the front doors to pick up their tickets for the evening's demonstration. What they must have thought, seeing the star of the show hanging out of the back of a car, retching in despair and distress, is anybody's guess. Needless to say, Stephen was totally mortified and although he pulled himself together with sufficient sang froid to do the demonstration, by his own admission, it wasn't the best performance he'd ever presented.

Both Rob and I can see the humorous side of this story: Stephen, alas, cannot, and ever since this incident all coffee cups, Starbucks or otherwise, have been banned from the car.

Chapter Twenty
The Island

The island in question is The Isle of Wight. Some of you might have hoped for somewhere a little more exotic, but the IOW has its own unique charm and subtle charisma and is full of Old English Magick that can easily trap the unwary within the folds of its enchantment.

I honestly can't remember who first suggested that we promote Stephen on the island... I think it might have been me, on the strength of his successful demonstrations in Portsmouth and Southampton... but either way, I was well pleased with the decision. The Isle of Wight had played a seminal role in my distant past and had always owned a piece of my heart, so much so that in a parallel life, I could easily envision a scenario in which I would have made it my permanent home.

Back in my show business days, I had done four summer seasons on the island, one of them fairly disastrous, the other three remarkably happy and successful. I hadn't been back for many years and was eager to see how much the place might have changed in my absence.

The fact of the matter was that it hadn't changed much at all. It was still a slice of England as it might have been back in the 1950s and, if one removed the presence of the summer tourists, the pace of life was still parochially slow. On the down side, I was saddened to see that Royal Squadron Hotel in Ryde had become a noisy disco pub, especially when I recalled some of my very special and happy memories associated with that particular establishment. A holiday camp which had been my home back in 1964 was now a forest of tangled trees and overgrown vegetation, while another had transformed itself into a posh private chalet hotel, with security guards on the gate! All vestiges of Woodside Bay and St Clare holiday centres were lost and gone for ever, except in the memory banks of my mind.

Nevertheless, setting foot on the quay in Fishbourne for the first time in 35 years, I felt a sense of homecoming and was saddened that it had taken me so long to renew my acquaintance with this precious little corner of England.

Stephen fell in love with the island and I think it's fair to say that the people of the island fell in love with him. Our initial opening was a two night stint at The Winter Gardens Theatre in Ventnor: the theatre was packed to the rafters and on both evenings Steve received a standing ovation from the enthusiastic audience. Standing ovations are not totally unusual, but it *is* unusual for a clairvoyant to receive such a response.

After this successful debut, we were eager to return, but found ourselves in the position of having to find another venue. The Winter Gardens was closing for some much needed renovations so, after a lot of hunting and shunting, we chose The Gurnard Pines Holiday Village over in East Cowes. It had a small but very modern theatre complex which could seat about 200 people and was no further out of the way than Ventnor had been.

Our first night there was in the middle of winter and for the sake of convenience, we had arranged to hire a couple of chalets. In the spring or summer months this would have been fine, but at the beginning of March the chalets were freezing cold, and I have a memory of Steve and Jo and myself huddled round a one bar electric fire eating a takeaway Indian meal out of the cartons, using a couple of plastic spoons Jo had found in the glove box of the car.

Despite this, Stephen was in high spirits. As we had driven up the driveway earlier in the afternoon he'd been amazed and delighted by the hordes of red squirrels which scampered and bounced around the pine trees. He was also extremely pleased with the evening's demonstration, not only by the detail and accuracy of the messages he brought through, but again by the enthusiastic responses of the audience.*

The Gurnard Pines became our IOW base for the next few years, but then we had to switch to another venue. It became increasingly difficult to find dates that were compatible to the Gurnard Pines' schedule and, like many other venues we have had to deal with, once they've got you on their hook there is a tendency to hike the prices to a point where one is forced to look at other options. We ended up at the Cowes Yacht Club... a bigger and much grander place (big enough to house a couple of Sunderland Flying Boats) and I suppose this is where the point of this chapter really begins.

Stephen facilitates all kinds of different messages from the spirit world to thousands of people from all walks of life. Each 'link' is unique to the individuals involved, but the initial contact seems to follow a familiar pattern; from the platform or the stage Stephen is made aware of a spiritual presence who wishes to pass a message through to a member of the audience... Sometimes these spiritual presences are brought to Steve through one of his spirit guides and occasionally they come through on their own, jumping the queue so to speak in their eagerness to make contact. Once in a blue moon, something else happens, which Stephen has never fully understood and finds extremely difficult to explain. One such message occurred at the Cowes Yacht Club on a warm sultry night in July.

The first half of the evening ran true to form and then about ten minutes before the interval Steve paused, looking slightly puzzled and confused.

"I think I've got a message here for a lady, probably sitting somewhere in the back of the room, and the only way I can identify her is through a blue caravan. So, is there a lady here tonight who knows anything about a blue caravan?"

"That would be me, I think," a female voice called out from the very back row. It was a strong confident voice and, although the lady in question didn't shout, her words carried clearly across the auditorium suggesting that she was no stranger to public speaking. She was sitting less than ten feet from where I was standing by the staircase which led up to the bar and I honed in on her immediately.

I found myself studying a very smartly dressed woman, probably in her mid-forties. She wore a simple grey dress, but it was beautifully cut and probably had cost her a lot of money. Apart from a silver streak above one ear, her hair was raven-wing black, cut in a short curly bob and accenting a pair of dangling diamante ear-rings. Her lips were a deep red and, judging by the rest of her make-up, she was an expert in its application. In a really weird and odd way, she reminded me of my mother as my mother had looked when she was about the same age and combining the visual impact with the projection of the voice, I immediately started thinking in terms of 'theatre'.

"Can you tell me the significance of a blue caravan?" Steve asked tentatively.

"Certainly…" the lady smiled, almost mischievously, showing even white teeth which spoke of big bills from private dentists. "I live in blue caravan… or at least I do for about seven months of the year."

"Okay… Er… Who is Arnold?"

"Arnold was my father."

"And what about Daisy?"

"Daisy was my mother."

"And they're both on the other side?"

"Yes, they both passed over many years ago."

"Ummm…" Stephen paused, and I sensed that he was struggling with this one. His usual flow of information was missing and he seemed to be groping round for something to say. Finally, somewhat tentatively… "And am I right in thinking that there is someone in particular you wanted to get a message from tonight?"

"Possibly, but then again, possibly not." The woman's smile had faded, her eyes had narrowed slightly, and she was studying Stephen quite intently.

"Who is Marion?" Steve asked.

"That would be me. My name is Marion."

"Good… In which case, can I ask what the significance of Friday might be? I don't know why, but Friday seems to be very important in some way."

"My cat is called Friday."

"Your cat?"

"Yes. He's a little stray tabby and I found him on a Friday, so I ended up calling him Friday."

I noticed that she was using the word 'I' and not 'we', which caused a resonant connection in my own mind.

"Okay madam…" There was none of the usual M'love or M'dear here, but instead, that very formal "madam", which also pricked my interest. "This might seem like an odd question, but do you work in a casino?"

"No, I have nothing to do with casinos."

"Oh, it's just that I see you dealing cards…"

"I like the odd game of cards," she admitted, "but I've got nothing to do with the gambling industry."

Here I had a sudden and rare flash of perception. I am not clairvoyant, but I do have some psychic ability, and I would have bet my Granny's crystal ball that he cards Stephen was referring to were Tarot cards. I moved a step closer to the woman who was giving Steve such a hard time and, although she was not wearing much jewellery other than the earrings I've mentioned, I now noticed that there was a delicate chain around her neck upon which hung a silver pentagram.

There is frequently some confusion about this emblem. It is a five pointed star embraced in a circle which connects the star points. It is a long established amulet of protection favoured by wiccans, psychics and magicians and should not be confused with the pentacle, which is the five pointed star *without* the connecting outer rim. In general terms (although there is some controversy and misinformation here) the connected star circle of the pentagram is a powerful symbol of protection while the pentacle is a talisman of attraction.

Stephen was looking agitated. He was pacing the stage in an obvious state of frustration. "Why is Spain important to you?" he called out, "and I don't mean just as a holiday destination!"

The lady called Marion emitted a throaty chuckle. "It's part of my name," she admitted.

"Your name is Spain?" Stephen sounded confused.

"My full name is Marion Spain-Cavendish," she told him, "and if you want to know the story behind that oddity I'll be happy to tell you, but it would probably take up the rest of the evening, so maybe it's not such a good idea."

Steve nodded, looking, I thought, rather grateful. "Yes, well, just take heart in the knowledge that your Mum and Dad have been here with you this evening and that they're watching out for you from the other side and, much as you might love your little cat, they're reminding you that there is a big wide world out there and maybe you need to do something to reconnect with it. Anyway, thank you and goodnight."

I could see that Stephen was glad to be done with this link and that he was looking forward to the interval which would give him a much needed breathing space.

We spent the next 20 minutes selling books while the majority of the audience crowded into the bar on the mezzanine floor at the back of the room.

"That last link was a pig in a poke," Stephen complained between signings. "Couldn't get much at all. There was lots of energy there, but something was blocking the messages and," he looked at me directly, "have you ever heard of anyone called Spain?"

As a matter of fact I had, because it was the nick-name of the poet Pete Morgan's mum. He dedicated one of his anthologies to her, simply writing 'For Spain' on the frontispiece beneath the legals. This was picked up by a fan at the Spanish Embassy in London, which led to Pete being invited to do a long poetry tour of Spain. It was an extremely advantageous piece of misinterpretation and helped to establish Pete's reputation back in the 1970s as one of England's leading new poets.

"I reckon that there might have been a lot more to that link than met the ear," I offered carefully, "and if she's still around at the end of the evening, I'll go and have a quiet word and see if I can get the back story."

Stephen suddenly laughed. "I've got to tell you I nearly dropped a major bollock out there tonight. I was about to say 'much as you love your little pussy' and changed it to 'cat' at the very last second. Can you imagine how the audience might have reacted to that!"

I imagined only too well, and it would have been up there with "you're hot in bed" and "it's nice to meet a man who comes more than once". Strangely, though, I didn't think that Marion Spain-Cavendish would have been particularly offended.

When the audience took their places for the second half I noticed that the lady in question was missing from her seat. Then out of the corner of my eye, I noticed her leaning on the balcony rail which overlooked the auditorium. Even as I watched, she slung a long coat over her shoulders and walked out onto the terrace which overlooked the harbour. I knew that this wasn't an exit from the building, so maybe she'd just gone outside to get some air or to admire the view. Either way, I strolled up onto the mezzanine and looked out of the glass door. Sure enough, there she was, gazing out across the yacht club and smoking a cigarette. Oh well, there was no time like the present, so I pushed the door open and went and stood next to her.

"That was an interesting message you got," I said cheerfully as an opening gambit, "though maybe a bit unusual. Stephen said that there was lots of energy around, but he thought something was blocking him, so maybe there wasn't as much evidence as usual."

She looked at me in a rather cool, but not totally unfriendly way. "You're James Christie, right? The man who writes the books with all the typos and spelling mistakes?"

"Yes," I admitted ruefully, "I guess that's me."

"They're quite good books," she offered, "but for God's sake, the next time you write one, make sure you get the services of a professional editor."

"Duly noted. Spell-check does leave a lot to be desired."

"Anyway, what's your interest in the message Mr Holbrook gave me?"

"We're working on a new book," I volunteered, "and because your message was unusual I thought it might be interesting."

"Yes, I suppose it was. In a way."

She left it hanging and struggling with a response, I said, "Well at least your Mum and Dad came through. That must have been reassuring."

She gave a short laugh, but there wasn't much humour in it. "They needn't have bothered. They were awful bloody parents! I didn't like them and they didn't like me!" Then her voice softened. "But at least, Mr Christie, I got what I came for."

"Dare I ask what that was?"

She shrugged. "Basically, I wanted to know if someone was dead or if they were still alive. If they'd been dead, then they would have been here for me tonight making contact. The fact that they didn't tells me that wherever they are, they're still living."

"Er, I'm not sure it works like that," I said hesitantly.

She smiled at me, and I thought with some degree of sympathy. Maybe even pity. "No," she eventually

252

replied, "if they had passed over, they would have come through this evening and I know that for a fact!"

"How do you know that?" I challenged – in a very unchallenging way.

"Perhaps because I know as much about the subject as you do," she said, and then "maybe even *more* than you do."

"That," I smiled into the warm blustering breeze, "is entirely possible." Then, to defuse the situation... "So what's the story behind the blue caravan?"

"I live in the caravan between April and October, maybe sometimes a bit longer depending on the weather, but then for the winter months I move over to Mallorca and rent a little finca just outside Palma. Usually time my arrival here for when the spring time buds are coming through on the trees."

"You've got the gypsy in your soul," I grinned.

"You don't know the half of it," she laughed quietly.

"Are you a reader?" I asked directly, remembering that Stephen had mentioned 'cards' and it took no stretch of my imagination to link her with the psychic arts. "It's just that I get the impression that you might be familiar with the Tarot."

"I *know* about the Tarot," she confirmed, "and if push comes to shove I'm a half decent astrologer, but my link with cards has got nothing to do with anything like that. If you really need to know, then I write verses for Christmas and birthday cards; anniversaries, weddings, even sympathy cards. There's not a lot of money in it, but at least it pays the rent. Sorry if that's a disappointment to you."

I was bemused and, yes, slightly disappointed by her answer, then, acting on impulse, I said something to her in *Dideckie* which is a western dialect of the old

Romani language used by gypsies everywhere across Europe. I had the satisfaction of seeing her raise an eyebrow in surprise.

"Ah, well," she conceded, "maybe you know a bit more than I thought you did." She then said something in the old Romani tongue which vaguely meant 'it takes one to know one'.

"I certainly know that you're someone with some psychic energy and maybe more than a passing interest in the paranormal," I said.

"Oh, and how do you know that?"

"The pentagram around your neck is one thing, and your general aura is another. Like you say, it takes one to know one."

She ground out the cigarette stub beneath her foot and looked at me with a very frank expression. "So, you really want to know why I came here tonight?"

"Yes, if you want to tell me. I have to admit that I'm very curious, especially about what you said earlier."

"All right then. I'm married to a man called Danny. We were together for 15 years. Then four years ago he went down to the village store to buy a newspaper and some cigarettes and, basically, he never came back. The police mounted a search, both locally and then nationally, I contacted every friend we'd ever had, but there was never so much as a sighting, never a clue. He left wearing a pair of shorts and a T shirt, with £8 in his pocket, so in theory he couldn't have got very far. For the last four years I've been wondering where he went and what happened to him. As a couple we were very close, both emotionally and on a psychic level as well, and I know beyond any shadow of doubt that if he had died, he would have come through for me tonight. Your Mr Holbrook is very good – I mean, to pick up on my cat Friday was quite remarkable – and if Danny had been around, he'd have honed in on this gathering tonight like a shot from a gun. The fact that he didn't, tells me that somewhere he is still alive, and that gives me my mandate to keep on hoping and to carry on searching."

"He might still come through in the second part of the evening," I suggested, "which, incidentally, you're missing out here on the terrace."

She shook her head sadly, sadly, but with an odd vibration of satisfaction and defiance. "No, if he was going to come through at all, it would have been in the first half."

"Maybe you could have a quiet word with Stephen at the end of the evening. He might be able to point you in the right direction."

For the first time in our conversation she looked unsure. "Do you think he would do that?"

"Yes, I think so. Especially if I ask him nicely. So, hang around for half an hour, then come down to the stage at the end of the demonstration."

Marion Spain-Cavendish spent ten minutes with Steve at the end of the night. He has never told me what passed between them, despite my frequent and sometimes insistent requests. I never saw Marion again and I have never heard from her. I think of her sometimes, in admiration of her faith and her spirit, and can only hope that she has either found her beloved Danny or, if not, has found some consolation and closure. So, Marion, if by some fluke you are reading this, please get in touch and let me know what has happened since that night we exchanged those few words at the Cowes Yacht Club on The Isle of Wight.

If nothing else, the message Marion received from Steve indicates that God does sometimes work in mysterious ways, that it is not always easy for Steve to bridge the gap between the two worlds and there are no scripts or pre-ordained patterns associated with messages from that other realm of existence.

Finally, a request here to Danny Cavendish... If you're reading this and you haven't already done it, you know what you've got to do.

Not everyone in the audience that night enjoyed the demonstration. There was a reporter who had barged her way in at the last minute, claiming to be with the local newspaper. She wrote a scathing review, making the usual claims of 'plants in the audience' and deploring the way in which Stephen was obviously conning people out of their hard earned cash. I was absolutely furious and, although Steve wanted to let it go, I felt I had to do something to rebut this scurrilous piece of gutter journalism. I was even more determined when, after some investigation, I learned that (a) she was not a staffer on the IOW County Press, but a free-lance who submitted various articles and show reviews, (b) that she had a reputation for being ill-informed and destructively cavalier in her opinions and (c) that she was a leading light in the local Catholic Mother's Union.

I lodged a formal complaint with the newspaper on the basis that, while we welcomed bona-fide journalists at Stephen's demonstrations, biased religious opinions constituted not only a conflict of loyalties between the reporter and her editor, but also a breach of trust and objectivity. On the basis that we had just paid the aforementioned newspaper more than £1000 in advertising fees, I demanded that they print a disclaimer to the effect that the views of a free-lance reporter did not necessarily reflect the views of the newspaper and, furthermore, that they should publish my own submitted article of rebuttal. This they did very quickly and from that point on we developed a very cordial relationship with the IOW County Press which continued for many years thereafter.

Chapter Twenty One
The Press

Dealing with the media and, in particular, regional newspapers can sometimes be a profoundly frustrating and irritating business. A few years ago, when I was still acting as Stephen's tour manager and promoter, I sat reading a copy of The Stratford Herald becoming more and more annoyed with the turn of every page. While Steve's advert was there (4x3 reverse block with star border) quite prominently in the entertainments section of the paper, nowhere was there any editorial coverage of Stephen's impending visit to The Falcon Hotel. From past experience I've learned that ten centimetres of editorial coverage is worth fifty centimetres of advertising and therefore, as well as being annoyed, I was also disappointed.

Just because a newspaper accepts a 'paid for' advertisement, there is no guarantee that it will run an editorial story – that is, it won't unless you're prepared to pay for half a page which inevitably costs many hundreds of pounds and in which case the paper simply 'writes off' the editorial coverage as part of the paid for advert.

From a small advertiser's point of view, working on a very limited budget, it seems most unfair that you can spend £800 on your half page and get a few lines of editorial, but spend the same £800 on four smaller ads each costing a couple of hundred quid and spread over a month, and you don't!

In the case of The Stratford Herald we'd spent a small fortune over a two year period advertising Stephen's demonstrations at the fabulous old Falcon Hotel – we'd been diligent in providing press releases with up to date information and as always we'd been generous in offering complimentary tickets, either to be used by the newspaper staff or as prizes for any competition the paper might want to run. And still not one bloody word!

I threw the paper down in disgust and pondered on the professionalism of provincial newspaper editors. This august body of people is responsible for providing you, the reader who has bought their newspaper, with THE NEWS! While there can be no doubt that two points off the interest rate is news, as might be the Prime Minister's decision to resign, or Israeli tanks blowing up a Palestinian village, these items are mainly dealt with by the national press, and the provincial editor's task is to provide you with the local news – the plans, say, for a new by-pass, or the Council's decision to increase local taxes, or possibly the conviction in court of a high profile resident who's been caught with their fingers in the till. If a Hollywood film company decided to use your town in which to film its next epic blockbuster, this would be news, or if the rock band from round the corner had a hit record or if the local 4th division football team beat Manchester United, if someone found a treasure trove of Roman coins or Nazi gold in Farmer Giles' forgotten acres, then, yes, these items would all be highly newsworthy.

But it doesn't quite work like that, does it? I mean, when was the last time *your* local football team beat Manchester United seven nil?

Time after time I've toiled through the pages of local journals to be assailed by stories of a gold watch being presented to Fred Smith for thirty years loyal service down at the gas works – I've celebrated the fact that Bernard Bloggs has been successful in breeding a champion ferret and thrilled at the news that Mary Brown (47 from 32 Acacia Avenue) has been reunited with the purse she thought she'd lost in Tesco's supermarket, containing £19 and last week's (losing) lottery tickets... Oh how I've frowned with sympathy to learn how a whole family was *totally devastated* when the Council refused them permission to paint their front door sky blue pink and how often have I felt a sense of disbelief to learn that some idiot has been fined fifty quid (fifty whole pounds!) for dangerous driving, especially when he's been doing it without tax or insurance and has asked for ninety three other offences to be taken into consideration.

The question is, IS THIS NEWS? – And I suppose the answer must be yes it is, if there's nothing else happening. But hey, hang on a minute! There *is* something else happening. Someone is coming to town who can hear the voices of dead people and who can communicate messages from beyond the grave and, my God, if he can do that, hasn't that got to be front page news? And even if he can't do it (although he's got a proven track record that suggests that he can), hasn't the fact that he *claims* that he can got be more newsworthy than ferrets, gold watches and lost purses?

Of course it has!

But there is a hidden agenda here maintained and promoted by the establishment that seeks to avoid rocking any kind of boat, that seeks not to offend what it perceives as being its orthodox readership, that stands upon the rock of Christian fundamentalism and lumps clairvoyance and clairvoyants into the same basket as fakirs, fortune tellers and hypnotists. This does not stop them from taking your money to run the adverts, but be damned if they are going to run any kind of story which might (a) upset the local vicar, (b) challenge the orthodox church, (c) offend the sensibilities of a few bigoted but quietly influential individuals in any given town who don't hold with anything to do with spiritualism and (d) go against the editor's personal prejudices. If, for example, your local editor is a staunch catholic or Calvinist, then bugger the principles of newsworthiness, equality and free speech, there's *no way* that a story about clairvoyance or spiritualism is going to get past that editor's desk and your press release is going to end up in his bin faster than it takes to open the envelope which contains it.

We came across this attitude very forcibly with a newspaper called The Glaswegian. On three separate occasions we'd spent what for us was some very serious money advertising Stephen's visits to Glasgow. On each occasion we'd sent off press releases along with photographs and complimentary copies of his book – all to no avail. Never a single line of editorial. In the end, my wife Joanna decided to take the bull by the horns and took it upon herself to telephone the editor in question to find out why The Glaswegian seemed so reticent to run a story on Stephen. The telephone conversation was not a success. It went like this:

"Good afternoon, is that Mr ------"

"Yep!"

"Oh hello, my name is Joanna and I'm with JCP and I'm just calling to ask if there might be any chance at all of a few lines of editorial to back up our advertising campaign for Stephen Holbrook's evening of clairvoyance at The Swallow Hotel?"

"No."

"Oh... Er, that seems to be a little bit final... I mean, can you give me any reason for this?"

"No."

"Er, can I just point out, sir, that we have actually spent an awful lot of money on advertising and if this next evening doesn't work, then we…"

"The answer's still no."

"You do realise –" there's a note of steel making its presence felt in Jo's voice in response to the editor's peremptory and somewhat belligerent tone, "– you do realise that this might mean we have to put our advertising budget with another newspaper that *will* give us a few lines of editorial?"

"That's up to you. Put your money wherever you like!" said the editor, then he terminated the call by hanging up on Jo, leaving my poor wife seething at this gentleman's lack of manners and undisguised aggression.

I'd intended writing to the press complaints commission and kicking up all hell, but I'd just come out of hospital and was supposed to be avoiding stress. Also, we were incredibly busy at that time arranging Stephen's 2001 tour, so I let it go for the time being. But this editor's attitude rankled to the extent that when we went back to Glasgow a few months later I did switch the bulk of our advertising budget over to another newspaper and when The Glaswegian's advertising sales manager phoned me asking to know why, I wasn't backwards in coming forwards in letting her know the reason. My critics might call me petty but as far as I was concerned there was a matter of principle at stake and the editor in question might do well to remember the old adage about the pen being mightier than the sword. After digging around I discovered that the editor was a leading light in the local Presbyterian Church and I suppose that explains it all.

To be fair, there are some newspapers that do carry our press releases and report (frequently with much praise and enthusiasm) on Stephen's activities. Ladies and gentlemen of the press, you know who you are, and we thank you very sincerely for your open mindedness, your professionalism and your integrity.

However... even the most dedicated and fair minded reporter can be forgiven for having a sense of humour, even if it borders on mischief. Stephen remembers a demonstration in Gainsborough when he forged a particularly strong link with a lady member of the audience.

It was March 17th 2011 and Doreen Slater had been feeling both excited and optimistic about going to watch Steve Holbrook's demonstration of mediumship at the Trinity Arts Centre in Gainsborough. This would have been her third visit in 18 months and she always attended on her own, and always got the front seats as she always booked them as soon as she saw them being advertised!

Doreen had lost her husband two and a half years earlier, on September 20th 2008. They had been celebrating their wedding anniversary and, although they would seldom venture out for meals, Frank had treated Doreen to a surprise dinner at a wonderful little pub on the outskirts of Gainsborough. Sadly, they hadn't even got through the starter when disaster struck.

Frank started to cough and went extremely red in the face. It wasn't long before Doreen was out of her chair frantically patting Frank's back in the vain hope of dislodging whatever it was that was causing the obstruction. None of the other diners seemed concerned, but people are often reluctant to get involved, either through embarrassment or that typical

British adherence to the value of privacy. It was only as she was starting to panic, that the waiter came over and realised that this was more than just Frank choking; he was holding his chest and by now had gone visibly grey. Leo, the waiter, was only 23 and probably very inexperienced, but his gut feeling told him that Frank was in serious trouble. He dashed to the bar and called over Brian, his Manager. As Brian approached, a very lifeless Frank laid limply on a nearby two-seater settee, while a young couple were trying to give their support to both a very poorly Frank and a distraught Doreen. Brian took one look and immediately called 999 requesting an ambulance. The ambulance arrived seven and a half minutes later and Frank was whisked off to the hospital.

Whatever good intentions Frank had had that day of treating Doreen on their 52nd wedding anniversary, it had had disastrous consequences. Frank never made it to the hospital: he was pronounced dead just over four minutes into the journey.

Fast forward two and a half years, Doreen was sat in her seat at 7.12pm. She always thought it silly that they had to stand around in the bar area, waiting to be told when the doors opened to the theatre, then it was a mad dash for seats, rather than letting people in earlier with a steady flow. She had been in the queue since 6.40pm, eagerly waiting! Steve was on form tonight, it had been an emotional evening but also highly entertaining, especially when a gentleman received a message from his ex-wife and seemed extremely reluctant to admit to anything, since he was there with his latest in a long line of new partners! Whilst sitting there listening, Doreen felt a slight charge of energy, she felt different, becoming aware of waves of peace and calm which seemed to settle around her like a protective veil.

It was at this point that the lady sat two seats along the row leaned forward and tapped Doreen on the knee, saying "I think he means you love!" Doreen looked up and suddenly became aware of Steve gazing steadily at her from the stage.

"Oh goodness! Sorry, so sorry, I was in a world of my own," Doreen stuttered.

Steve grinned. "Well, I couldn't have been that interesting can I?" he joked. "Anyway, my love, I have a gentleman here who says he is Albert…?"

Doreen gasped. "Oh my! That is my Dad's name!"

Steve: "Yes love, he says he has been with you all day and he has wanted to get through tonight, with it being such a special day."

Doreen looked a little confused.

Steve: "Is it your birthday, m'love? He's just shown me a birthday card."

Instantly, Doreen knew. How could she have forgotten? It was the 17th March, which had been *her father's birthday!* She was exhilarated and also quite embarrassed that she had only just realised. In her defence, her Dad had passed away when she was only eight years old and a whole host of other, seemingly more significant anniversaries, had crept into her life since then.

Steven carried on… "He says that he has literally only popped in quickly, because he wants to let Frank speak."

Instantly, Doreen's eyes glazed over and she began to sob, "Yes, yes, that is my husband."

Having established the link, Steve's voice became stronger and more confident. "He has just said

September 19th, is this date significant to you? Oh, yes it must be, because he's laughing as he's saying it."

Doreen confirmed the date. "Yes, he would be laughing, because for the first five years of our marriage, he got our anniversary date wrong. He always thought it was the 19th, then it finally sunk in that it was actually the 20th!"

Steve: "Are there two different meanings to the 20th though? He's telling me *two*! So are there two different anniversaries connected with the 20th?"

Doreen "Yes Steve, he also died on our anniversary, the 20th September!"

From that point on, Steve delivered many more pieces of information to Doreen, including the name of Oscar (their first cat they had shortly after marrying) and the scar Frank had behind his left ear where he had fallen off a ladder whilst clearing the guttering! But it was the last remark that caught Doreen totally off guard.

Steven exclaimed with a huge smile. "He is mentioning sweet corn and corn on the cob! I know that sounds unusual, but that's what he's said!"

Doreen felt a surge of relief and disbelief. "Oh my God! Yes, corn on the cob makes perfect sense and...." and then she just couldn't say any more.

Steve's voice softened. "Oh, it's alright my love, don't you trouble yourself. It's often the most seemingly trivial thing that comes through in the message that causes the most emotion. Frank loves you and is with your Dad, and they both miss you so much. I will say goodnight love, and thank you."

It was at the end of the evening that Steve approached the edge of the stage and called over to Doreen. He was very surprised to see how small she was; obviously Steve was a lot higher up, being on stage, but clearly her head didn't even reach the top of the stage, so he went down to her. Doreen was so very grateful and almost apologetic about being so upset, but Steve re-assured her it was only natural, but what she said next stopped Steve in his tracks! Doreen said "The sweetcorn you mentioned and the corn on the cob, that is what he was choking on when he died."

Straight away, Steve knew the significance and why it had caused so much emotion. Doreen continued "He died on our anniversary, he had corn on the cob for his starter; he hadn't even finished it, when he started to choke and triggered the heart attack straight after." Doreen had tears streaming down her face. Steve provided as much comfort as he could, telling Doreen that he always likes to have things confirmed because, as he says, it's very much a one-way communication; he repeats what he hears, but doesn't always understand the meaning behind it.

A fortnight later, Steve was on the phone arranging adverts for an evening in Doncaster, speaking with Lily, a lady who Steve was very friendly with and who had worked at the newspaper for many years. When she said, quite matter-of-factly, "That article in the Gainsborough edition wasn't very fair, but I suppose you get used to it!" Stephen had no idea what she was referring to.

"Sorry" Steve said, "what article?"

She replied with "That one about the corn."

Steve hadn't a clue what she was talking about, and she continued "I think it was last week, or the week before. Hang on while I look through the office copies." At that, Lily left her seat and started to flick through the back copies. "Here it is!" she exclaimed!

The headline read 'CORNY CLAIRVOYANT AT THE ARTS CENTRE'.

Steve was in shock, "Can you please send me a copy Lily, I haven't seen it." Naturally, she could, and she put a copy of the offending edition in that night's post. These days of course, she could easily have zapped over a pdf or jpeg of the page, but back in the day, things were very different!

Steve eagerly awaited the back copy, but it was two days later when he received it. Amid the review that did make many positive points, one thing really stood out, and really annoyed him. The review read – *'I was very impressed with the detail of the communication to the recipients of the messages, but my interest started to wane when Mr Holbrook started to communicate with a corn on the cob!'*

This, he understood, was probably the reporter's way of putting her own humour into the article, but the very fact that she had picked up on something she thought was incredibly insignificant, was actually the most important part of the message, providing Doreen with the proof that it *was* Frank delivering that message, as nobody else would have ever have thought to mention corn on the cob.

At the time Stephen was angry and dismayed in equal measure, but with the passage of time I think perhaps he has come to see the funny side of the story. For my part, if I was a junior reporter on a small provincial newspaper and I wanted to impress my editor, then I cannot honestly say I would not have done the same thing, however unprofessional it might have been. Either the reporter had fallen asleep and had missed the point of the message, or she had deliberately slanted her article to score a cheap point and get a quick laugh with the 'corny clairvoyant' headline.

However it is strange that no matter how good the evenings have been, with the many hundreds of reviews Steve has read about himself, the demonstrations which he has really enjoyed the most are the ones usually 'played down', or even ripped apart by the press. Conversely, when he has had a night where he hasn't felt on top form, he gets rave reviews! So, what's that all about?

Stephen is quite right when he says that it is the 'little things' which are the proof of the evidence he is providing. Doreen's corn on the cob is a fine example, but I can think of many others. A lady in Tamworth was told that her new fridge had a broken seal. She pointed out that it was a brand new fridge, only delivered and installed that same afternoon and quite openly told Steve that she didn't believe him. Steve asked her to check the top seal of the fridge door as soon as she got home and to contact him if she found anything wrong. An hour later as we were driving up the A1, Steve's phone jangled and it was the lady telling Steve that she had just got home, had checked the door of the fridge and indeed the top seal *was* broken!

On the subject of fridges Stephen told a lady in Leicester that "her pope kept falling off the fridge door" which was quite bizarre until it was established that a fridge magnet with the image of His Holiness The Pope, did, in fact, refuse to stick to the fridge door and, no matter where the lady put it, it inevitably came unstuck and fell to the kitchen floor within a few seconds!

In Lowestoft he told a lady that her husband "had two left feet". He assumed that he was referring to the gentleman's clumsiness and even made a joke about finding two left shoes to fit, but on interviewing the recipient of the message after the demonstration I learned that the gentleman quite literally did have two left feet as the result of a birth defect and that he had to have an orthopaedic shoemaker make him special shoes – with two left feet!

At The Cochrane Theatre in London he told a very elderly gentleman who had recently lost his wife, that she was alive and well on the other side and that the old tattoo had been removed. This meant nothing to Stephen and nor did it really mean anything to the rest of the audience, but it certainly meant everything to Jacob Steiner. His own tattoo, a vicious memory of the Dachau concentration camp still remained, albeit faded, on the inside of his left arm. His wife Helena's tattoo, also an unwelcome gift from Dachau – had been 'removed'!

In Bury St Edmunds Stephen was winding up a message he'd been giving to an attractive lady on the second row from the front. Her name was Christina and she'd recently lost her newly married husband in a car accident. Steve mentioned her husband by name and made links with both of her parents who had passed over, and he also mentioned someone called Fritz who was being looked after by her late husband. The lady confessed that Fritz was the name of a pet dog, which had been in the car with Tony when he'd had his accident.

That was the only information she gave to Stephen, but after a few seconds of pondering while he paced up and down the stage, he turned to look at her and asked her if Fritz had been a Dachshund. She confirmed that this was so and then Stephen came out with the clincher, telling her that long before the accident Fritz had been living a compromised life as a result of an earlier accident which had required the amputation of his rear left leg. The lady confirmed these facts, so in effect Stephen had identified the breed of the dog, the fact that one of his legs was missing and indeed that it had been the rear left leg.

I don't think you can get more specific than that and these few examples of the 'little' snippets of detail that Stephen brings through as evidence, are just five of the most memorable incidents which spring to mind. There are dozens and dozens more, each in their own way, providing a unique element of proof.

Chapter Twenty Two
Interviews

Much earlier in this book, reference was made to an interview conducted by a lady called Sue Farrow of The Psychic News magazine, which was followed up by a significantly more detailed piece, published in August of 2019. I thought it might be illuminating to have a look at Stephen's responses to PN's questions – and then to ask a few of my own! I have to tell you that Steve absolutely hates all this, but I've told him he's got to co-operate or I'll tell the story about the haunted toilet, the rubber duck and the melted cheese. Thus, I can assure you, Mr Holbrook is co-operating! Therefore we might as well start with the Psychic News interview.

PN: *What was your first psychic experience?*
Stephen: My Granddad came to visit me in the early hours of the morning saying "go and tell your mother – I've gone!" I found out the next day that he had visited me within five minutes of his transition to the spirit world.

PN: *Where are you living at the moment?*
Stephen: I live in Castleford in West Yorkshire, in a minimalist three story town house. It's a nice modern estate with excellent links to the motorway.

PN: *Who is in the rest of your family?*
Stephen: My partner, Rob, and my three children, Robbie, Bradley and Ellie.

PN: *Do any of your children show any signs of being psychic?*

Stephen: As a child, Robbie, who is now 25, showed many signs of becoming a budding medium. I always remember that when we were on holiday in Norfolk and he was running his toy car across the carpet of our caravan, he suddenly stopped what he was doing and looked up at me. "Dad," he asked, "what would happen if a helicopter crashed into the sea with seven people on board?" Bradley, my other little boy, had got his hand stuck in the safety gate and I was distracted, so didn't give Robbie the attention he should have had. Well, later that day we decided to drive to Cromer – this, I might add, was about five hours later. A news bulletin came on the local radio station saying that a helicopter had just gone down off the Norfolk coast, with seven people on board. So, Robbie had had a clear vision of this incident half a day before it had actually happened.

PN: *What psychic gifts do you possess and where did you develop your mediumship?*

Stephen: I'm a clairaudient and I was trained and nurtured by the Spiritualist Church.

PN: *Before becoming a full time medium you ran a hairdressing salon for eighteen years. Were you worried about making ends meet after leaving your day time job?*

Stephen: Yes, I was! I ran a very busy hairdressing salon in Leeds city centre. Without wanting to sound conceited we were so busy that if clients didn't re-book before leaving they probably would never get another appointment. As it was, my first client was usually at 7.30 in the morning, the last being around 6 in the evening, which just about gave me time to jump in my car and get to wherever I was demonstrating that night.

Looking back on those times now I reckon that a lot of clients came not so much for their hair but because they were hoping for a snippet of information from the 'other side'. I always remember giving a message to Nell McAndrew who came in for an appointment when she was still only 14. She was very quiet and shy and, bless her, she was dressed in her school uniform. Anyway, spirit inspired me to tell her that she was going to be a very famous model and travel all over the world.

She was totally embarrassed by this and never came back, until one day, five or six years later, she came to see me in the salon and handed over a portfolio of all her best known pictures. By that time she wasn't only on the books of Elite Model Management in London, but she'd also been used as the Lara Croft model for the Tomb Raider video game. Amazing to think that this was the shy 14 year old I'd met a few years earlier, and since she became so famous she's frequently spoken of the message I gave her in many of her magazine interviews.

PN: *You're currently touring the UK. How many venues are you visiting and how do you travel? Car, train or plane?*

Stephen: Some months I do 26 nights out of 30. I travel by car, but thankfully I don't have to do any of the driving. I leave that to Rob, my partner and manager, who gets me wherever I'm going, safe and sound. It gives me time to catch up on my bookwork, but a lot of the time I just catch up on my sleep. We do between 40 and

50 thousand miles a year and it can be very exhausting. We end up living out of suitcases and staying in a whole host of different hotels, but after doing it for years and years, eventually you get used to it. Some people think it's a glamorous lifestyle but, believe me, it isn't!

PN: *You're demonstrating not just in hotels and spiritualist churches, but also in libraries, golf clubs, bowls clubs, town halls and masonic halls, and even a conservative club. Do you believe it's important that you try and reach people who would never enter a spiritualist church or attend a body mind and spirit centre?*

Stephen: Yes, I do think it is extremely important to connect with new people and spread the gospel. In the past I've been promoted by several national newspaper groups and have even done a few clairvoyant cruises in the Mediterranean and the Caribbean, but it is so easy to lose contact with your roots and these days I feel the need to get back to basics. When you're working in front of a crowd of 500 people you lose the personal touch, if you like, the intimacy, and quite honestly the clairvoyance can suffer. So, I have consciously chosen to work to smaller audiences, although, of course, it does mean working a lot more nights of the year.

PN: *Why have you always shunned working on TV?*

Stephen: I haven't gone down the TV route, despite the BBC coming to Hull one night to watch a demonstration arranged by Henrik Briksen,

274

Jane's former husband. If it had gone ahead, it would have been an interesting format and I did think about it for a while, but then very shortly after the Hull demonstration I was mulling it over and while I was waiting to go on stage there was some piped music playing "Please Don't Go" by KC and The Sunshine Band, and as soon as the demonstration was over I phoned Jane and told her I was very sorry but I didn't want to do the TV thing, and would she try and explain why to Henrik. I think that my decision was influenced by knowing Jane, because I realised what power TV has and how it can change your life beyond all recognition. I like my privacy and I demand it for my family, and TV exposure would have changed all that.

PN: *Can you tell us something about the work you do for charity?*

Stephen: I'm passionate about combining my evenings of clairvoyance with fundraising opportunities and so far I've managed to raise £30,000 for my local hospice and another £27,000 for PACT, which is a Sheffield based charity that raises money for kids under 13 who are suffering from terminal cancer and counselling for bereaved parents. This year alone we have committed ourselves to doing more than 20 demonstrations for various local good causes, including dementia and breast cancer...

There were a lot more questions asked in this in-depth interview which I have deliberately edited out because elsewhere in this book Stephen has already answered them in one form or another. I asked him a lot more *personal* questions, verging on the mundane, and in so doing hoped to show something of Stephen The Man rather than Stephen The Clairvoyant. For example, I wanted to know what was the best film he'd seen recently...?

Best Film? I would say that the best film I ever watched was The Call, starring Halle Berry, a fantastic film that kept me on the edge of my seat all the way through. However, just recently, on the very RARE occurrence I actually have time to go to the cinema, I saw a film called The Good Liar with Helen Mirren and Ian McKellen. Two British greats together, which made for a fascinating film, with so many twists. One of those films that you're left remembering days afterwards. This leads me to my favourite actress – Helen Mirren. Although, for the younger generation amongst you, I also admire the talents of Suranne Jones and Sarah Lancashire. What inspires me about these two in particular is their versatility. As for my favourite actor, I have to go with both Anthony Hopkins and Harrison Ford – can't decide!

Favourite Food? If I eat out, I have to say it is 75% Indian food and the simple reason for this is that by the time we finish demonstrations in the evening, finding anywhere else open is hard work. Especially after 10.30pm. I do enjoy Indian food, I love the variety of flavours and there is not much on the menu I haven't tried! But I think I have to say my real favourite, if I had the choice, would be Italian food. I absolutely adore pizza and also Lasagne. As long as it's with some form of salad, perhaps my way of making it appear healthy! But to be honest, anyone who knows me knows that I am a real food lover, it's a real passion in my life. My favourite starter would be deep-fried Camembert with cranberry jelly. There aren't many things I don't eat! And, naturally, all washed down with a dry white wine. To be honest I am no connoisseur of wine, just dry white, not sweet or even medium, simply the drier the better.

The best demonstration of Mediumship I have ever seen?
This was one by the formidable Gordon Higginson. He was
a true master of his craft - with his irrefutable evidence and
his inner showman, he was so inspiring to watch. The way
he used to present his fantastic survival evidence, tinged
with humour, was something that I will always remember.
Also, my wonderful, wonderful friend, Una Pearce. Una had
an amazing natural ability to channel Spirit and was always
happy to sit in the background. I used to be fascinated as
she would turn full grown men to emotional wrecks within
minutes of channelling their loved ones. However, more
recently, I visited Woolston Spiritualist Church (Heart Sent
Messages), run by Colin and Annette Blann. Annette has,
over the last 18 months, provided me with outstanding
evidence that my Mum is truly around me. She gave such
wonderful details that nobody would ever know, apart from
me – and of course, Spirit. It has happened more than
once, and after we got to Southampton on one occasion,
she presented me with a piece of paper, telling me that 3
days previously my Mum was enjoying watching me write
this book about the stories that have unfolded, and many
other things. At the time, NOBODY knew I was writing this
book, after a 12 year gap since my last book 'Survival'. So
my heartfelt thanks to Annette – it is so nice to actually
receive a message myself, especially when the evidence is
so amazing.

Favourite female vocalist? Obviously the answer is Jane
McDonald. I have been Jane's most ardent fan ever since I
first heard her perform, back in the days before she was
famous. I also have great respect for Barbra Streisand. I
like this woman's voice. I was once listening to Radio 2 and
it was an interview with Brian Epstein and he summed it up
perfectly when he said "Barbra's voice is like listening to an
orchestra, with all the different instruments coming
together in harmony". I love 'Papa, Can You Hear Me?'

from Yentl, and 'Don't Rain On My Parade' – both amazing, emotionally charged songs.

Having said that, I have been watching my best friend Jane for over 30 years now and over the course of time I have seen her perform night after night in clubs, theatres, open air venues, cruises and even arenas, and I have yet to meet anyone who can go out there again and again, and deliver such outstanding vocals. I have always said, from day one, that she has a special quality, something so utterly distinctive, and that she would, one day, be recognised for her voice. Now, finally, she has. Yes, a wonderful TV personality, but to me, more than anything, it is her amazing voice. I am so proud of what she has achieved. James, I know you're not a great Streisand fan, but maybe you've got a point when you say that Streisand sings from her head while Jane sings from her heart.

What song or piece of music would you like played at your own funeral? The song I would like playing at my funeral is 'Compass' by Sam Bailey. I honestly don't know who wrote the lyrics – (think it's Dianne Warren – Rob!)

The happiest moment of your life? I can't say which was THE happiest moment of my life, but there are three, all of which are of equal significance – that is when my three children were born. There have been many wonderful things which I could recount, but none of them have any comparison to the feeling of how I felt when 3 new lives came into this world.

Motor vehicles? To be truthful, I'm not that bothered about cars, they aren't my 'thing'. I see a vehicle merely as a way of getting from A to B. We currently have a Vauxhall Insignia, I think it's our 7th one now! It's practical because of the boot capacity and big back seats that fold down. When we are away on our longer seven to nine day tours, it is often packed to the rafters. I am a creature of habit, so when I come to renew my car, I make a phone call to Chris

Hudson at Evans Halshaw Vauxhall in Wakefield, and ask him to get me yet another Insignia with low mileage. And within three weeks, I am sat at his desk signing for my newest car. He knows exactly what I like, a really great no-fuss guy and has never let me down. Rob, however, got quite a shock when we went to pick up a new car a couple of years ago, as when we were exchanging all the paperwork, he noticed the registration number ended in 'OAP'. He said "Surely you can NOT be serious!" I can still see that look on his face as he drove out the forecourt and I can remember me saying "Well, you know I'm dyslexic, how could I know?" However, if I really had to choose my next car (if I wasn't dashing all over the country), I would probably choose a Range Rover. I did have an old BMW X3, which I loved, and I loved the feeling of being higher up, maybe it felt safer somehow. One day, when I finally slow down, I may just treat myself!

Most important message you've ever received? I remember many years ago, at the Town Hall in Leeds, the guest medium was Gordon Higginson and it was hosted by The Greater World Spiritualist Church. He gave me a wonderfully evidential message and said that "One day, you will be up here, doing what I am doing". I was only 16 years old at the time and my friend forced my hand up in the air, and I am so glad she did, because it changed everything. Suffice to say, five years later, The Greater World hosted another demonstration at the Town Hall, which was supposed to have been led by Steven O'Brien, a wonderful, well respected Welsh medium, but unfortunately for some reason, he had to cancel. So, I was asked to step in at the last minute and do the demonstration. So there I was, at Leeds Town Hall, doing exactly what Gordon had told me I would be doing, addressing an audience of over 500 people. Coincidentally, Gordon was a huge friend of Eric Hatton, who also incidentally stated earlier in this book, came through and gave me startling evidence and words of wisdom and guidance, which have been of paramount importance in my mediumistic journey.

What is the most important message you've ever given? That's impossible to say, because you don't always know the significance of the message you've given. But something which happened quite recently is worth passing on. A few days ago we were doing a demonstration at The Capricorn Restaurant in Goole and I met up with a lady who'd had a message from me three years ago. This lady had recently lost her sister Christine to breast cancer and Christine had come through, saying, among other things, "you need to push them for a check". She understood the message and got the drift of what Christine was trying to say. She waited two days and called the doctor to arrange an appointment and, even though she had no tell-tale signs, she couldn't ignore what her sister had said, despite the fact that she absolutely hated doctor's surgeries. She had the examination and had a referral two weeks later, only to find she had stage three breast cancer. She then went on to have a mastectomy and, although the cancer had already gone on to the lymph nodes, now, in February 2020, thanks to her sister's intervention, she is 100% clear of cancer.

Politics and Brexit? With regard to Brexit, these are uncertain times. It is obviously going to have its pro's and con's for everyone, but only time will give us a true indication of whether the move was a good one. I think there was a total lack of understanding with many of the general public as to what Brexit actually meant. And to be truthful, its guidelines and headlines never made for simple understanding. Politics has never been a strong point for me, so I just try and take a bird's eye view of everything, but like everyone else, I'll have to sit back and watch things unfold over the next few months and years to really see the bigger picture. It just goes to show how consumed everybody was with the word Brexit; it seems like ALL we heard about! One day, after a short visit to Rob's Mum, she was waving us goodbye on the doorstep, as she always does, and suddenly she frantically waved at her arms at us to stop and shouted "Ooh hang on, I've got something for you, it's some of those Brexit biscuits I got from the Co-Op". Dot often provided us with snacks for our journey. As Rob went back into the house with a bemused expression on his face, wondering what on earth 'Brexit Biscuits' were, he was handed two packs of Belvita biscuits!!! An easy mistake to make I'm sure, when it's been engrained into you every minute of every day!

What is your take on the coronavirus pandemic? To be quite honest it took me by surprise. Some might say I should have seen it coming, you know, being clairvoyant and all that, but the fact of the matter is that I simply didn't!* The cost of it all, both in terms of the number of lives that have been lost and, of course, the economic effects, have been horrendous, but I think that maybe there might be a bit of truth in the old saying that 'every dark cloud has a silver lining' because when this is all over, I think our world will be just a little bit different. Maybe a very big bit different! For one thing, I think that people might find themselves being a lot nicer to each other, that maybe the NHS will stop being a political football, that people and governments might be a bit more caring towards elderly folk who need lots more support in the community than they've traditionally had. Maybe our country will become a lot greener and perhaps people will be more mindful about what they eat and where they dump their rubbish. So, like I say, 'every dark cloud' and all that. One thing is for sure, and that is we won't go back to being exactly the same as we were before and I think that might be a very good thing!

On a very personal level, I had to cancel 90% of my demonstrations in 2020 and, although that has hurt me financially, my greater concern has been in letting other people down... People who've needed some contact with departed loved ones. And there is another aspect to all of this. I was meditating (*dozing – Rob*) in the garden, aware of all the beautiful perfume and scents from the flowers, when I became aware of a spiritual energy around me. It wasn't hostile, but it was certainly a bit critical. It seemed to say "you think you've got problems down there? Well, spare a thought for us up here! You might be in lockdown, but you've got telephones and computers; you've got skype and iPads and iPods, etc., etc. All we've got is you and the few who are like you, and right now all our lines of communication are on hold until you get back to work and open up the telephone exchanges between the earth plane and spirit world. We've got thousands and thousands of people wanting to make contact with their families, but it's as though all the telephone exchanges have suddenly become unplugged. So, you've got your lockdown and we've got ours!"**

Any plans to move permanently abroad? You asked me whether, in the future, I could see myself taking up permanent residence overseas and the answer is no, definitely not! Travelling abroad has taught me one thing, I love Great Britain, and although it is nice to have some time somewhere hot and sunny and spend some time relaxing, it's just as lovely to come home!

Where do you see yourself 15 years from now? Where do I see myself in 15 years' time? Well, providing I am actually still breathing (and this may seem a real cop-out and, to some people, a boring answer, but as I have got older, I have realised to just go with the tide and wherever it takes me), it has become clear to me that we only ever have a rough guide line of where our lives are headed. Therefore, I live in the 'here and now'. What has happened has happened, and I have learned many valuable lessons in life and I am in no doubt that I am about to learn many more and, quite frankly, looking forward to doing so. However, there is one thing that I hope for... and that is, even if, at any given point, I am physically unable to walk out on to the stage, someone will kindly wheel me on and let's hope mentally I am still able to maintain a link with Spirit. Because, throughout my journey of life so far, it is the sheer love of my work that has been a constant, and has always somehow managed to keep me going.

And that will do very nicely, thank you very much, and if you *really* want to know about that haunted toilet, rubber ducks and melted cheese, I'm always open to a bribe! Incidentally, *I did see it coming, but not in the way that it came, and **I saw Stephen after three months in lockdown, three months in which he hadn't done any demonstrations and had spent his time decorating the house and attending the garden. He looked fit and well and 15 years younger than he'd looked when I'd seen him at the beginning of the year. This illustrated the pressure and tension that six nights a week, 50 weeks a year, imposed upon him. Night after night on the road to one demonstration after another comes at a tremendous cost to both physical health and mental energy, and to my mind this personal aspect of lockdown was a very good example of the 'ill wind' scenario.

Chapter Twenty Three
Evidence III

I finished writing the first draft of this book on the 31st of January 2020 then went out to celebrate this country's long overdue divorce from the EU (not from Europe, please note, but just the flaming EU!) I was feeling quite buoyant, not just because of the Brexit situation, but also because I'd just had the results from a recent cardiogram which told me I was a lot fitter than I had any right to be. As another example of the frequent synchronicity which makes its presence felt in all aspects of Man's interaction with the spirit world, on the morning of February 1st 2020 I received a long email from Rob Green outlining an incident involving heart attacks and cardiac arrests. So, let me introduce you to Paul and Fiona, and I quote from Rob's email more or less *ad verbatim*.

The couple had been together for seven years. It had been a standing joke that they had been engaged for five years and, since then, Paul had never even so much as mentioned the Big Day. I think Fiona just went along with this, knowing Paul's laid back attitude and just expected it to suddenly happen sooner or later. Patience was Fiona's virtue, she had never been the pushy type and never expected too much from anyone.

It was April 2017 and Fiona was preparing for their five day caravan holiday in Devon. As usual everything but the kitchen sink was ready to pile in the car the next day. She had literally just finished the bulk of the packing and was about to start making an evening meal, when the phone rang.

"Hi Fiona, it's Beryl. Can you and Paul meet us at the hospital? Ian has been taken ill. I can't talk right now, just get there as fast as you can, bye, bye."

Fiona's heart pounded so rapidly, she felt it was about to jump out of her chest.

"Paul!" she shouted. "It's your Dad, he's had to go to hospital. That was your Mum on the phone. Don't ask me anymore because I don't know anything, she just said we had to meet her at the hospital straight away."

Paul quickly put on a coat and slipped a pair of trainers on, and they were off.

Beryl and Ian had also been looking forward to their short break at the caravan in Devon; they were going to go down for the week and were to meet Paul and Fiona down there. But, Ian's mate from work, Peter, was having a leaving party at a local club that night, so plans changed and that's where they were heading... Until Ian became breathless and sweaty, with pains to the chest!

Beryl hadn't bothered with an ambulance, as she couldn't bear the thought of being alone with Ian, waiting for the emergency services. She got him into the front seat of their VW Passat, put her foot down and was at A&E within seven minutes. Ian was deteriorating rapidly and trying to control the pain. He seemed to be fighting consciousness and as they drew up to the main entrance Beryl stopped the car, opened her door and at the speed of light had Ian up with his arms around her shoulder. Desperately trying to rush through the main doors, she left the car running and the doors wide open on double-yellow lines.

She got to the Reception and, between pitiful wails, said "You have to help me, something is wrong with my husband, he can't breathe!"

Beryl tried to regain her composure, just as a Security Guard grabbed Ian and took him over to a spare wheelchair next to the ladies toilet. Beryl quickly gave all Ian's details and within minutes he was taken by a nurse to the Acute Assessment Unit. There, she tried to fight back the tears and explain what had happened. At that moment Beryl knew she had to find Fiona and Paul, so knowing Ian was in safe hands, she told the nurse she would be literally two minutes and hurried through to A&E to see if she could see her son and daughter-in-law, as Beryl knew they wouldn't know where to go.

The nurse reassured her not to worry and she would keep an eye on Ian. As she rushed through to the reception area, she was surprised to see how quickly it had filled up… or was it that she was so intent on getting help for Ian, that she hadn't noticed how busy it was? There was no sign of Paul or Fiona, so she walked to the front door, across the tarmac to see if they were on their way. She couldn't see anyone and was just about to turn back, when she heard Paul's voice.

"Mum, Mum, sorry, we went to the wrong car park!"

The three had a brief group hug and Beryl quickly tried to explain what had happened. With that, they went on their way to the Assessment Room. Just as they got through the A&E reception, Beryl saw the same nurse who had been with Ian. She was calling something out but Beryl didn't quite catch it. The nurse, on seeing Beryl, signalled her to come quickly. The nurse explained she had been calling for Beryl and looking for her. It was at that moment she saw the look on the nurses' face and knew there was something seriously wrong.

"What is it, what is it?" she spluttered.

"Mrs Wood, would you like to take a seat over here with your family, the Doctor would like to talk to you."

Those were the last words that would resound in Beryl's head. From that point forward, Beryl felt like she was on freefall, every single part of her mind and body had been consumed and she felt like she was in a vacuum. Her normal senses seemed to have shut down, she seemed unable to function, couldn't see or hear anything. She seemed to lose all recollection of Paul, Fiona, or even Ian. Her husband had suffered a massive heart attack, literally within seconds of Beryl leaving to look for Paul and Fiona. Even though he had been surrounded by all the medical professionals, sadly they were still unable to resuscitate him. Ian had been pronounced dead at 6.15pm Friday 14th April 2017.

The following days for Beryl, Paul and Fiona were devastating. Ian was only 58 years old and still had the rest of his life in front of him. He and Beryl lived a normal, low-key lifestyle, happy for just being in each other's company. Everything about their lifestyle revolved around their tightly knit family unit, including, of course, Fiona and Paul.

Ian had been really looking forward to the holiday break, even though it was only going to be for a few days. He had hoped to get a couple fishing trips in and he had been looking forward to cooking the four of them some lovely meals. These were the simple things that Beryl and Ian loved.

But what was to follow was Beryl and Paul trying to put one foot in front of the other, and try to start to get things sorted. The Death Certificate, letting the family know, arranging the funeral but, most of all, trying to let this horrendous situation sink in.

Life was never to return to normal for Beryl or, for that matter, Paul and Fiona. They had been a wonderful team, they obviously had their squabbles and a few harsh words now and again when they didn't view things in the same light but, as family went, they were incredibly close. Paul seemed to be in a world of his own, not really showing the same emotion as Fiona who would be bursting into tears most days, and it was Paul who comforted her, even though it was *his* Dad who had passed away.

Fiona knew it should be the other way round, but couldn't help herself. She also knew Paul well enough to know that he did his grieving in private and God only knows what turmoil he had been going through. It was nearly two weeks now and they were getting impatient with a number of delays which were holding up Ian's funeral; it wasn't just because of the Easter Holidays that things were going so slowly... Beryl had had a real fight to get the Death Certificate, because there seemed to be some hoohaa as to what was the cause of death. She was sure she had been told it was heart related, so why the hold up? She was just keen to give Ian the best send-off ever.

It was now Sunday 30th April and finally the funeral was sorted for the following Thursday, the 4th of May. Fiona was settled on the settee, whilst Paul had met Harry, his mate of 15 years, for a couple of hours fishing at the local lake. She was just browsing through the Birmingham Mail and as she turned the 4th page, she was drawn to an advert for An Evening of Clairvoyance at the Village Hotel in Solihull, literally three minutes from their house. Knowing that Ian hadn't even been buried, she stared at it and read the words 'prove the spirit survives bodily death'. This reminded her of her previous visits to the local

Spiritualist Church, but Fiona had never attended a public meeting. She then got up to make a coffee, leaving the paper open at that page. A couple of minutes later, Paul walked in, very happy that he had had a good catch and proceeded to tell Fiona about a 3lb Carp and a 1.5lb Perch. In return, Fiona made all the right noises and made them both a drink. She was pleased that Paul had had his mind taken off things, even for just a couple of hours. As she wandered back into the lounge, she said to Paul "Take a look in that paper".

"What bit?" he replied.

"The spiritualist advert" and, to her surprise, he picked up the paper and started to read it. She hadn't expected that.

Paul said "What are you saying? It's tonight!"

"What?" replied Fiona, as she took the paper. She hadn't even read the date and there clearly in front of her was the date, Sunday 30th April. "Oh my God, I hadn't realised it was tonight, I didn't read the date, just the other bits." She couldn't read the look on Paul's face, as he pulled out his mobile and started to dial. It took a while to answer, but Beryl finally picked up.

"Hi Mum, it's me, fancy a night out with me and Fiona?"

After a long pause, Beryl said "Oh well, erm, I hadn't expected you to call asking me that, I've got my hair colour on, that's why it took me so long to answer."

"Mum, it's 2.30 in the afternoon, it doesn't start until 7.30."

"What doesn't?" replied Beryl.

"A medium is on at the Village Hotel in Solihull."

"What, tonight?"

"Yes" said Paul, "I have a weird feeling."

"What sort of feeling?"

"Oh, I can't explain."

At this, Fiona piped up, "Oh Paul, it may be too soon, you haven't had the funeral yet."

Paul ignored this and said to Beryl, "Well, me and Fiona are going, so let me know later if you want to come along, it says just pay on the door. We will need to leave here at 7pm to get there for 7.15pm. Have a think about it and let me know later."

"Okay love, let me see how this hair colour turns out and I'll call you back."

Fiona looked bemused, "God Paul, I had no idea you would want to go, let alone ring your Mum to come along too. Are you sure about this?"

He replied "Well, it can't do any harm. It's funny, when I was fishing today, I got a feeling I couldn't explain, like Dad was trying to tell me something. Then I come home and the first thing you do is show me that advert, and of all the nights it could be on, it's tonight. And we never even usually get that paper!"

Fiona was still apprehensive, she had mixed feelings; she didn't want to open a can of worms, or indeed make things any more painful than they already were.

Fast forward to 7pm and Paul and Fiona were locking up the house and ready to set off on the three minute journey by car to the hotel. They were meeting Beryl in the car park, only when they arrived the car park was full and they had trouble getting a space. It was at that point that Fiona's mobile started ringing.

"Where are you?" asked Beryl.

"We're in the car park" replied Fiona.

"I'm coming in the main entrance to the car park, but there's a queue, it starts in 15 minutes!"

Again, Fiona was starting to think this wasn't such a good idea. They eventually parked up and told Beryl that they would meet her in the main reception. After waiting for what seemed like forever for Beryl, eventually she turned up. She'd had to park up on the roadside and looked a little exasperated. Paul immediately noticed that his Mum had lightened her hair, but didn't waste time talking about it, as they were already five minutes late by now. They quickly hurried across to the function room and, to their surprise, there were still one or two people going in. The evening on the door for Rob had been stop/start all night down to people having trouble parking. The evening was clearly underway, but they were still allowed in. Rob explained that it was very busy in the hall, but there were a few seats left.

Paul paid for the tickets and, a little tentatively, they entered the room. Everyone was listening to the medium who was in full flow, giving a message to a lady near the front. There was a main walkway between the front of the room and the back, and Paul could see three seats together on the far side. So, they made their way across, looking more than a bit self-conscious and embarrassed.

"Stop!" Steve called out to them. "No sorry, *don't* stop, keep walking m'loves and take your seats, I need to talk to you straight away!"

But they *did* stop and looked at Steve in total shock. There they were, trying to sneak in quietly and he'd just drawn all the attention to them!

Steve said thank you to the recipient of the first message of the night and he knew this was an amazingly charged evening, and he was full of energy.

"I would like to talk to the three people who just came in." He waved in the direction of the trio. "The lady there," he said, pointing directly at Beryl, "I have a gentlemen here that has only just passed away, he's desperate to get your attention."

Beryl looked gob-smacked, her face paled.

"Can I hear your voice please, love?"

"Yee-e-s?"

"He's talking about Paul."

"That's me!" shouted Paul.

"He is mentioning the caravan."

"Oh God" said Paul.

"No, it's Steve Holbrook mate, not God!" The audience laughed.

"Who is Beryl?"

"Me!" said Beryl, "I'm his wife." And with that she burst into tears.

"Okay love, just relax and try to concentrate on my voice, because if you let yourself got too upset, you won't hear me."

"All right, yes," said Beryl.

"He likes your hair lighter, love."

"Aagh! I only did it today!"

"He's telling me about fishing..."

"Yes, I've been fishing today," said Paul.

Beryl butted in "And he was going to go fishing with his Dad at the caravan."

"He's just mentioned three pounds, have you lost some weight, Paul?"

"No, but I caught a three pound carp today, Jesus!"

"He is mentioning a number four, is it a date? Or a house number?"

"I'm not sure," replied Paul.

"He says Thursday."

"Thursday the 4th May! We are burying him then!"

The audience gasped.

"At two pm?" Steve asked.

Beryl... "Yes, it is two o'clock. It was one o'clock but we had to change it."

"Is someone talking about proposing?"

Paul: "Yes, me! I was thinking about proposing to my fiancée, when I was fishing today. I had a weird feeling Dad was trying to tell me something."

Fiona's face went pale.

"It's about time, sir, if you don't mind me saying so!"

Fiona gasped "Even I didn't know that!"

"Well, you do now!" Steve laughed out loud.

"He's also telling me about 'The Power of Love'."

Beryl... "That's the song we are playing at the funeral, he liked the version by Frankie goes to Hollywood, but I like the Jennifer Rush version better."

"He is sending his wishes to Peter."

Beryl: "We were supposed to be at Peter's leaving party the night he passed away."

"Who is Fee?"

Fiona... "That's me! He was the only one who called me that, and I let him, even though I hate it!"

"Well sweetheart, looks like he's still winding you up. He says you are too bloody patient and he will 'be there' for you. Do you know what that means?"

Fiona: "Yes, I always said I wanted him to give me away at my wedding."

"He will be there love!! Is your birthday the 11th August?"

It was now Fiona's turn to break down "No, but my Dad died on the 11th August, 9 years ago."

"Well, your Dad says he is with Brian."

Fiona tried to stop the tears as she said "That's my Granddad."

"Well it looks to me like they all want to give you away love!" Once again, the audience laughed.

"Does someone drive a VW Passat?"

Beryl: "That's our car."

"Not now, he says, you have to give it to Paul."

Beryl: "Yes, I had thought of that a couple of days ago, it's too big for me to drive."

"Who is Ian?"

Beryl: "That is my husband you're speaking to."

Stephen: "Well, he says he didn't say goodbye to any of you, but he wants me to let you know he will stay around you and always give you that guidance from the other side of life. Just before I leave you, he's told me to mention Devon."

Beryl: "That is where we were due to go the day after he died."

Stephen: "He says he is there already and he went for free!"

Beryl was crying and laughing at the same time.

Stephen: "I will say goodnight and God Bless to you all, and he says he will be with you on Thursday at two pm for the funeral."

Paul, Beryl and Fiona said in unison, "Thank you so much, goodnight".

The rest of the evening was just as fully charged, with the emotional roller-coaster of tears and laughter. Steve ran over a little, on purpose, as he had a bit of a late start due to the car park being full. Steve had gone through two pints of water that evening and was desperate for the loo, but as always after the show, people like to come and chat and Steve always likes to give them that time. So, he stood there, cross-legged, chatting to the people who had either had a message or just wanted to ask a question. After 15 minutes, he left the room and outside was Beryl, Paul and Fiona.

As Steve passed, he said "Good luck for Thursday love, I really hope that message has helped you."

As Steve has said so many times, it's not uncommon for people to receive messages from family members that have only recently passed away, many even before their own funerals. There appears to be no time threshold between us and the spirit. Nevertheless, it always seems to shock everyone, including Steve!

Paul took Steve's hand, shook it and said "Can I just say what you said was absolutely bang on... Devon, the caravan, the three pound carp, Thursday the 4th, the funeral, me thinking about proposing, the fishing and that weird feeling I had, the car, The Power of Love, I am gob-smacked, mate."

Beryl chirped in, "And even my hair! I only coloured it today and the fact that we should have been at Peter's party the night he passed away. Thank you so much, it's too much to take in right now, but I so *so* glad we came."

Stephen gave her hand a squeeze. "It's a pleasure love, I am really pleased for you all, but I must go, I've been trying to get to the loo for the last 25 minutes! Goodnight, see you again."

Steve rushed to the loo and, as always, headed straight for the cubicle, because the last thing he wanted to do was have a conversation at the urinal. He felt relieved to be there after drinking those two pints of water. He heard the loo door go and became aware of a conversation being struck up by two men who had just come in, both with really strong accents.

"Hey mate," said the first. "What you doing here?"

"Oh, our lass booked the tickets but it's not really my cup of tea."

"Shame I didn't know you were in there, we could have had a drink in the interval."

"Yeah, or even better, we could have slipped off down to the pub. What a pile of crap that was, tonight."

"Yeah mate, you're absolutely right. I only came for our lass."

Steve listened intently and realised that to save any embarrassment, he would have to stay in the cubicle until these two men had left.

He tried to stifle a laugh because it just went to show that if your communication with Spirit is clear and the messages you convey are accurate, you are still met with scepticism and disbelief or are accused of planting people in the audience. Some people will sit and listen to the mound of evidence and watch the recipient be reduced to tears, yet if it's not their *own* message, then in the lad's words 'It's a pile of crap'. Steve learned a long time ago that you can't please everyone, so now, the only people he likes to please are the loved ones in Spirit.

It's true that both Rob Green and I can get very defensive and uptight when Stephen has to face any kind of crude and critical comment, frequently verging on slander and invariably based on ignorance. Nor are we the only ones, for Stephen has many friends and allies, all of whom would leap to his defence in the face of such ill-informed negativity. Stephen, however, just laughs at it and shrugs it off. He can't actually *do* anything about it, other than to carry on with his work, secure in the knowledge that he has friends in the spirit world who are also very much on his side, guiding him through the 'slings and arrows of outrageous fortune'.

Chapter Twenty Four
Dying

Oddly, perhaps because of the story just narrated in the previous chapter, combined with my own on-going battle with heart failure, I started thinking about dying – and not just dying, but the actual *process* of dying. It crossed my mind that whether you live in Bournemouth, Bermuda or Beijing, no matter whether you are Christian, Moslem or Jew, regardless of your cast, colour and tradition, be you rich or be you poor, you are a member of the human race and as such you have one thing in common with every living thing on this planet. You are going to die! There is no escape. One day, for whatever reason, your heart will stop beating and that will be the end of it.

This life, the only life you have ever known, will be over – and then the mystery begins. Do you fall into the black void of forgetfulness – a permanent hole of dreamless sleep, a scenario where your life spark is snuffed out for ever and everything you have done with that life, the triumphs, the disasters, the successes, the failures, the lessons, the loving, the myriad experiences that have formed your thoughts, beliefs and actions – all count for nothing? Are meaningless and without point? Or is there something else? And if there is something else, what is it? Where is it and how does it work, and will that 'something else' be the same for all of us or will there be variations depending upon our faith and creed?

Many people from a variety of different cultures believe that Death is not the end of the story but merely a gateway of transition from one life to another. A better life, lived on a different plane of existence. This place, called Heaven in many languages and appropriately enough derived from the word 'haven', is supposedly the place of peace and personal enlightenment, of spiritual grace and tranquillity where all inequalities are equalled, all wounds and hurts are healed and we all, in our different ways, come closer to the source energy that created us. Furthermore, as an added bonus, we are reunited with our loved ones and ancestors who have gone before.

Sounds divine, doesn't it? So why is it that even the most hard pressed of us, from the lowliest untouchable in the back streets of New Delhi to the loneliest drug addict in the back streets of New York, does not want to die – and fights tooth and nail to hang on to the last vestiges of life, no matter how awful and untenable that life might be? Why is it that our most enlightened spiritual pundits from Archbishops to Imams, New Age Angelics to evangelists of any creed, are not in any great hurry to go to this other 'better' life?

And yet there is an even more fundamental question to be asked. Given that death is such an intrinsic part of our lives and always has been, and given that we all, as it were, are in the same boat, and given its absolute inevitability, why do we fear it so much? And make no mistake, despite all religious faiths and platitudes, we are terrified witless by the thought of dying – and if not in our intellectual conversations with our fellow men, then certainly within the recesses of our private imaginings, we rail and recoil against the concept. A fundamental human fear is, and always has been and always will be, the fear of the unknown. Someone else's death we can deal with, albeit not always easily, but dealing with the prospect of our own death is a different matter entirely. It causes some of us to dismiss the idea completely, others it impales upon the crutch of religion, while others find their salvation by spending their lives in preparation for the event.

Of course, there are the exceptions to the rule. The person locked into a wheelchair, the person who lives with severe physical or mental pain... The person in an ongoing state of emotional crucifixion... all might prefer the uncertainty of death rather than face the continuation of their earthly suffering. To my mind, this validates the concept of suicide and is a good reason for a change in the law to allow assisted dying without prosecution.

Man is the only species alive on this planet with an awareness of his own mortality: there are theories which hold that elephants and some of the big whales also have foreknowledge of their impending demise, but until one can have an intellectual conversation with an elephant or a whale, they must remain nothing more than theories. This awareness within humanity is both a blessing and a curse. The blessing comes in knowing that our human suffering is not infinite, the curse comes in knowing that we only have our allotted number of years to do all the things we would like to do and achieve all those things we would like to achieve. There is a law of diminishing returns here, for the older we get, the more we become aware of the speed of our passing years. It pushes some of us into reckless impulsiveness as we seek to make up for lost time and opportunities, others it cossets in a veil of tired depression as we lose the will to fight and we hang on, counting the days as we hurtle towards our inevitable exit.

I had an Aunt who firmly believed that "when you're dead you're dead", that there was nothing after death other than a long dreamless void of permanent sleep. No dreams, no spiritual reunions, no awareness of self or of anything which had gone before during the span of life. She was not alone in this belief, for there are many who share in this opinion, seeing it, in scientific terms, as the logical outcome of death. To me, however, it seems totally *illogical*. The human spirit is the vital spark of all creativity and I find it hard to accept that all our human experiences are simply obliterated with our passing from this world to the next. It *feels* wrong and goes against the fundamental laws of reason and common sense.

Another thought to be kept in mind here is that from the very beginning of recorded time there have always been references to Man communicating with Spirit and, of course, vice versa. If this phenomenon is to be accepted, then logically those spiritual communications must come from somewhere. Sceptics would argue that they emanate from Man's own mind and subconscious, but the evidence clearly suggests that this is not the case, especially when we bring the efforts of third parties into this, in the form of mediums and clairvoyants.

All of the mediums I have ever spoken to are quietly convinced that the messages they convey do *not* come from the recipient's subconscious, but from direct communication with the spiritual energy of a departed loved one. The evidence provided earlier in this book, and indeed in the other three books I have written about the work of Stephen Holbrook, present this as a self-evident truth and therefore it is clear to me that if a medium like Steve can provide hard evidence for life after death, then he is doing the world a great service in removing much of the fear associated with the process of dying... And for goodness sake, what a better, brighter, happier world this might be if that fear was obliterated altogether.

I suppose there are many ways in which a person can die and lucky are those who simply pass away in their sleep or who are suddenly struck by a bolt of lightning. They go without any foreknowledge of their impending transition which, tragic though it might be, has got to be a damned sight better than withering away degree by degree in a hospital or hospice bed or staggering along the bleak corridors of a care home, clinging to a Zimmer frame while dribbling down the front of your shirt.

Speaking to soldiers who have returned from Iraq and Afghanistan, they know they are taking risks and accept the possibility of death: they are not too worried about the bullet in the back of the head and actually their greater fear is that of being maimed by some indiscriminate IED. This information got me thinking and I spent the better part of a year doing some research. The conclusions were reasonably clear. The fear of dying was a very real fear, but the *greater* fear was concerned (a) with the manner of the passing over, (b) the physical pain of that transition (c), what might be on the other side of life and, more importantly, (d) how loved ones left behind might cope with the loss and bereavement.

Here again the work of mediums like Stephen Holbrook must be seen as invaluable if it gives people the chance to say goodbye, and even more invaluable if it provides evidence of post mortem survival. The sceptics may scoff, but I have seen so much sublime relief in the hearts of those who have received messages from the spirit world and if the evidence they have received enables them to move on, to find some calm and tranquillity and perhaps also a modicum of faith, then Stephen has served them well and done them no harm.

The actual process of dying is unique to the individual and there is an erudite and sympathetic guide to be found on the HOSPICE UK website which I thought was very sensitive, but perhaps of slightly more use to relatives and carers than to their patients. So, in search of greater insight I talked to three nurses, all of whom were involved in palliative end-of-life care. Across the board, their opinions and observations were almost exactly the same.

First of all, it has to be said that the majority of people being admitted to a hospice know that it is going to be a one way journey. Those who do not are those who have lapsed into such a mental state that concepts like time and place no longer have very much meaning. Of those who are all too well aware of their situation, some deal with it with calm stoicism while others can experience depression, distress and agitation. However, in the very last days or even hours of life, a quality of peace and tranquillity descends upon the patient and in nine out of ten cases they slip away without drama or trauma.

While I found this vaguely reassuring, it still did not provide an answer to the question that was nagging away at the back of my mind... namely what does it actually feel like to die? Does the dying person know what is happening and, if they do, how do they feel about it – if indeed they feel anything at all?

There are many well documented stories from those who have had near-death experiences in which they talk of travelling with growing velocity along a dark tunnel towards a shining bright light, only to be halted in their tracks before they can enter the 'light'.

Medical science suggests that this is simply a process of the mental synapses 'letting go', which is as good a theory as you're going to get from a scientist, but which does not explain why this vision of travelling along a tunnel towards a bright light is so comprehensively endorsed by so many different people, from so many different cultures and countries across the world. Either way, it still doesn't answer the fundamental question of what is it like to die? Perhaps we are not meant to know and perhaps the only way we are going to find out is when we ourselves take that final step into the unknown.

Unless...

Unless you could talk to someone who had travelled into the Light and had then come back to tell the tale!

The next two parts of this chapter deal with two separate events, which seem totally disconnected until you step back and join up the dots. The first concerns a message which Stephen gave to a lady at the Ramada Jarvis Hotel in Loughborough more than a dozen years ago. In those days I was still travelling with Steve and still keeping copious notes of most of the messages.

It was a hot sticky evening in July. The small function room was packed to the gills with 120 people, all sitting cheek by jowl. There was no air conditioning and, despite the fact that all the windows were wide open giving us an exciting view of red brick walls and a slab grey car park, we were all uncomfortable with the heat and perspiring profusely. Stephen decided he wanted to go through the evening without an interval so that we could get out of the room as quickly as we could, and the message in question went to a woman sitting vaguely in the middle of the room.

"I want," he began carefully, "to talk to a lady who lost her husband only last year and I think as a result of some kind of prolonged health condition. As for the gentleman, I don't think he knew he was ill, but I think he might have had a sudden heart attack and he passed over in the hospital a few hours later."

Initially the room was silent with no response, but then the lady I've just mentioned put up her hand and waved it tentatively. "I think that might just be me," she said nervously.

She was a slightly older woman, possibly in her fifties, with fair greying hair and glasses. In many ways she was quite unremarkable and seemed ill at ease, almost as though one part of her was desperately keen to get a message, while at the same time being very nervous at having been singled out from the 100 plus audience.

"Who is Gary or Barry?" Stephen asked.

"Barry's my husband," the lady answered tentatively, "but..."

"And who is June?"

"June is my sister."

"Well, June has just pushed her way through and she's telling me something about September. Can you understand that, m'love?"

"Yes, she died in September, three years ago."

"And when she was down here was she a kind of, well, you know, a pushy person? Always demanding to be heard and wanting to be at the front of the queue?"

"Yes, she was very much like that, I'm afraid." The lady gave a sad little smile in embarrassed admission of her sister's shortcomings.

"She's telling me something about a house..." Steve paused, and then, "she's saying that she's sorry about what she did about the house and that you'll understand what she means?"

"I know exactly what she means," the lady confirmed, now looking a bit upset and that sad little smile disappearing somewhere off into the sunset.

"Who's Doris?" Stephen wanted to know.

"That's my name. I'm Doris."

"And what's the significance of a cart wheel?"

"I don't really know, except that my second name is Carter."

"And what's the link with Australia?"

"My son and his wife both live in Australia."

"Well," Steve joked, "you'd better make up an extra bed, because they'll be coming home soon."

"That's quite right," Doris confirmed. "They're coming over next month for a few weeks for an extended holiday."

"I think that maybe you'll be pleased to see them when they arrive," Stephen laughed gently, "but I reckon you'll be even more pleased to wave them goodbye when they go. I think they might be with you for a bit longer than just a few weeks!"

The audience laughed at this humour but the woman called Doris remained impassive.

"Now..." Stephen slowed his words, "I've got the gentleman here with a heart condition... Can you understand this, m'love? This gentleman would have been quite poorly for quite a long time before he passed over...?"

"Yes, that would be my husband Barry."

"Well, he just wants you to know that he's all right now."

"I flaming well hope so," Doris retorted briskly, "because while I'm sitting here he's at home painting the bathroom!"

There was another laugh from the audience but Stephen looked at Doris in blank incomprehension. "No, there's something wrong here, m'love, because the gentleman I'm talking about here would have passed over in the autumn of last year."

"That's quite right," Doris told him. "My husband Barry did pass over last October and he was dead for more than four minutes before the medical team were able to resuscitate him. Thank God, he's made a full recovery and, although he's retired from his job, he's still got enough energy left to paint the bathroom and last week he built a garden shed in our back yard!"

This is one of those quirky messages which potentially gets lost in the many hundreds of messages which Stephen will bring over in any given year. I remember it quite clearly however because (a) I had a long talk with Doris Carter at the end of the evening, which (b) led to me interviewing her husband Barry a few weeks later. In some ways Barry was as unremarkable as his wife; he was a short tubby little man with thin grey hair and a round open face – and it was a face blessed with twinkling blue eyes and a ready smile which seldom left his lips. He was an avid aficionado of country music and had, until recently, taken great pleasure in smoking a stained old meerschaum pipe. For someone who had 'died' the year before, he exuded vitality and optimism. When I met him he had finished the bathroom project and was now in the process of laminating the kitchen floor. I think he saw me as an excuse to take a long break from his task and he was happy, eager even, to talk to me. Therefore, in his own words…

Transcript of taped interview with Barry Carter

I'd just had my 50th birthday and I suppose you might say I pushed the boat out a bit with all the booze and fags and rich food. I remember having a really restless night's sleep with lots of indigestion and heart burn, and the following day, which would have been the Sunday, I felt completely washed out and knackered. I was sick a couple of times and was running to the loo every couple of hours, but by bedtime I was feeling a bit better, so I turned in for an early night around ten o'clock and fell asleep without having to count a single sheep.

I woke up again around two o'clock in the morning and I've got to say I was feeling really weird. It was as though someone was sitting on my chest and I was finding it a bit hard to breathe. Also, my cheeks felt hollow and I remember thinking "oh hell, I'm going to be sick again". So I thought I'd better get myself to the bathroom and I tried pushing myself up into a sitting position, but then the weird feeling got even weirder because it felt like there was a herd of Wildebeest galloping around inside my chest and as clear as day I can remember thinking "oh shit, I'm having a sodding heart attack!"

So I nudged Doris and told her to phone for an ambulance because I was seriously not very well. So Doris made the call and then helped me to sit up on the edge of the bed and I suppose this was when I started getting really worried because there was this bloody awful pain right across my chest and all the way down my left arm. I've got to say I knew what was happening to me and, to tell you the truth, rather than being scared I was downright flaming angry. I thought "this can't be happening to me. I've never had a day's illness in my life!"

To give the ambulance lads their due, they were there within ten minutes and, even as the ambulance was pulling away from outside our front door, one of the crew was fitting me up with an oxygen mask while another was shoving a cannula thing into my left arm. To tell the truth, by that time I was only half aware of what was going on and the next thing I remember with any clarity is being wheeled on a gurney out of the ambulance and whisked into the A&E department of Loughborough Hospital. I kept looking round for Doris and started panicking a bit when she wasn't there.

You hear all these stories about the state of the NHS but even as I was wheeled into this little curtained cubicle, there was a nurse and a doctor fitting me up with all these wires and tubes and then, most important of all, Doris was there too, sitting on a chair and looking as worried as I felt. I wanted to tell her not to worry because everything was going to be okay, but I think it was maybe around then that I lost consciousness and I don't remember anything 'till I woke up in a hospital bed with all these wires attached to my chest and a TV monitor going ping pong ping pong somewhere over to my left.

I can't say that I felt ill or in any pain because to tell the truth I wasn't feeling anything very much at all, except that I was very worried for my wife. She was sitting in a chair at the end of the bed, fast asleep, and looking absolutely shattered. Apart from the fact that it was daylight, I had no idea what time it was, or even what day it was.

Anyway, a bit later on a doctor came to see me and told me that I'd had a heart attack, which was something I'd already worked out for myself. What he told me next made my blood run cold. Apparently I was going to be transferred over to the Leicester hospital because I needed a heart by-pass operation and I needed it pretty damn quick.

Cutting a long story short, I was transferred over to Leicester that evening – don't remember much about the mechanics of the journey – and after I'd been there for about an hour, I was told that I'd be going in for the surgery the following morning. At that time I wasn't in any real pain (apparently I was pumped full of morphine so I suppose that's hardly surprising) and I started wondering if they'd made some kind of mistake with the diagnosis. Lying in the Leicester bed, I felt really ill and groggy, but not anything like what I'd imagined I might feel after having had a heart attack. I suppose I was in no position to complain or ask any questions, so I just lay there thinking that the medical staff knew what they were doing, so I might as well let them get on with it.

Anyway, the following morning arrived and I was told that the operation had been postponed until that evening because they were short of the bloke who gave you the anaesthetic. Doris was there with me for most of the morning, but then had to go home to feed the dog and catch up on some sleep. She promised she'd be back in the early evening, but it turned out to be a wee while longer than that before I saw her again.

On the one hand, I wasn't in any great hurry to go through open heart surgery, but, on the other, the delay gave me plenty of time to fret and worry about it. I suppose I must have dozed off a few times, but then at some time during the afternoon, something changed and I was suddenly wide awake. Well, sort of wide awake. I had a tickling feeling in my feet, a bit like a mild case of pins and needles, and then the sensation moved slowly up my legs, over my tummy and my chest and all down my arms. While all this was happening there was a feeling of pressure inside my chest, and in my head as well come to think of it, and when I tried to open my eyes everything was very blurry. I knew there was a big red button that I was supposed to press if I needed assistance, but when I tried to reach for it, I couldn't move my arm. In fact, I couldn't move anything at all!

I was hoping that one of the nurses would pop in to see me, you know, just to find out if I was still in one piece, but rather than there being any nurses on hand, there were two other figures standing either side of the bed. Now, they weren't ghostly apparitions or anything like that, but I'll admit that I couldn't see them all that clearly because my eyes were feeling very stingy, you know, like they get when you've been crying. One was a young lad, who looked familiar, although I didn't know who he was. The other figure I recognised straight away and it was then that I knew I was in real trouble. This was my Dad, and he'd been dead for more than 30 years!

The pins and needles covered my head and shoulders and I heard a kind of tearing sound – you know, like when you rip a sheet of paper or a bit of old cloth, and then there was this tingling feeling in my throat and I tried to cough – and then I was being thrown upwards and out of bed and I was sort of pinned with my back to the ceiling, looking down at myself on the bed beneath me. I could see myself as grey as the North Sea and as still as a rock, and all the time there was this beeper blaring away in the distance. All of a sudden the room seemed to be full of people all fussing around, but I don't know what happened next because by then I was out of the hospital and moving up in the sky. One minute is was a lovely sunny afternoon and the next I was floating through a beautiful dark blue sky full of stars... Well, I say dark blue, but maybe it was an *evening* blue, if you know what I mean...

I was aware of the young lad walking to one side of me, and my Dad was walking on the other side with his hand resting on my shoulder. As clear as day I remember him saying "Nearly there now, son. We'll soon have you home!" I was also aware that there were other people watching us. I couldn't see any of them and it was more a case of just sensing their presence. Anyway, they were all clapping their hands, just like my mates giving me a round of applause down at my local pub when I won the karaoke, then as clear as day I heard my mother's voice asking "Have you got him, John?"

My Dad sounded very pleased with himself. "Yes Peggy," he said, "all safe and sound!"

I looked round trying to see where my Mum might be and then something like an express train hit me right in the middle of my shoulder blades and sent me tumbling arse over tit back the way I'd come. Out of the blue, into the sunshine, and then doing a nose dive down towards the hospital like a paratrooper without a bloody parachute.

I had the fleeting impression of hitting the hospital roof then I was back in the ward, looking at my body prostrate on the bed. There were at least half a dozen people round the bed and there was this one nurse who was holding those big electric paddle things that you see in the movies. She pressed them against my chest then, wham, something else hit me in the middle of the back, only this wasn't like an express train, it was more like a V2 rocket. Then everything went still and black and I woke up 36 hours later, still in the hospital bed, but now with even more wires sprouting out of my body. Thank God, Doris was sitting next to me, and I've got to tell you I was bloody pleased to see her. She was chattering away cheerfully but to be honest, I couldn't understand a word she was saying. I was just so pleased that she was there.

Quite a while later I was told that I'd had another heart attack. That I'd been clinically dead for nearly five minutes. They'd managed to bring me back and had done a double heart by-pass almost straight away. I remember lying in the bed and longing for a pint... I didn't know it then but my days of downing pints were over – maybe just *half* a pint at the weekend – and, as for my pipe, well Doris made sure I never smoked it ever again. I know I shouldn't but, God knows, I really miss my old pipe!

Anyway Mr Christie, that's my story. That's what happened to me. I know some people will pooh pooh the tale, but I remember it all very clearly and it's something I'm never going to forget. Well, I mean, you wouldn't, would you? Not if it had happened to you!

The thing that puzzled me for ages afterwards was the identity of the young lad who'd been with my Dad and, although it didn't happen quickly it gradually dawned on me that the boy might have been me, as I'd been when I was 15 years old, which is the age I was when my Dad passed away. I can't explain why I think that or how it might even be possible, but that's what I *think*...

Barry Carter was a down to earth working class man, gifted with dry wit and a vibrant sense of humour. If he was occasionally given to flights of fancy, it would be in the context of imagining himself as a successful country and western singer and certainly not as any kind of spiritual traveller. And yet, because it is so similar to other stories I have heard or have read about, I find it easy to believe his words, and you must make your own decision as to their veracity. It has to be said that Barry has not 'dined out' on this story and I was only the third person he'd ever shared it with, the first being his wife and the second being his local vicar.

I suppose, if I am going to be brutally honest, I believe Barry not only because I *want* to believe Barry, but because his story coincides perfectly with my own preconception of what it might be like to experience that moment when the spirit departs the body.

There was a very important research document published more than 40 years ago (not on sale to the general public) which suggested that the pins and needles sensation that Barry experienced was representative of the nerve endings within the body letting go of the spiritual connections which binds body and soul together and although there were no 'tunnels leading towards a bright light' the concept of elevating upwards towards another realm or dimension is well documented by many other people who have had near-death experiences. However, as I say, while I believe Barry's story, you must make your own decision.

One thing I can tell you with absolute authority is that I think Barry Carter was being totally honest in his report; he wasn't making anything up and *he* certainly believes it to be totally true. The heart attack and subsequent surgery has helped him to change his lifestyle for the better, and the experience of his temporary passing and the brief spiritual connection with his parents has ignited an element of spiritual faith within him which had previously been absent from his life.

Epilogue in the form of some final thoughts from Stephen

Before this book is concluded, I have to confess that it was as much of a surprise to me, as anyone else, that I even started it! There wasn't going to be a 'Book Four'. I didn't see the point in churning out much of the same stuff as you might have found in my earlier books. However, this book has ended up being a life-changing experience for me. I didn't really appreciate the changes as they took place and basically I think that's because of all the emotion that was attached to each synchronised event, therefore I was not able to enjoy the experiences they had created.

I was cleaning my car out one Saturday morning. The evening before I had had a demonstration at the Metropole Hotel in Leeds and Mel, a neighbour from across the road, came up behind me, tapped me on the shoulder and made me jump. I literally jumped a foot in the air as I was fully absorbed in the noise of the car vac. I shrieked and then said "Bloody hell, I was in a world of my own, you scared the living daylights out of me!"

"Sorry Steve, but I just wanted to say we really enjoyed last night and to thank you for the tickets."

"Oh, that's great, pleased you enjoyed it" I replied.

Mel's husband, who's also called Steve (so it gets a bit confusing sometimes), looks after the maintenance of our car and is a real diamond; he is always pleased to help and stops us from getting ripped off. A couple of years previously, I had offered tickets to any of my evenings to them, but they had never approached me with regard to this. Until just recently, when Steve said that Mel and her Mum would like to go to the Leeds evening, so I arranged this for them. Lo and behold, near the end of the evening, both her and her Mum received wonderful confirmation from their loved one. I am so glad this all happened because it is really down to Mel that I found the title of this book.

As Mel turned to walk home, I promptly opened the front door and shouted to Rob "Write this down – 'In a world of my own'". He did as I asked and never said a thing. By now, I think Rob is so used to me that he never bats an eyelid, or questions anything. Probably because he doesn't want to know the reason!

Going back to writing the first few chapters of this book, I have dredged every part of my mind and been totally honest, not just with you, The Reader, but with myself. I now know that my Mum was the inspiration for this book, *and* the instigator, and has been working diligently behind the scenes, because (1) she wanted me to be as open as I could be, to literally bare my soul, as Mum was the most open, warm person I have ever met, and (2) which I now understand fully, because she wanted to help me grieve for her. I hadn't even realised that I hadn't, as yet, actually grieved for my Mum. It may sound strange, but when I look back, when did I actually have time to grieve? I was even working the night of her funeral and every night right up to her passing, I had commitments and would never let anyone down. Helping others with their grief took my mind off the pain that I was suffering. After writing these chapters freehand, when I was reading this back to Rob to be typed up, I couldn't get through a few lines without breaking down emotionally. It was clear I was registering, for the first time, the pain. It hit me like a ton of bricks.

Without going into the finer details, the next day, I was physically ill. And after three days of running to the loo, at least 20 times per day, I had no choice but to see my doctor. I explained my sudden demise to him; I just couldn't understand it, because I felt okay mentally.

I spent three weeks sleeping on the settee because I was up between 15 and 20 times a night going to the

315

bathroom, my stomach was bloated and I couldn't eat. Working away so much, I couldn't see my own doctor, so twice I went to hospitals for scans, a colonoscopy, bladder x-rays, blood tests, you name it – I had it! I really thought I had something seriously wrong. Yet still, I never missed one evening.

Some nights I felt like crawling out of the demonstration on my knees, but my Mum had drilled it in to me, "Never let people down, never have time off unless you are dying" she would say. So therefore, from the 12th July 2019, when I started this book, it had to be put on hold until now, the 27th January 2020. I just could not face writing one more word that I would have to re-read, digest and re-live. So when I say that Mum was instrumental in the writing of this book, on a purely selfish level, I am so glad I did. Because I would still be living in a false sense of security thinking that I had got over my Mum's passing and presuming I was fine, when obviously this was far from the truth.

Something I learned from this is that we need to take time to let things sink in and balance our minds in order to go through the grieving process. This process obviously affects everyone in a different way. Because I hadn't taken that time to mentally deal with Mum's passing, grief dealt me a physical blow which almost grounded me. This goes to show that if we don't grieve initially, the grief is free to resurface at any given point, hitting you like a sledgehammer.

Hindsight is a wonderful thing, if only we had the privilege to see around the next corner of our lives, we could negotiate the bend more easily, but that is not the case. I suppose it is like reading a novel that takes you on so many twists and turns, you start to wonder who could ever imagine writing something so complex. But the author has the advantage of hindsight as, before they start the novel, they know the end of the story, therefore making it a much easier process to plot out.

One thing is certain, I now feel strong again, both physically and mentally, and I can say, with conviction, that I have never been as happy with my focus and commitment to Spirit. It's as if a cleansing has taken place and I have opened up to a whole new level. My family are rapidly growing up and moving on in their chosen directions, and for the first time in years, I feel a true sense of freedom. Also, with the knowledge that a Mother's love cannot be severed, I now know that Mum can continue with her own spiritual journey. Knowing that she was not just an amazing Mum in this world, but she is continuing her maternal duties by helping me with my own grief for losing her and gently forcing me to confront things head on.

Therefore, Mum, I thank you for sharing your journey with me and just hope that anyone reading this book will be able to take one sentence, one chapter, or even just a few words, and feel that it has somehow made you realise that we may all look different and, indeed, think differently, but at the end of the day, we are all one. All we ever truly own is our personal responsibility. As I finish off this book, a brief memory of Robbie, my eldest, when he was four years old, filters into my mind.

As a child, he always had a runny nose and, typical of toddlers, he would wipe it on the nearest thing to hand, usually a sleeve. On one occasion I remember saying to him "Robbie, don't wipe your nose on your arm, you need a tissue". His reply was childlike but also very challenging. He simply said, "But Dad, I can't help it, that's how God made me!"

Curiously, when I was talking to him the other day, telling him that his words had taken on a greater degree of importance for me, he mischievously pointed out that they were not really his words at all, but those of his Grandmother, who would frequently say to him "that's how

God made you" when he'd failed at something or had done something that he was later unhappy about. So, as far as I'm concerned this is another affirmation from my Mum delivered through my eldest son!

It makes my heart melt even now, just thinking about it. But I want to quote those five words back to my now adult family and I dedicate this book to you all, for the love and support you have shown me in this new chapter of my life. To anyone who dares challenge it, my reply would be quite simple –

I can't help it. That's how God made me!

Mage Publishing
By the same author

Biographies:

THE LIGHT IN THE DARKNESS
The Stephen Holbrook Story, Part I
ISBN: 978-0-9527109-1-2

OUT OF THIS WORLD
The Stephen Holbrook Story, Part II
ISBN: 0-9527109-2-7

SURVIVAL
The Stephen Holbrook Story, Part III
ISBN: 0-9527109-6-7

THE PSYCHIC ART OF SANDY INGHAM
ISBN: 9-7809527109-8-1

IN THE ARMS OF THE WIND
Anthony Zander's Experiment with Death
ISBN: 0-9527109-3-5

Fiction:

THE OPENING
Horror and Magic
ISBN: 9-7809527109-7-4

Fiction on Kindle:

THE VAMPIRE OF YORK
ROYAL DEMON
CISNE DEL LARGO
KONTIKI NIGHTS
THE SUMMER OF '63

Spring 2022
FAT MEN FEEL THE COLD
Poetry

www.magepublishing.co.uk